CASTA Plays in Translation (Belgian Series)

FOUR WORKS FOR THE THEATRE
BY HUGO CLAUS

Edited with an introduction by David Willinger

Translated by David Willinger, Luk Truyts and Luc Deneulin

T0125225

CASTA (Center for Advanced Study in Theatre Arts)

THE GRADUATE SCHOOL AND UNIVERSITY CENTER
of the City University of New York

INTRODUCTION

The success in recent years of such entertainments as *Agnes of God*, *Sister Mary Ignatius, The Name of the Rose,* and *Ghostbusters II* gives ample evidence of how the sacred continues to exert a fascination on the contemporary mind and be a fit subject for theatre, cinema, and fiction. Behind this popular front line of films, plays, and novels lurks a second bastion of more penetrating productions, such as Joseph Chaikin's *The Dybbuk*, Richard Foreman's *The Golem*, and Peter Brook's *Meetings With Remarkable Men* and *The Mahabarata*. The latter works, while not in themselves esoteric exercises, bring both participating artists and audiences closer to an echo of the mystical experience; they whisper an assurance that esoteric practice and phenomena are available even in these profane times. It is in the ranks of the latter grouping of, let us say, mesoteric works (standing midway between the esoterica of secret mystical practice and exoterica, which exists as an outward plane of mysticism for the consumption of the uninitiated) that Hugo Claus' *The Temptation* is properly situated.

Flanders, the northern half of Belgium, where Claus was born, is inhabited by an intensely Catholic people and has long been a seedbed for theatre issuing from a religious or anti-religious impulse. The Middle Ages brought to the Lowlands an extremely active sectarian theatre of mysteries, moralities, and processionals. The forerunner of the classic *Everyman*, *Elckerlyc*, originated in Flanders. In our century, Maurice Maeterlinck, like Claus a native of Ghent (although a French-speaker, whereas Claus is a Dutch-speaker), wrote a series of plays, including *The Blind, The Death of Tintagiles*, and *Sister Beatrice* which are mystical allegories of man's position vis a vis the numenous. And Michel de Ghelderode, both in his early maeterlinkian static dramas such as *The Old Men* and *The Strange Rider* as well as in mature classics like *The Chronicles of Hell* and *The Siege of Ostend*, was in fevered dialectic with Catholic dogma and institutions.

The latest in this line of Flemish theatre writers, Hugo Claus, is a 60 year old playwright, novelist, stage and film director, and (along with Willem Frederik Hermans) the poet laureate in the Dutch language. Belgian by citizenship, Flemish by culture, Claus is author of over forty plays, twenty-five novels, and twenty-five volumes of poetry. His recent epic tale of Flemish collaboration under the Nazis, *The Sorrow of the Belgium* (*Het Verdriet van België*) garnered tremendous success in both France and Germany (and is soon to come out in English in the Pantheon series), which repeats Claus' triumph of the '50s when his play *A Bride in the Morning* (*Een bruid in de morgen*) took Paris by storm. Claus, an *enfant terrible* no matter what his age, captured the Belgian imagination as a member of Cobra, the art movement led by Karel Appel and Pierre Alechinsky; his long-term liaison with porn-star Sylvia Kristel did nothing to bleach his scandalous public image. His private life is continually a source of avid interest to the Belgian public, which eats up news of Claus' amorous attachments, the latest being with Veirla DeWit, a charming person half his age.

The same public figure who treats with porn stars and evades the tax service, has a strong Catholic vein running through his work. His 1963 novel *Regarding Deedee* (*Omtrent Deedee*), which he just adapted into the film *The Sacrament*, had to do with a priest's relations with his family. And in his play *Maskeroon* (*Masscheroen*, 1968), inspired by the medieval legend of Mariken van Nieumeghen, performed only once at the seaside resort of Knokke, Claus assigned the roles of the New Testament Wise Men to three overweight naked gents. This latter affront to the Church's good name caused Claus to be arrested and the play banned forever. Perhaps it is the inevitable lot of writers growing up in circumstances dominated by the Church to endure a lasting ambivalence toward religious pursuits. Faced with the hypocrisy and materialism of the Church establishment, they abhor what they see. And while the Church pulls a firm reign on creativity, it gives the artist an especially fecund creative source from which to draw, positing itself as the object of the artist's inspiration.

But it was not until his first-person narrative, *The Temptation* (*De Verzoeking*, 1981) that mystical or religious subtext bursts onto the foreground of Claus' world in all its darkly glowing glory. *The Temptation* is about a hundred year-old blind nun whom the church is about to beatify, offering her sainthood in reward for her intense holiness and -- more than that -- because she is in direct communication with angels, God the Son, and Saint Joseph. We learn of all these matters through Sister Mechtild's own mouth, directed by her distracted mind. The text contains no third-person description, but her ramblings are interlaced with snatches of dialogue with the nuns and priests who surround and unintentionally torment her.

The Temptation, while written as a prose work, has been performed several times since its publication, first in a production directed by Claus himself, in which Sister Mechtild was played by a male actor. The opportunity for a tour de force turn has not been overlooked by the other theatre practitioners who have staged it either, for Claus' histrionic talents in no way desert him when bent to prose. As a play *The Temptation* invites the actress (or actor) playing the part to speak in the many voices within Mechtild's head as well as the voices closing in on her, those of the enemies to the poor nun's enlightenment.

One cannot ignore that, despite the buffo theatrical opportunities admixed with grotesque satire on the contemporary church, *The Temptation* is a sincere record of the inner torment of a soul's mystical quest. There is no question but that Hugo Claus has steeped himself in mystical doctrine. Sister Mechtild most closely resembles the character of the medieval Flemish beguine Hadewijch (1200-1260). The latter wrote many poems in closely rhymed couplets which, inasmuch as they are saturated with talk of Hadewijch's love for the deity, represent an intense mystical experience. Her commentator N. DePaepe describes this love as "that which does, wants, demands, refuses, bestows, or deprives." Her poems have titles like "Let Me Go, I Beg of You, Let Me Go." While Claus doesn't try to copy Hadewijch's style her fervent, florid, obsessive love finds an echo in Sister Mechtild. DePaepe refers to the 13th century devout as "One of the most valuable pearls in the . . . crown of Dutch poetry, " a practically verbatim description by the Canon of Sister Mechtild in *The Temptation*.

But Sister Mechtild's struggles, restrictions, and aspirations accurately reflect those that mystics of all ages have undergone. Consulting, for example, the classical mystic texts from the Middle Ages, *The Dark Night of the Soul*, by the Spaniard, Saint John of the Cross, or *The Adornment of the Spiritual Marriage* by Jan Van Ruusbroeck (or Ruysbruyck), a native of Claus' Flanders, one is struck by how close they come to anticipating Sister Mechtild's own "dark night" and spiritual merging with a higher being.

The mystical writers speak of the ladder of spiritual development as a "going forth to meet the Bridegroom." In *The Temptation* this notion of spiritual marriage has been incarnated quite literally; Sister Mechtild is having a sado-masochistic *engagement* with the Deity. She flirts with Him, pines away for Him, and is in general no different from any adolescent waiting for her boyfriend to call on Saturday night. She drops bait with which to entice Him to come to her and mortifies her body with the same end in sight as has a southern belle primping before the mirror. She derives lascivious pleasure from Him even in her dreams: "When I see You in the dark of my sleep, then I make in my bed." The ascetic Mechtild is actually a romantic who has personified the Higher Power and probably engages in more libidinous preoccupation and activity than most other women her age (how many are there?).

Sister Mechtild often finds herself longing for a God who appears infinitely cruel in His abandonment of His most loyal subject;

but this is apparently a very necessary phase in spiritual development for the adept. Sister Mechtild likens her position to " . . . running through a desert, a chasm, and straying we throw ourselves into
the cesspool and then must become what we are." The implicit
portrait of a capricious God that Claus paints here is not appreciably
different, however, from that found in the mystic texts where the
favors God grants

> do not depend on any good works performed by the
> soul, nor upon its meditations, although both of
> these things tend to dispose the soul for them. But
> God grants these favors to whom He wills and for
> whatever reason He wills. For it may happen that a
> person will have performed many good works, and
> yet he will not be granted these touches of Divine
> favor; and another will have done far fewer good
> works, and he will receive the most sublime favors
> and in great abundance. (Saint John of the Cross,
> p.102)

God has apparently thrust Sister Mechtild into a state of
permanent longing -- one more keen that any common yearning for
an absent partner. Mechtild's longing brings water to her eyes with
sorrow and water to her mouth as though in anticipation of some
unforgettable celestial repast which is forever out of reach. "And
therefrom there often spring in such a man tears and great longings."
(Ruusbroeck, p.76) This God, by modern interpretation, would be
considered a sadistic, love-denying, withholding macho male; but the
medieval Ruusbroeck approves the state of unbearable longing He
engenders as essential for inner growth:

> Here begins an eternal hunger, which shall never
> more be satisfied; it is an inward craving and hanker-
> ing of the loving power and the created spirit after an
> uncreated Good. And since the spirit longs for frui-
> tion, and is invited and urged thereto by God, it must
> always desire its fulfillment.
>
> Though God gave to such a man all the gifts which
> are possessed by all the saints, and everything that
> He is able to give, but withheld Himself, the gaping
> desire of the spirit would remain hungry and
> unsatisfied. The inward stirring and touching of God
> makes us hungry and yearning; for the Spirit of God
> hunts our spirit: and the more it touches it, the
> greater our hunger and our craving. And this is the
> life of love in its highest working, above reason and
> above understanding. . . . (Ruusbroeck, pp.121-122)

And Mechtild is conscious enough of her path that she willingly accepts the prolongation of her hunger.

It would at first sight seem paradoxical that one attending to the highest and most pure union with God would be satisfied to remain filthy of habit, covered with sores, pimples, carbuncles, and in such a general state of physical degradation as is Sister Mechtild. The first image of her in the play is of one afflicted by a dire need to scratch her infected skin eruptions. John of the Cross notes the frailty of the body and the resistance it puts up against spiritual progress:

> But owing to the fact that the sensual part of the soul is still too weak and thus incapable of receiving into itself the full power of the spirit, these advanced souls -- because of the interaction and communication between spirit and sense -- suffer as a rule from many physical weaknesses or digestive disturbances, and in consequence also from spiritual fatigue. For, as the Wise Man says: 'The soul is weighed down by a corruptible body.' (Wisdom, IX,15).
> (Saint John of the Cross, p.84)

Odder than Mechtild's physical condition is that God who willed her ultimate triumph in this quest would set Sister Mechtild down amongst those least equipped to comprehend and encourage her on her path; indeed the sisters and Mother Superior thwart her efforts at every turn, although they bask in the glory of being associated with one reputed to be a virtual saint and who brings such notoriety to their convent.

However, looking at the example of Saint John of the Cross' life as it neared *its* end, we see that the situation was not so different. Covered with sores and suffering from pulmonary distress, he was given the choice of passing his last days in sympathetic surroundings among clerics at the university he had founded or under the authority of one of his fiercest, most ruthless opponents. He chose the latter inhospitable domicile as the place he would end his days on earth. And in his state of physical decrepitude he *voluntarily* had himself laid over an ass and delivered to his enemy. The neglect and mortification of the body, then, is intended to contribute to a purification of the soul. Alien and unsympathetic surroundings are a test of faith and charity.

Sister Mechtild must, at every turn, forgive her tormentors their depredations. What torments her more than any other person, however, is her conviction that she suffers from the sin of spiritual pride, a self-satisfaction with her works and herself and a con-

v

comitant condescension to those around her ("It is the pride of joy [at having been chosen] and that joy must be crushed."). But her condescension is quite one-sided. While she certainly feels superior to the other sisters, Mother Superior, the priests, and even to the Bishop when it comes to spiritual works, yet she is absolutely abject when her physical person is in question; she treats herself to unremitting abuse for her earthly casement. She is grateful to God when he absents Himself and turns a deaf ear to her prayers, for then her faith is tested and her longings intensified. She is a model of those referred to in *The Long Night of the Soul* who:

> desire to be despised and . . . their work held in no esteem. And they think it very strange that anyone should say good things of them. These are all signs of the spirit that is simple, pure, sincere, and very pleasing to God. (p.164)

Physical blindness reinforces spiritual sight. Yet another aspect of the abnegation of the fleshly, Sister Mechtild's blindness derives from the classical notion that those blind to the temporal world are capable of far greater vision of the numinous. But the soul itself may be blind.

> The third evil which the desires cause in the soul is they darken it and make it blind. David, speaking of this matter, says: 'My iniquities have taken hold of me, and I have lost my power of sight.' (Psalms, VI,4). And when the soul is thus darkened in its understanding, it is also blunted in its will, and the faculty of memory becomes dull and disordered in its proper functions. For, as these latter faculties in their operations depend on the understanding, it is clear that, when the understanding is blurred, they too will become disordered and disturbed. Desire thus makes the soul dark and blind; for desire, as such, is blind. And this is the reason why, whenever the soul allows itself to be guided by its desires, it becomes blind also.
> (Saint John of the Cross, pp.17-18)

Sister Mechtild has thus been plunged into darkness as a penalty for desiring God's immanence. And her understanding has been proportionately blurred that she may better apprehend God when He comes to her. Darkness in Sister Mechtild's cell removes the impediments from the in-flooding of mystical light. In his chapter on "The Silencing of the Passions," Saint John of the Cross enunciates the credo which Sister Mechtild has supernaturally received and follows to the letter:

Take care that you always choose
Not the easiest, but the hardest;
Not the most delectable, but the most distasteful;
Not what gives most pleasure, but is less pleasing;
Not what allows you much rest, but what requires great exertion;
Not what consoles, but what deprives you of consolation;
Not the loftiest and most precious, but the lowest and most despised;
Not the desire for anything, but a desire for nothing.
Do not go about seeking the best of temporal things but the worst;
Desire nothing but to enter for Christ's sake into total nakedness, emptiness, and poverty with respect to all things of this world. (p.25)

It is therefore especially terrible when, abhorring temporal light, she is forced to tolerate its introduction into her cell in the name of keeping up with the times. Mechtild must forever resist her tendency to condemn those around her; rather she must remind herself that their pecadilloes are, in fact, useful aids to her renewed resolve. Claus masterfully plunges us into the blind nun's dark world through the extremely gradual disordered, and fragmentary exposition of her surrounding circumstances.

What is particularly baffling about Sister Mechtild's dilemma--and revealing about the exigencies of mystical practice--is that many of Mechtild's torments come in the form of kindnesses and comforts. A soft bed, light in the cell, clean habit and hood, cheerful companions, priests who urge her to abandon painful self-mortification and who forgive each exaggerated transgression--those are anathema to her practice and thus the work of the devil. Her bind tightens in that she must nonetheless act in total obedience to her ecclesiastical superiors even if their dicta run directly counter to the most intimate and direct instructions she received from God and the angels.

Both author and principal character know that the penitent's trials must go well beyond the bounds of common decency. Christ's own mortification is, of course, the greatest model. Saint John of the Cross cites the experience of Job whom God left naked on dunghill; only then did he "come down and speak with Job face to face." (p.177) It is not entirely, then, the Flemish proclivity for scatology which prompted Claus to lavish details of Sister Mechtild's physical degeneration.

Sister Mechtild has been doubly plunged into profound darkness, first by physical blindness, then by the insidious introduction of light into her cell. But she is further handicapped by being stripped of "means." Sister Mechtild often fells herself to be devoid of means to call upon God, particularly later in the play, when prayer, divine images, and faith desert her.

For the advanced mystical student, striving to attain to God with no help from the usual tools is a normal, if despairing, phase to undergo. "Christ comes into us and in us, both with means and without means, that is with the virtues and above the virtues. And He impresses His image and His likeness in us, namely Himself and His gifts." (Ruusbroeck, p.28) Thus is Sister Mechtild left bereft by her Bridegroom. even on the doorstep of spiritual attainment. She endures her Calvary of abandonment in the public toilet in skewed imitation of Christ, and in imitating Him, merges with Him in spiritual marriage. Claus, then, has created a mystical document which treads a very fine line between deep piety (and certainly the text betrays great erudition concerning the various stages on the mystic's path, many of which Sister Mechtild reproduces) and absolute mockery of the religious life.

****

"And he came and took her by the hand, and lifted her up." (Mark, I,31).

If one were to seek out a saint-like person in contemporary times, however unlikely the success of such a search, a convent would still be a more probable repository for her than a brothel. Unless you're Hugo Claus. The perverse Claus, imbued with that love of overturning conventional morality so prevalent in Flemish dramatists, has reincarnated the savior of humankind in the person of a small-time hooker who works out of a road-side bordello. *The Hair of the Dog* (1982) is riddled with references, images, and action segments that invoke the New Testament Gospels. Hung on the fragile hook of a detective thriller, the story of Mira Davids would be an unsatisfying, fragmentary one, if considered autonomously from her identification with Christ. *The Hair of the Dog* actually has two simultaneous actions unfurling alongside each other--that of the whore who foresees her end and goes to it with eyes open, and the other invisible one of a human/god making a sacrifice for all mankind. The former anecdote is enacted in passing time on the temporal plane, whereas the latter takes place in eternal time, is in fact an infinitely repeated, ever-present occurrence that has no beginning or end. Claus intimates Mechtild's immersion in eternal time in *The Temptation* by continually shifting verb tenses and the reenactment of Calvary. In *Hair of the Dog* he substitutes "real life" events as analogues for the stages of Christ's martyrdom and invests his characters with super-human prescience of events to come.

Spiritual significance is embedded in every detail of *The Hair of the Dog*. Structured, like the German expressionist dramas, as a station play in which each terse "station" or scene represents a stage in the hero's (not necessarily Christian or even spiritual) development, the segments here regain their full connotation of the Christian stations of the cross. Claus divides the play into fourteen vignettes, fourteen being a mystical number from the New Testament:

> So all the generations from Abraham to David are fourteen generations; and from David until the carrying away into Babylon are fourteen generations." (Matthew, I,17).

The hints begin even in the cast list. Mira Davids--"Jesus Christ, the son of David" (Matthew, I,1)--her name contains her hidden identity. Mira, like Christ at the time of His death, is thirty years old, and sees her profession as a mission to bring love to mankind. Her mother, an old reprobate whore, insists, "Our Lord cares for the sick. We care for the sick," which proposition echoes Jesus' very own words when he was berated for eating with publicans and sinners: "They that be whole need not a physician, but they that are sick." (Matthew, X,12). Indeed, Mira loves all her clients and gives herself to them with a love tempered by detachment and self-sacrifice.

The premise of likening a wretched whore to the greatest religious prophet who ever lived has its justifications, however far-fetched it may at first appear. A whore's is an analogous calling to a prophet's in the renunciations it exacts--no husband, no home, or family for a whore. A whore can never really call her possessions her own. She shares outcast status with the spiritual prophet, as well as holding an irresistible attraction for those who come to adore her. Attraction, however, is counterbalanced by physical peril, which is an incessant occupational hazard both to prostitute and to prophet; they become targets for the most exalted adulation and the most squalid attacks on their person. And the spiritual leader, like the whore, may *serve as stand-ins*--the former for the god whose gospel they are preaching and the latter for the personal human fantasy.

One of the play's most important characters, Janine, another whore from a neighboring bordello, is already dead at the curtain's rise; and it is her death which provides the precipitating push to the events which ensue. Her recent demise, a brutal murder, has engendered an ambiance of danger, since the murderer, not yet identified, is still on the prowl and may follow up with murders of other prostitutes.

If Mira is the Christ, then who is Janine in the parallel, hidden action? We know that her throat was slit and quickly learn that calve's head in tomato sauce was her favorite dish. Through this gruesome, comic information, we identify her with John the Baptist. The tomato sauce is a reminder of the prophet's bloody end; her head swam in a pool of her own blood. Piero, Janine's pimp and a likely suspect in her murder, now "sees blood everywhere."

Janine is said to have been desirable for the "special tricks" she used to perform, sexual parlance for fetishistic acts clients with idiosyncratic desires dote on, jocosely analogous to the miracle of baptism performed by John. And Claus cleverly has her wearing leather, a tip-off; for while a whore who wears leather does so to signal a penchant for sado-masochism, "John [the Baptist also] had . . . a leathery girdle about his loins." (Matthew, III,4) It is significant that there is an important concubine, Salome, in John the Baptist's story, who bore his head on a platter; in *Hair of the Dog* John *is* a concubine who has been deprived of her own head. In Christ's story, Mary Magdalene and the woman taken in adultery were all recipients of Christ's mercy; in *The Hair of the Dog*, Christ and whore are one.

Janine is known to have owned a sheep, which is now masterless. Mira wants to take it in. A strange pet for a whore, a profession more often identified with bright-colored birds, luxuriantly haired cats, or (as with Mimi) poodles and other lap dogs. Yet the anomaly is set to naught when the lamb of the New Testament, traditionally an archetypal image of the mild, charitable Jesus, is brought into the picture. "And look upon Jesus as he walked, he saith, Behold the Lamb of God!" (John, I,36) "And he shall set the sheep on his right hand . . . ." (Matthew, XXV,33) " . . . I will smite the shepherd, and the sheep of the flock shall be scattered abroad." (Matthew, XXVI,31) And that is precisely the situation the sheep finds itself in in *Hair of the Dog*: shepherd dead and flock in disarray. Mira's longing to give the poor animal asylum is a signal both that she identifies with the sheep and that she is prepared to pick up and bear Janine's fallen sceptre, a responsibility which entails living out the role of the martyr. " . . . the good shepherd giveth his life for the sheep." (John, X,11)

Another absent character who yet visits Mira during her epileptic seizures (akin to bouts of divine transport) is her absent father, Puma. "And, lo, a spirit taketh him, and he suddenly crieth out; and it teareth him that he foameth again . . . ." (Luke, IX,39) The seizures have been genetically passed down to Mira from Puma's side of the family. Puma is a mysterious figure about whom we receive scant information apart from that he was supposed to have perished during the Korean War. The sobriquet Puma replaces an earlier name, Joseph. We also know that during his life he lied and cheated "because things were supposed to be different" and that Mira yearns to be reunited with him. He is, thus, a composite of God the Father and the terrestrial father of the baby Jesus, Joseph. On those occasions when Mira rejoins him during her *grand mals*, he is silent, impassive, and remote; his sole definite act is to strike her with the butt of his rifle and repeatedly abandon her.

The Virgin Mary of the play, Mira's mother Mimi, is just about as antithetical to the traditional portrait of Jesus' mother as possible. George introduces Mimi as "Consoler to the Afflicted, Mother of Sorrows," but the woman who answers to those august titles is actually an overweight, loquacious, coarse, and blousy old hooker. She is no virgin, and she surely wasn't one before Mira's conception either. Her conceit is to carry a stuffed dog; she is thus a debased version of the Virgin Mary, whom frequent medieval images depict accompanied by miniature sheep.

"The Son of man came eating and drinking, and they say, Behold a man gluttonous, and a winebibber, a friend of publicans and sinners." (Matthew, XI,19) The above is a perfect description of Mira's constant companion and sometime pimp--George, the embodiment of appetitive, sinning man. He is a slave to his fleshly desires--those for food (he is forever imagining what his next meal will be), marijuana, cocaine, and voyeuristic sex (And violent crime? Suspicions turn on him, as the play progresses, as the murderer of Janine). This character takes on added complexity, as he is a self-styled art critic for the local paper and a socialist, attributes uncommon among pimps. His erudition turns out to be buffoonery, however; his misquotes of the Bible, for example, give him away. And his socialism is highly theoretical, deeply engaged as he is in capitalist enterprise--human flesh being the commodity.

Even George's last name describes his function and identity--Herremans, men of the lord. He is both a composite of the disciples (adoring as he is of Mira) and unredeemed sinner, the very epitome of he for whose sake Mira must die: all of sinning humanity. One of Mira's earliest gestures is to remove George's shoes, an inverted version of Mary Magdalene wiping Christ's feet with her hair.

The cast of characters is completed with Mira's nemesis, Frans and Bob De Sloter. Frans, her erstwhile lover, eventually turns her in, fulfilling the role of Judas, betraying her with a kiss. And De Sloter, wittily embodying the New Testament homily that ". . . a corrupt tree bringeth forth evil fruit," (Matthew, VII,17) as well as the Old Testament image of the serpent, drops spryly out of a tree and thus enters the action. "Are you . . . the Queen of the Road to Kortrijk?" Bob, now on solid ground, inquires of Mira if she is the Queen of the Road to Kortrijk, just as Pilate demanded of Jesus if he were King of the Jews and the Son of God; both of them laconically reply "You say so." "Pilate said unto him, Art thou a king then? Jesus answered, Thou sayest that I am . . ." (John XVIII,37) Bob is as bold in his evil as he is censorious of the evil he presumes to root out in others. A violent, profane individual, he doesn't hesitate to crush his foes inasmuch as he sees himself as a scourge of wrong-doing. But his vision is faulty in that he takes Mira at face value as a low-life hooker, failing to see her exalted inner self. And he is guilty of the greatest wrong in the play, the immediate death of Mira, with a blow to her ear. Thus, he is the representative of that "corrupt tree," society and her institutions. As such, he is Herod, Pilate, Annas, Caiaphus, the Roman centurions, and all the Pharisees combined.

And just in case there is room for doubt of the play's allegorical nature, Claus sets the whorehouse in the neighborhood of the River Lys which George doesn't fail to characterize as "the River Jordan of my heart." This quaint estuary, biblically smelling of flax, is a touch of ancient Galilee running through modern Flanders. And to this bucolic spot, Mimi fondly recalls, used to come all sorts of notables, particularly the real-life celebrated prose writer (of regional novels), Stijn Streuvels, along with a landscape painter, and a furniture maker, unmistakably the three "wise men [who came] east to Jerusalem," (Matthew, II,2) to bless the infant Jesus. Puma actually drew his daughter's name from a novel by Streuvels. The parallel is unmistakable: The Wise Men gave the infant (Mira) its name through the intermediary of its earthly father, Joseph (Puma).

The action of the play is rudimentary enough but, as remarked above, contains a series of, sometimes unobtrusive, sometimes incongruous details, which asequentially but cumulatively intimate the parallel one--Christ's progressive steps to Calvary. Poor Janine (John the Baptist) is dead, and all her clients (converts) have gone respectably underground. Mira repeatedly foresees her own immanent end, and somewhat systematically prepares for it.

Jesus preached "Therefore take no thought saying, What shall we eat? or, What shall we drink? or Wherewithal shall we be clothed?" (Matthew, VI,31), and Mira acts accordingly, rejecting all care to her bodily needs. She will not eat, nor will she conduct business; she explicitly renounces her physical requirements. Her Golgotha commences as she is overtaken by a searing headache, in itself innocuous, but when compared to Jesus' crown of thorns it becomes apparent that her sacrifice has been set into motion. When she goes into her epileptic seizure, George rubs her face with vinegar, an irritating substance that is administered twice to Jesus: "They gave him vinegar to drink . . . ." (Matthew, XXVII,34) and ". . . straightaway one of them ran and took a sponge, and filled it with vinegar, and put it on a reed, and gave him to drink." (Matthew,

XXVII,48). Then an insignificant event for the episode at Golgotha is here repeated in a fashion to heighten Mira's humiliation: her dress tears down the middle. "And they crucified him, and parted his garments. . . ." (Matthew, XXVII,35).

Blood spurts from Jesus' side when assaulted. "But one of the soldiers with a spear pierced his side, and forthwith came there out blood and water." Claus merely resituates the blow from the side to Mira's ear. George knows well that what Mira wants to wear when she is laid out--her dark blue dress. And indeed, it was in a purple robe that they clad Jesus before crucifying him (John, IX,2).

And after her death, despite the play's seemingly naturalistic trappings, the natural world participates in acknowledging the enormity of Mira's sacrifice. A wind rises up and glass shatters. "Now from the sixth hour there was darkness over all the land unto the ninth hour." (Matthew, XVII,45) "And behold, the veil of the temple was rent in twain from the top to the bottom; and the earth did quake, and the rocks rent." (Matthew, XXVII,5) And Bob hastens to effect a cover-up; but Mimi cackles as the stink of the crime must perforce fly back in his own face, implicating him before all the world.

****

The Christ story, apparently ubiquitous in these few dramas by Claus, crops up also in the sober, naturalistic domestic drama, *Friday* (1969). While Claus had had prior success in the theatre, notably with his play *A Bride in the Morning* (Een bruid in de morgen, 1955) which received a production by the famed Pitoëff family in Paris and for his social drama on the subject of labor unions, *Sugar* (Suiker, 1958), yet the 1966 emergence of *Friday* clinched his reputation as a writer for the stage. His own film version of the play (1974) on the touchy subject of father/daughter incest, did nothing to diminish that reputation. Though, perhaps, less adventurous structurally that the other works presented here (and more like other plays of this genre he has essayed (including the two mentioned above as well as *Interieur* (1971) and *Back Home* (Thuis, 1975)), yet it reveals a dramaturgical stolidity and penchant for unflinchingly facing the complexities of painful human interactions that belie Claus' frequent flippant and clever distantiation from suffering deployed in many other works.

Immediately upon curtain's rise, *Friday*'s genre is given away by the "tasteless parlor" that greets the audience's eyes. The Christ story, paralleled through structural units embedded just below the play's action in *The Hair of the Dog* and reenacted wholesale in *The Temptation*, is here present in small, self-effacing details of stage design, sound effect, and casually uttered verbal image.

A statuette of Our Lady that can be lit up from inside presides over the parlor, and George's homecoming is accompanied by a hymn about the Virgin Mary, coincidentally broadcast over the radio. The cosmos subtly invades this drab kitchen of dimly conscious people, adhering even to their dishware. "Yes, the design's [on a new cup] the tree of life they say. A hundred and fifty margarine coupons for the whole set." Just as Eliot's Prufrock measured out his life with coffee spoons, the Vermeersch family's divine accounts are tallied in margarine coupons.

The main characters of the play, George, Jane, and Eric, have committed acts whose enormity is so great, according to the scale of the play, that they cannot be forgiven; and each of them must shoulder the consequences in guilt and humiliation. George has committed adultery with his and Jane's daughter, Christine, who spilled the beans, sending him off for a spell in jail. The prison term was, however, preceded by a sensational trial and visitations by lynch mobs who came to the Vermeerschs' door to revile the whole family. Jane's beauty parlor business has since dried up, and she has been obliged to go to work in a factory, laboring for a minimum wage. While George has been away in prison, Jane has taken revenge with the family friend, Eric, with whom she has produced a child. Through George's unpardonable infidelity to Jane with his own daughter, Jane's unpardonable infidelity to George with his best friend, and Eric's seduction of George's wife--they have thereby all most publicly brought shame down on each other's and their own heads and yet must somehow continue to look each other in the eye and carry on with their lives.

Friday, then, is about forgiveness for the unforgivable--forgiveness of others and forgiveness of self. These people, for whom religion, as is customary in modern times, is a social duty to be acquitted as peremptorily and mechanically as possible, yet, Job-like, are dragged through the spiritual fire of suffering and dropped on the other side, cleansed. George confides that his time in jail has been a spiritual preparation "for the next life," and Jane finds him, now that he is out of it, "like a priest." As he laments:

> You're nothing there, in the dark, and when you breathe too loud there's no one can hear you. And when you drop dead there's no one to help you in that darkest of dark pits. Go ahead and scream. Shriek all you want. Concrete walls and a hole in the ground and you're lying there naked as a worm, screaming until the Dear Lord comes with His hammer and nails and hammers the nails right into your belly.

The George Jane is now surprised to discover home from prison is one who has forsworn eating meat on Fridays and who hangs a crayon drawing of the suffering Christ up on the living room wall, replacing the kitchy advertisement for hair products that had hung there formerly.

The common denominator for all George, Jane, and Eric's shame-ridden acts is sexuality. As George succinctly puts it when referring to the customs inspector, his co-inhabitant in prison, he was also arrested "for his dick." In fact, the sexual organ, in Claus's universe, the organ non pareil of temptation, is what gets everyone in trouble; its removal is the penalty of choice for its wrongful deployment. The lynch mob which came to Vermeersch's door during the hottest days of the incest scandal called out that they'd "cut off his pecker." George, recriminating with Eric for making a cuckold of him, complains, "No sooner do I have my back turned, but you swipe one of my balls." And he jocularly proposes castrating himself so he can get his old job back. If his penis got him into trouble in the first place, then he will have to sacrifice it (figuratively) to make amends.

The "dick," concrete embodiment of irresistible, forbidden passions, gets you into trouble which lead to unbearable trials; but it can also be a catalyst toward spiritual elevation through a chastening, saint-like inner struggle. For George is not entirely cured of his lust for his daughter. The fear of his backsliding haunts both he and Jane even now.

Back on the scene of his old haunts, memories of the past rush in on George, dramatically realized as flashbacks. From the first, in these flashbacks, it becomes clear that Christine, already well into her precocious teens, flirted with George as much as he seduced her. What is especially peculiar about this twisted coupling is the religious tone both George and Christine invest it with. George sings a little church ditty and compares himself with God watching over his little ones. Then he imagines her as a Christ figure, who offers her body to others, not for pleasure or money, but "out of compassion. To wipe out misery." And Christine, too, longs for a way out of her overpowering desires. She dreams of her aunt, who would tell her how to rise above her own impulses. And when George and Christine ultimately do perform the "carnal act," once and once only, the first thing they do is get down on their knees to beg God's forgiveness. Their whole courtship is permeated with theme and variations on sin, redemption, and forgiveness--a peculiar ambient mood for seduction, but one apparently quite enticing to them.

In *The Hair of the Dog* and *The Temptation*, a single character is endowed with Christ-like features and travail. In *Friday*, however, the Christ role is passed from hand to hand, and they all assume it for a time. Throughout the trial and its aftermath, Jane attested up and down to George's innocence. She repeatedly went to visit him in prison, despite his refusal to see her; and she suffered the depredations of public humiliation for a crime she didn't commit. All this she did for George's sake, for during the play's action she admits she was aware of the incest, and that it caused her great suffering to acknowledge it.

George is an obvious Christ figure, as is the customs inspector who goes literally crazy imagining himself to be Christ; and the arrival of the new baby, fresh from Jane and Eric's adulterous relationship, is akin to a Nativity. Is this baby, born of their sin, uncontrolled compulsions, and weakness the Christ child?

> George: Is it [the baby] really ours?
> Eric: Well, it's not the Holy Ghost's, is it?

Certainly, the child born of an adulterous union is traditionally one which calls down the world's pity on it; its very illegitimacy elicits an extra measure of Christian compassion for its vulnerable, helpless status. But to get beyond their sin and suffering for it, the infant's parents must cleanse themselves through a series of personal revelations and literal washing; these latter represent a purging of their temptations and lead to a restoration of the previous order, with George and Jane unifying into a couple once more and Eric taking off for the south of France leaving his job to George. George washes his hands innumerable times. And absolution is sought when Jane and Eric have one last [though pretended] bout of love-making, stage-managed by George, after which he declares: "You're all clean now." It takes this improvised ritual of purgation before he can once again claim his wife as his own. The last gesture of the play is Jane preparing to wash George's hair; and the audience leaves with the biblical resonance of cleansing hanging in the air.

****

Serenade (1984), in contrast to the other plays in this volume, takes a committed dive into the profane figure of modern existence without postulating a sacred ground against which to contrast it. Within the technological wasteland of t.v.'s and walkmen, the only trace of sacred activity is a crazed bag man raving on, reciting the Acts of the Apostles at the top of his voice. Once the sacred element is removed, all that is left is perversity; and *Serenade* is indeed an encyclopedic catalogue of heterosexual depravity: pederasty, incest, castration, overturning sex roles, necrophilia, bestiality, cannibalism, sadism, masochism, and a landscape which puts one in mind of Claus' forbear and countryman, Heironymous Bosch's canvasses of Hell.

Originally written from dreams of four Dutch actresses, Claus extracted each dream's dramatic element and concatenated the resultant vignettes into a comprehensive whole dramatic event, which he originally directed himself. The series of independent, but interlocking scenes has the structure of a surrealist *cadavre exquise*--seemingly disparate parts are connected, but what links them may only be deduced a *posteriori*. The narrative scenes are interspersed with a recurrent one depicting women wheeling shopping carts through a supermarket, spouting disconnected nonsense phrases. The phrases refract microcosmically the seemingly haphazard relationship between the play's scenes. But like the play's single (evincing great restraint for Claus) biblical reference, "In my father's house are many rooms," *Serenade* may, through room-by-room increments be weaving an image of a large house whose contours take some time to resolve to coherence.

The disparate episodes are yet subliminally connected, not only by the strands to the growing web of perversity which is taking form, but by an accumulating complex of images and associations that crop up in one vignette after another. For example, the t.v. program, "Miss Wild World," that is broadcast from the vantage point of the broadcasting studio in one scene is the same program being watched in the living room of a character in an unrelated scene later. Characters in two different, again unrelated, scenes are watching Rod Stewart sing "Passion" on t.v. An airplane (perhaps the same one) inexplicably and irrelevantly flies overhead in two scenes. Likewise Chopin's "Sérénade Mélancolique" is heard in several scenes. A character smells horsemeat in one scene and a character in a different scene is a horsemeat salesman. People continually know each other or remind each other of other people they know.

The first scene, again, though ostensibly unrelated to the subsequent ones, has a kind of connection in that it indirectly kicks off those that follow. A discontented mother is standing on her porch voyeuristically taking in hers and the neighboring children, who are playing out the parts of cartoon characters in a tent; but through all the child's play they are precociously awakening to sex play.

The mother vacillates in her attitude to what she gleans is going on. But following a visit from her respectable, conformity-obsessed neighbor and her husband's return home from work, she dives into the tent with the children to join them in their sexual antics. Her entry into the tent is akin to Alice's down the rabbit hole. And although the character of the mother never explicitly reappears (her name, Monica does, several times), it is her metaphorical dive into the world of the inclusive, unbowdlerized, juvenile imagination which unleashes the torrent of perversity that opens before us in *Serenade*.

The play's sources, dreams, are the keys to the improbable events which are enacted within it. Very often a plausible premise takes an unexpected turn into the world of unconscious wish-fulfillment and the concomitant fear of realization which we associate with dreams; the forbidden or feared inexorably comes to pass, and this includes instances forbidden by conventional morality, as when a bishop starts making love to a cuddly duckling in the middle of a solemn procession. No less are those that might be frowned upon by the Women's Liberation Movement, as when the actress who has been tormented by the male lead playing opposite her deliberately takes his thumb and presses it painfully into her crotch.

This is, in fact, a landscape literally littered with phallic imagery. George Vermeesch's "dick" which represents the congenital curse destined to get him into trouble, is here replicated a thousand-fold. Not only is it to be found in the actor's finger which gets sadistically pressed into the actress' crotch, but it disguises itself as a hot dog eaten by the woman in the railroad car; she calmly munches it as a strange man obnoxiously comes on to her. The hot dog imagistically leads to the man's own penis, which elastically stretches across the entire car and then snaps off his body, pulled by the enraged, molested woman. The phallus reappears in the scene of the young woman who is tricked into looking at her brother's and father's erections beneath the breakfast table, the same young woman whose boyfriend had his penis painted blue, his team color; in another scene, a woman's fondest fantasy is to be able to urinate standing up in imitation of her male relatives; a little girl has to phallically stick her finger in her grandfather's mouth for him to suck on, a desperate measure taken to stifle the profanities pouring out of his mouth. And the radio commentator in yet another scene, reporting on the parade passing by, blithely comments on the Ardennes Rifle Brigade whose "flies are standing open so that the summer evening breeze that's blowing down the street and park, making our flag wave, has free reign up and down its staff. . . ."

Claus, in *Serenade*, as in *The Hair of the Dog* and *Temptation*, sends his characters into seizures. But whereas in the former two plays, the seizures are intervention from divine sources or pathways to divinity, in *Serenade* they serve multiple functions: they may lead to death or orgasm, or revelations. The seizure for Claus is a modern-day equivalent of the classical Greek catharsis. It is clinical but spiritual as well.

****

xviii

I would like to thank the following individuals for their invaluable help in the creation of this book: Bob Elsen, Pol Arias, Clara Haesaert and Diapason, Jack and Magda Van Schoor, Marvin Carlson, Anna Van der Wee, Edwin Wilson, Richard Brad Medoff, Daniel Gerould, Felicia Ruff, and especially to Gretel Cummings, the great actress who first created Sister Mechtild in English.

1990, New York City

CONTENTS

Introduction

THE TEMPTATION

Translated By
David Willinger and Luc Deneulin

Bread is baked every day. Now, so soon? I smell bread. How come no hosts? Every day? The scorched wood, the ovens smell, the sisters sweating.

The matins and the terce. Then later, at long last, the eucharist. And then, O my desire, the inner prayers. Now's the time for the inner self, a quarter past eight, any minute now. And after that in the old days came. . . I remember the old days real good, the knitting, the sewing, the crocheting for the sisters far away on the equator and their shiny-jetsoot-nightblack children who don't have clothes. Chorus prayer. Sext. Chorus prayer. Nones. Compline. Come on.

A robin redbreast in a cage
Puts all heaven in a rage.
My baby didn't have no red breast, it wasn't a baby, it was nothing but a bloodstain. The blood on the floor of the car got washed away, the slimy slit got washed in the hospital.

Hey, I'm awake.
My pallet creaks. I have not merited my bread on this earth. The bread smells warm.
In the sweat of Thy brow. I have not merited. Forgive me.

Back then--you felt a blanket on you. Like for instance when you were cold. Remember, Mechtild? First your skin with the cold lumps, all of a sudden like warts, and your own teensy-weensy hairs, and then after a while something warm, wooly, and stinking hot, real nice even. Every so often, I think.
I confessed it. "Father, I feel the blanket sometimes, and it is. . .I think. . . real nice."
"Yes, so?" he said, gruff. With tobacco on his voice.
"Like a second skin," I said. "Like the skin on milk but then. . . with hair."

"Who?"

"Hair. Hair. Hair." I said, young like I was, angry.

"Sister Mechtild, the stones are popping out of the ground it's so cold. Make sure you stay well under the blankets. We're not talking about mortification here. That's an order. And at your age too! Use your head woman."

"No, Father."

"You want to find yourself back at the Lord's side so soon? Don't tell me that that's what you really want. Please Sister Mechtild."

"Yes Father, it is."

"Do you want to catch pneumonia, is that what you want?"

"If I only could."

"Away. Out of my sight."

The little sliding door slammed shut.

"Yes, Father."

Birds. I lived in farm country back then.

They say that when you lose one sense, the others double up and work twice as hard.

When I could still see things. Robin Redbreast.

Magpies. White and Black. A little lighting bolt with a shadow. He fired. The magpie fell down, plumetting down flapping. Pigeons too. My sister's baby: sick just like a pigeon, pounds dropping off before your very eyes, doctors couldn't even figure it out.

I was in the refectory scrubbing when Sister Colette came to tell me. Sick just like a pigeon.

The sisters are singing. Sister Paula said: "The very, very beautiful-lest thing in the world is my sisters singing." Sister Paula-of-the-Holy-Heart, the dumb goat. What kind of nonsense is that? The beautiful-lest! And that from someone who took the vow years ago.

There can only be one beautifullest.

In the Garden, singing on His hands and knees, clammy from fear and sorrow, and all on account of us, that night when the soldiers will come and take Him.

Forgive me, Sister Paula-of-the-Holy-Heart.

And don't you forget it, you goat! Forgive me, Sister.

In the Garden, daybreak, same as now. He lies there now, sobbing. The day has started. Thanks Mechtild. You can still tell the difference. Thanks for the difference between light and less light.

Sisters singing. I have to scratch, but I don't. First intention of the day.

The Tract for the common mass for a virgin martyr.

Today it's for Clara. Third-rate mass.

Clara ran away from home. To the Benedictines.
It was Saint Francis himself who cut her hair off. You can still see the scissors on a velvet cushion in Italy. Clara did so much self-mortification that everybody got scared, and they didn't scare so easy back then in the time of Saint Francis. It was what was that year? I used to know the year. She was sick for thirty years, Clara was.
So don't you complain, Mechtild. Not you.
Veni, sposa Christi, they sang.
Mud in my ears. So many pigeons. The water runs out of my eyes.

Can't see, but shrieks enough for three. I'm supposed to say "shriek-ing," says Sister Clarissa. I'm not supposed to say "bawling." It's indecent.
"What does a dog on a chain do?" says I.
"The dog barks," says Sister Clarissa.
"No, no, no, dogs bawl," say I.
She just stood there with her mouth full of teeth. "You're being diffi-cult, Sister Mechtild."
For a hundred years now I've been saying "bawling." Father said it, Mother said it, everyone around where we lived in Heule said it. Bawling, that's what we said for dogs.
But everything changes so quick. Me too. Even though I don't want to. Only He doesn't change. Never. Thanks.

It's going to rain, I can feel it in my fat legs. They're killing me. Thanks.
I need to scratch, but I don't. Ankles, knees, calves, they're killing me. It is good so. It gets worse every day, every hour. Sometimes I think I've got seven blankets on me, and that all seven are rubbing, sanding me down. Against my carbunkles.

Back in the days when I could still see my toes, they were blue, almost black.
Sometimes I see glass, milky, dull glass. Light. A parel-lel-o-gram. Light. It must be Spring.
Veni, veni, veni. In May, in May, in May.
"Mechtild," my husband said, "you can't carry a tune at all!"
"No, Joseph."
He didn't actually call me Mechtild. I was called something else back then. Now I'm Sister Mechtild. I used to be somebody else back then. My cell changed me.
I'm not supposed to use the word "cell." It's a "room" now. The room smells of me. Even though I can't smell. A nose like a stone. A stone packed with cotton wool.

Your hair falls out, lies next to you, and then your cheek feels it. Fingernails rip, petals from a flower.
Flowers are little pieces of skin with prickles on 'em, that much I still know. Lo-be-lia.
Elbow broke. Other elbow broke too.
And I'm seeping out from all sides.
They say they can sew guts back together.
What are you doing, Mechtild? Drawing up an inventory, hmm? Thighs burst open, sugar in the blood. Haha! And the ruined thymus, the bruised glands, the mashed ear.
It is good so. Thanks.

The last thing I saw, the shadow of a shrub on the pebbles.
Then everything went gray before my very eyes.

I used to have brows, lashes. They held back the sweat. Many winters back, through the little window, an airplane. Winters further back, whole nights full of airplanes and sirens.

The sisters cluck, chatter. It was unbearable in the beginning when we were first permitted to speak. After all those happy times, the silent time, to have to get used to words again: month and man and moon and mouth.'The sisters laugh. That's the worst part. Satan laughs. The lamb doesn't laugh. It bleats, it weeps.

He revealed His fiery heart to Lutgardis in the 13th century, to Gertrudis in the 14th century, and to Mechtildis, the one from Helfede. Sweet Heart.

The sisters babble, they tell jokes, they over-sleep, drive cars, eat spaghetti. And one of them, who shall remain nameless, smoked a cigar, and she got it from a reverend father too.

I can see You better than with my eyes. When I see You in the dark of my sleep, then I make in my bed. It's all Your fault. I may not see You. I may not think on You. It is my pride.
Or should I store up all my thoughts of You in a little corner of my brain? Save You for later? The day is long. You won't wear out if I think on You, or if I think not on You. It's the pride of joy, and that joy must be crushed, otherwise there can be no atonement, and only atonement can please You.

Don't answer me. Not yet. Never. Because if You did, then I might stop hungering after You. Water in my eyes and my mouth like from a great hunger.
Enough! Away with You. Just for now, my Sweet Heart, just for

now.

Sister Bertken smells like a drugstore. I ask for no explanation on the subject. Nothing personal. We're not going to start in on that, now are we Mechtild? Even though I have dispensation, I will not talk.
The bed grunts, squeaks. Almost as loud as me. The bed is an object belonging to the world. Like me. Me, who was ordered not to be an object belonging to the world. "THEREFORE HATH GOD ANOINTED YOU WITH RADIANT OILS GLISTENING."
I *am* listening.
Wrists are killing me. I sit.
Relax. Teeth bleeding.
Filthy thing, Mechtild.

"All this self-mortification and over-doing of atonement gives us cause for worry, Sister."
"Yes, Father, yes, Father." (He was chewing tobacco, the smell from it seeped into the drenched wood of the confessional.) (He slammed the little door shut.)
I hauled myself up. Yes, Father. I'm crazy about Him and it doesn't matter to me that you didn't give me absolution (forgot to), since He, the one I love like a backward farm-girl, He never gives absolution either, He doesn't. And MAN DOESN'T BELONG TO HIMSELF.
I may be babbling, but at least I know I'm babbling.
"HAVING NOT THE MEANS,
NARY A STITCH,
HAVING NO DISTINCTIONS."

Novices, postulants, sisters, they all sing on account of my feast day. Name days, birthdays, you could count on them back then. I had another name back then. But I won't ever say it again. No, I will not burn myself on that glowing red-hot thread that runs from Mechtild to the one before.

"Your feet are totally black now," said Sister Bertken.
"You'll have to go see Doctor Bruyninckx," said Mother Superior, it can't go on like this. You hardly eat, and still you keep on gaining weight. Just look at that belly."
"It's water, Mother."
"Then that water has to go."
"Those black feet," said Sister Bertken, "it's black blood."
"It is good so." That's what I said.
Black and cold, every part of me like my feet, that's how I shall be, and it is good so. Warmth is for the others who think of Him as a source of pink, cozy, bright heat. But He is cold. Gaudete justi. I want to be as is His cold. Icicles for thoughts.

In the beginning. Not in the beginning of the beginning, because my soul was blind like a mole then, but in the beginning when my eyes started going blind at first. I laid my palm on the glowing pipe from the stove in the refectory, and then did I grieve over a lovely thing like the blindness of my body. It was a dumb, mad, silly grief, because not of Him.

And that feast day is today. Any minute now. In fact it's already started, because they're singing for me. But I mustn't keep on rattling around in my own self. He makes the day begin, the feast is for Him alone, even if He doesn't want it, because He alone is festive, with chorales and choirs. Temptation. Temptation.

The vegetable garden. I wore wooden shoes back then. The cloister garden. I knew the name of all the plants and shrubs. But that second Vatican Council, in ten years time they changed everything, sisters walk around in short dresses, and they don't say "Reverend Mother" anymore, just "Sister." The hosts are baked abroad.
There never used to be any light in my cell before. We never ate meat.
And yet You rejoice? (EVEN IN THE OCEAN OF SORROWS BOTH SUFFER AND REJOICE.)
Here in my stubborn darkness.
The darkness of the snow.
Because it pleaseth Him.
I'm tumbling through the dunes, sand in my eyes, on all fours, I sing, a squeaking sack of water and grease.
Expect nothing. No salvation. No order or comfort or security. Ah, that thirst.
With my knees broken, like a she-bitch, towards your odor.
And my teeth chattering.
Like she did, the whore, the bitch, when she washed His feet with her long, soft hair.

"Sister Mechtild."
"Sister Bertken. Now, so soon? What's that? Flowers, silver paper."
"Lilies."
(What I don't say is: "His body is a hill, white with lilies.)
I say: "Thanks."
She, Sister Bertken, pulls my sheets off. "It's the most beautiful day of our lives. Oh, if I didn't have a good grip on myself, would I ever be jealous of you! I couldn't sleep a wink on account of my nerves. I brought you a new veil. Can you feel it?"
"My own veil is good enough."
"No, Sister, it hasn't been ironed in years. Mother Superior says that

on this festive occasion. . . ."
(Back then: The Rule. The silence. A magpie.)
"Come now, Sister Mechtild. Upsy-daisy. One, two, two and a half makes three!"
I'm a bale of barren grass.

The cheery voice of little Sister Bertken is bubbling along. Sometimes it isn't love that makes people happy, but nature. Heaven can inflict this on some people. But these are not necessarily the best of the lot.
It's her, Sister Bertken. "All the sisters are waiting in the refectory. And there's chocolate sprinkles on the bread. And something very special for you, Sister Mechtild."
"I stink."
"Hah, you can say that again! When was the last time you set foot in a bathtub?"
"Mind your own business."
"Do you think this is pleasing to the Lord?"
(He turns away from me, holds His nose shut, and He proclaims: She is shit!)
(One day the sisters tried to drag me into the bathtub on orders from Mother Superior. I fought and bit. And then I froze in the icy water.)
(My sins, my sins.) "Go away, Sister, I'll get dressed."
(Fire brands in my skin, charcoal stains on my soul.)

My love, my cancer.
Rabboni, master. Keep away from me.
Hey? Where are You?
Do I disgust you? Good, I'm glad. Just go back to Your Father.

Right through the grease, the fire, and the ripping . . . Meeow! Who just meeowed? Ooh, it was me. Even my skeleton's killing me. It would be base and vile of me to ask You to cure me. I may not ask so trivial a thing of You.

"O Sister Mechtild."
There's that weak quavering voice, it's Sister Hildegarde, she comes from Alvoorde, her father was a flower grower. She's got gout and smells of straw.
I guess grace can come to just anyone.
"Oh Sister Mechtild, come now, give me your arm."
Get away from me. I'd rather break both my legs.
"Does it hurt?"
"No more than usual. I'm just not used to walking, that's all."
"Not so fast." Panting. Strumae.
"We killed a little lamb. For you. For your feast."

"I don't eat meat."

"But we sure do, don't we Sister Bertken? And especially today. In honor of Sister Mechtild's feast."

"And the lamb's mother, the sheep, was she there when the little lamb's throat was cut and when it was skinned?"

"Of course not."

The sheep saw it all from a distance, from the meadow, the stable. And she lost her fleece in sorrow. Thick swatches of wool lying in the grass, wads of wool blowing around the orchard.

In the year now what is it? Before the other war, something dropped out of me. It was living, quivering. It fell onto the floor of the car into the dust, and hung off me by a pink and yellow bloodbespattered gut.

My husband wanted to call it Anna.

Saint Ann carries a flowering branch in her hand and holds it out as an offering to anyone who will accept it. There's a little girl sitting on her lap.

I've seen Ann quite often, but my father confessor doesn't want me to tell anybody.

OBEDIENT, PURE, AND POOR, that's the Rule. I may not laugh at it. I couldn't laugh even if I wanted to. I can hardly breathe.

"Sister Mechtild, you don't have to hurry, but . . . keep moving, Sister. Ally-oop. Let's go. Come on. Right."

"Because we can't be late. Everything has to go according to the schedule, understand? The whole ceremony."

"Don't push."

"Stay off her back, Sister." "Forgive me. I forgot."

The rips down my back, the running sores, that she forgets. Ha! Some sisters! It is joy, sisters. There is the essence of love, and then there is the other thing, the act of love.

"Ten yards to go. Look, they're waiting for us."

You, help me to get through this silly march to that feast.

No, never mind. You keep Your hands to Yourself too.

"How old are you now, how old are you n-oo-ow?"

I can feel them looking at me. O, keep your sheep eyes to yourselves, you nuns who I must call sisters.

There are three tables; the second is the special one under the clock; the first table, the one they're bringing me, dragging me, hauling me to, is for the old people.

Then there are three clocks, the big one belongs to Jesus, a smaller one, the village clock belongs to Saint Teresa (who beat the tamborine and got her sisters to dance), and a shabby little clock, the one that plays the Angelus for the dead.

The first time I sat at the third table, I was so ashamed to see the skullery sisters, the sweat streaming out of them, silent and downtrodden, I can still see it now, ashamed, furious, sad. Because I was supposed to be a wise virgin, a clever one, and not like them, virgins, maids, cooks, frumps.

"You come sit on my right, Sister Mechtild. Do you want some honey? Chocolate milk?"
"I can't eat anything, Mother."
I could eat three loaves of bread, two jars of cherry jam. I have a mouth of tin and a cast-iron stomach. That's what my father said back on the farm when my mother told him to watch out, that the buttermilk mush was too hot.
I see him all the time, he is sitting on a smoking dungheap that's on fire, and he's sizzling.
"Sister Bertken, she hasn't set one foot in a bathtub.!"
"She didn't want to, Mother Superior."
I say: "I am very disobedient, Mother."
"Well, it's not so important today. Drink some chocolate milk. Here. Careful now."
(And she whispers: "Sister, in my room, on the sink to the left, you'll find a spray can, Bidex Deodorant in blue letters. Because she can't be around people the way she is!")
Evil all around me. Evil within me.
I am despair and I am evil.
They're just plain evil.

There's a radio playing while we eat.
The sister's go home every so often now. The time my mother died, I wasn't even allowed to go then.
Now we've got cells with wallpaper with flowers and puppets and garlands on it. They play cards or ping pong from time to time, I hear them enjoying themselves.
The window bars have been done away with. And the compline. And the invisible grace.
He scratches in my hair while I sleep.
And I don't take communion often enough, says Mother Superior, well, that makes her sad and Deacon Nachtergaele says so too, she says.
I had been difficult one particular Whitsuntide, and then I had to take communion in my cell. I shook and trembled. And that's when Deacon Nachtergaele said: "This is not a sacrament involving pain." And since then, never again. If I did take communion the way they think is so heavenly, then there'd be unity
HAVING NO DISTINCTIONS.
He must not come in me. Since then He'd be my child and I His

mother and His mother for to be is too small a thing for me.

"Sister Mechtild, it's time."

(I used to be called Madeleine, Madou, Malaise. When I had time. Time, unity, duration. What I went through, that never-ending movement. I thought that was real, that I, this creature, was real.) I thought that His whole life, from His infancy 'twixt ox and ass, till He turned into that hundred and twenty pounds of flesh and bones all went by on the cross in a single flash. And then His Father left Him grievously stuck up there on that mountain with the gallows.

That's not time. There is another kind of time. Or no time at all. (It's just an invention, a habit, a belief.) But I'm just rambling around in my head. Mother Superior sits me up straight. Sister Cecilia runs a damp cloth over my face.

"Mother, may I go back to my cell, I'm sorry, I mean my room?"

"Don't be difficult, Mechtild. No crying. Let's go."

She gives me her arm. Two fat farmers under one umbrella.

"We're behind schedule," says Sister Bertken. And sprays a sour vapor all over my clothes and my hands that prickles and itches. Mother Superior sticks a little pill in my mouth, makes me drink chocolate milk.

My stomach gurgles and tosses. Macula. Sposa Christi.

"Mommy, I want to go to my room."

"No, Madou, you stay here. Stand up straight."

"I don't want to set eyes on that man."

"Madou, he only has your interests at heart. He's got a shining future ahead of him. With shining jewels on your fingers too. And he's a member of the church fund.

"He strips me with his eyes, Mommy."

"Has he ever touched you?"

"Yes. No."

"It's a sacrament."

"He means to turn me inside out, Mommy!"

It was before the Germans came, for the first time. All those cold tight movements as night fell and he told me that I was the prettiest girl in town. His name was Joseph. Then in the mirror on my closet, I saw over my husband's shoulder, I saw it, that shiny sheep eye glaring out and not letting me go, it just kept looking. When he finished with his moving, my husband Joseph screamed like a peacock and rolled over.

Prussian soldiers in town. The car was driving to the hospital. Then the too-soft rubber wall in me broke and the warm water streamed out onto the floor and the thing fell out between my knees.

That little pill the treacherous Superior gave me is called Valium.
It calms you.
She says that they're going to pay tribute to all the sisters, surviving
and dead, in my name, at the Monument for the War Dead, and that
the whole town council will be there, and the bishop too, and that I'd
better still my pride. "Forgive me Mother." She talks about Lord
Jesus as if he was a whip cream cake. But I don't know that Lord.
His portrait's hanging in all the hallways, that much I still remember
from back then. And used to think, "he must be some distant rela-
tive." That's all.

It fell without any audible plop. It had purple hands and feet, and
wet, red hair. It rolled out of me like a turd. The car had iron wheels.
Every joint inside me cracked. I ripped.

"The Canon's got a Mercedes," says Sister Bertken. "My brother has
one just like it, only a little smaller."
Police sirens go along with us as we drive. Sister Bertken holds onto
my hand.
I can feel daylight. It's unbearably hot.
I can't make out what the Canon and the Mother Superior are going
on about. About the seating arrangements on the dais. Lift me by
my veil up out of this gliding seat. Grab my thin hair and drag me
away from them. Slam my ridiculous fat carcass onto the street
stones.
But the more I beg, the more you keep your distance. You promise
and You promise and it is good so. And believed, You are believed.
Thanks.
Let me stay the way I am, even if I suffocate here in my darkness, in
my dark existence that's riding in a Mercedes, in the smell from a
spray can and my diabetic body.

"Madeleine. Don't leave me.
"You've been good to me. But you should never have set foot in my
father's house.
And never poked around in my belly the way you did."
"Madeleine."
"You should never have spoken to me, because I bring people bad
luck. There is no room here for you anymore. Not one square inch
in my whole soul for you anymore.
Forgive me, Joseph."
"I can't."
"Pray for me."
"Are you trying to bury yourself alive?"
"I can't help it, Joseph."
"You're not the first woman to lose a child."

"Yes, but other women didn't lose their children because they were being punished, not because He was jealous as is His right. He had every right in the world to tear that baby out of me and bespatter my thighs."
"I always thought He was goodness itself!"
I laughed so hard I got a cramp. It was killing me, and wouldn't stop.
"Him? Him? Him? Goodness itself?"
"How can I go on living?"
"Then just die, Joseph."

The ridge in the distance was called Monte Calvario. Palm trees. Children playing with a fishbone-thin pig. In the sea there lay a silver war-ship. In the Bay of Naples. When I renounced affection. On account of You. Who I know not. Sweet Heart. You who promised. And then wanted no more to do with me. Even back then. You didn't stop punishing me. You left me lying like a dishcloth in a corner of the refectory, in with the brushes and brooms. And you still do.

Ceremony. Fanfares. Speeches. The bishop blesses the gathering. They said all sorts of things about me. As though I was a pastel colored picture, a holy card at a funeral, or a postage stamp. Not the tepid, gray cavern full of shit that I am, the grimy grave. When it was over, Sister Bertken wiped the sweat off my face with a kleenex that scraped my forehead. The car growled and glided along.
"There are going to be a lot of big shots," she whispered, and stuffed the hair under my cowl. "Sit up straight."
And I did. And spun my ring around my finger, the one from my cruel, unfaithful betrothed, who I hardly know. The one who spits on me while I sleep.
"Arthur," said the Canon, eating peppermints, "we're in no rush. Because we can't be too careful with Sister Mechtild, especially now that she's received the Order of Leopold II, right Sister?"
"Answer!" hissed Mother Superior into my ear.
The car cushions were soaking wet with fluid, the shit, and the blood.

"I don't mean to be presumptuous," says the Canon, "but I've heard from a reliable source that it occasionally pleases the Lord to offer you a glimpse of His mystery in the form of. . . ."
He waits. So do I. Car honking.
"Of angels, she says," says Mother Superior, the tattle-tale.
"Just so, just so," the Canon shouts triumphantly.
"I may say nothing about that."
"Did it seem to you that the angels were really there in the flesh and blood?" He laughs. On account of me.
I say: "Your Reverence, you're laughing your soul away."

"You hit the nail right on the head," he says. I hear his false teeth clacking and scratching.

"Have you got enough room for your legs?" he asks.

"Mind your own business."

"We can't take her anywhere," says Mother Superior in a low voice.

"Is she car-sick?" asks Arthur, the driver.

"Arthur, would you mind pulling up the window?"

"Your Reverence, we may not speak of Him, and we may not think on Him."

"Only pray? Just so, just so, Sister Mechtild."

"We must forget. . . all things in creation."

"Do you have to throw up, Sister?"

"Come, lean back against me. Quiet now," says little Bertken.

"Back then, almost from the first, He revealed Himself. And that He stayed hidden from me, that's my own fault. I was the cause of my own calamities."

"Just so, just so."

"And then the eyes of my soul opened wide."

"Then you are indeed blessed, Sister Mechtild."

"No!" Where'd he ever get that idea?

"Turn off by the City Hall, Arthur. And now Sister Mechtild, we have to put our best foot forward."

During the reception, they take hold of my hands and murmur things. Sister Bertken says: "Mind your manners, Sister. Still a half hour to go. Please."

"Is she car-sick?"

"At her age."

"Does she still have visions?"

"Stigmata?"

"A great honor, Sister, a pearl on the crown of our religious life here in our beautiful West Flanders."

"It's not only on account of your advanced age, however much that too is a sign of grace, but for your exemplary piety."

"His Eminence will be here any minute now."

"And other dignitaries too."

(Take not Your Name in vain. No, not idly.)

(We hasten to You. Days, nights without You.)

(Hunger and darkness, that is You.)

"Sister," says the voice.

That's all it says, and I wake up. Sister Bertken gives me a shove and tugs at my dress since I'm supposed to curtsy now, but I stay there stiff as a board, screwed into my veil. It's my husband's voice, I mean my brother, Joseph. "Your blessing be on us and on our convent, Eminence," says Mother Superior. "Forgive Sister Mechtild. Her health lately. . . ."

Because I called out, whinnied. I couldn't help it. The devil takes the shape of what we love (or have loved). O, UPROOT WHAT YOU LOVE.

He coughs politely, and says confidentially, like in a confessional or a bed: "We have heard so many fine things about you, Sister, more than about anyone else in our bishopric."

They present me to so many different personages that I don't have time to guess at who they all are. I'm getting too carried away, taken up with his voice, taken up with his being. And all the while I hear them talking about all different orders, veterans, missionaries, aldermen, strangers every one. But Joseph says, laughing, jolly as if he were in a café: "You're a bigger draw than the bishop, Sister. And that's the way it should be."

Sister Bertken or Mother Superior gives me a shove on the behind, means to make me fall. A bunch of lightening bolts. I gasp. Rustling, click, click, I feel the light snapping like a scissor, the photographers don't stop talking, I can't make out what my new-found Joseph is saying.

Has he gone?

"Joseph!"

"Quiet!" says Mother Superior.

"Maybe she's feeling closed in. It's pretty warm in here. Come along. The parlor's got air conditioning."

Somebody pushes me into a cold leather chair. I want to go back to my pallet and the chalky smell of the wall.

As the lightning shoots through the air--my little sister and me, we grabbed onto each other in the orchard. Daddy called us inside and swore at us, but we didn't budge--only at times like those do you see how pale, how humbled, how lost we are.

"Joseph."

Sister Bertken's cool, thin fingers hand me a glass. If I bit down on those fingers. . . I don't. If bit down on the glass. . . I don't.

"The devotion for Saint Joseph (the Canon, drawing out his words, peppermint) is a very rare occurrence."

"And yet he is the protector of our church."

"The patron saint of Belgium."

"He concerns himself with our good death." (Sister Carmen, a young foal.)

In the voice of a doctor examining a wound: "Didn't he have marital relations with Mary after Jesus's birth?"

"Not necessarily," says the Canon.

Hangmen have as much right to love as anyone. I say:

"We're supposed to burn a candle for him the third Wednesday after Easter."

"Just so, just so."

Then something happens that should never. He comes over and says: "Do you still remember me, Sister?"
"Yes, Brother."
The doctor, also right there chuckles: "Brother Eminence."
He clears his throat, he smokes too much. Just like before, in the many rooms of our house.
When we saw the volcano, the black water.
When he taught me about innocent lust.
When our child was saved from the hell of this world.
"I have sought you out." You didn't, you never sought me. The gentle disaster, the horrible disgrace, the happiness which unhappiness is, that's what sought me out, Him and no other!
"When you were eighty, I pinned His Holiness's medal on you."
I nod.
"There was a beautiful picture of you two together in the newsletter, Eminence," says Mother Superior, and drinks and slurps. Sisters read newspapers these days. In my day, when everything was silent: only clippings on religious subjects and ceremonies.
"I remember you very well," I say.
He growls, coughs. Turns away.
"It was the same year that Sister Anna Seton was beatified,"
says Sister Carmen almost inaudibly.
"Delicious petits fours."
"Sister, I'm Jules Hendriks from the land registry. May I be permitted to drink to your health with this Vouvray?" (He shouts at me as though I were deaf.) "May you live many more long and pious years."
"Don't say that."

"How much do you weigh now? Two hundred twenty? More?"
Doctor Steenhuizen scolds me. I'm not listening to him, he says, and I don't move around enough, he says. Hadn't I promised him to exercise ten minutes every day? Swedish gymnastics?
"You're letting yourself go, Sister, that's no good."
"No, doctor." I really tried, but my beloved didn't want me to. He saw me right through the chalk walls of my cell. How I was doing dumb things, and puffing, and trying to reach my toes, and my beloved hooted at me and stamped on my stomach and I fell down and broke my hip in three places.
My bridegroom here on this earth, my eternal light, my spy, my beleaguering love.

"Vanderveken from the County Government. To your health, Sister."
"Don't say that."
"I am Father Angelus, Sister."

"You?"

A mean laugh. "My black children call me N'gelus. Daddy N'gelus. They thought I was a dangerous man because I had blue eyes."

I want to go lie on the ground and eat chestnuts.

Sister Bertken holds onto my shoulder.

Magpie. Black and white lightning bolts. The thick water in my skull. I'm swaying, the wood of my chair is cracking.

"Please, Sister Mechtild. It won't be long now. Then we'll drive over to the Memorial for the War Dead. For the wreath-laying."

"And then?"

"Then we'll have lunch with the mayor."

I cry. I'm entitled to. He said: "Cry not for Me, but for yourselves and for your children."

Sister Carmen is wiping off my face with a cloth.

"Quiet," she says, she the quiet one, who's usually leaping down the hall like a foal. She's only a little girl. She lays eggs just like the birds, snakes, and crocodiles. I kiss her warm hand, my mouth glides along her wrist. I hear her wiping off her hand.

"Eminence."

"Joseph," I say. "Do you remember how I carved holes out of my hands and feet, and around my heart with a potato knife? You looked at me as if I was a mongoloid.

Why did you take me back? To test me? You who are jealous and rotten, taken up into His arms. You were spiteful and jealous, and you had every right to be. You didn't see it, you didn't see Him, you said. And you had every right not to. Because He is not a person. He can't be admired, He can't entrance you, He can't be known. That's what Saint Bernard said. If I knew Him, I'd know myself.

Noverim te, noverim me.

And yet is He closer than my closest close.

He hasn't changed, with his ears sticking out, his red worker's hands, I can see them as if I had eyes. He took care of me. Yes Mommy, you're right, he is good to me and the sacrament is valid after all.

But not for me, with my disgusting pride, with my hay fever, my stink, my God.

"Sister Mechtild?"

"She's sick."

"Or drunk. From that one little glass!"

"Yes, Mother. I am your servant."

"I'm ashamed for you, Sister."

"Don't worry about what others think, Mother."

Joseph, my dead husband of this earth, I'm sorry. I could never tell

you while you were on this earth. Don't turn away. Don't look at all those others, the ones who are perfectly happy just to kneel down before that Jew on the cross, those who give no offense as I do now. Gaudete justi!
Go look for him in the pictures of your prayerbook and be happy. Get working on your immortality kids, just like it was homework. I loved you, Joseph, like I loved the child I was expecting when my breasts were swollen up with milk. I chose Him because I could do no other. Like that old swine chose Saint Anthony.

He comes over and sits down next to me. He sends Mother Superior away.
He's talking like he used to in the café, not the way he did in our bedroom.
"Redemption," he says, "or temptation?
Or reconciliation between the spiritual and the world, between the rational and faith? "Faith," he says, "mustn't be kept under glass like a beautiful ornament. The three thrological virtues are possible for everyone, not just clergy. Leave off the folklore, Sister Mechtild.
We can even work alongside progressive and Jewish scholars to spread the word of God."
Only then I notice that he's not talking to me, but to the Canon, and the man from the land registry. And they're answering.
"Mount Olympus isn't so very far from the Gospel, all things considered."
"Christ was crucified with his back to the Arabs and Jews and His face to the North, in our direction, that of the Flemish people."

They're putting off my love.
My sin is that I hear rumors from the world.
SISTERA MAY NOT PREACH OR INSTRUCT, BUT MUST ASSIST MEN WHO DO SO WITH THEIR PRAYERS.
"Joseph," I say, "you wept for your child. So did I. Not for very long, but long enough. I wanted to bask in His impenetrable decreEs. But then I saw the perfection of His righteousness, and now am I the object of His will, that and nothing more. He's cooking me like mush. He who will comfort and console me is of the devil."

What are they talking about anyway?
"She is protected by her precious ignorance, Eminence."
"Secular utopias are not the answer for her either."
"While faith ought not to be a private matter, it must absolutely be a constituent element in any new social ordering."
Are they drunk? What was it? Vouvray? Wormwood? Vinegar?
"Not only desirous of being an element proper to God, but in fact. . . to be the unifying element proper to everyone. . . ."

"Holding out the universal justice not only to future generations, but also to the dead, those sacrificed to history."
"Christian hope is there for all, the hope for what we call resurrection, right or wrong?"
I shove the soft sister's hand away. I thought that I was the blind one, hopeless, closed-in, fat and lazy and dark, but it's they who are! I sing and the meeting comes to a halt, the reception grows silent. I'm singing at the top of my lungs, I can't hold a key and I can't keep time, but my voice echoes against the walls, against the Pharisees.

I am the vixen, I am the mourner,
I am the cord, I am the fox,
I am the hedge, I am the liver!

"That's what I like to see! At her age and still so full of piss and vinegar!"
"Saint Theresa was pretty spry too, don't forget."
"The next verse, Sister."
"Encore, encore."
The sisters hiss. The Canon cautions them. Mean, muffled laughing. I sink down into my chair, and cover over my blind eyes. Don't help me, don't pamper me, don't sedate me. I stick out my hand and a glass slips into it, I gulp it down, a biting cold.
"Hooray!"
"To your health."
"What a constitution. I'd trade mine for hers any day."
The sisters keep on whispering and hissing. I try to sit up, but too suddenly. Fall back down. Pain. Everywhere. It is good so.

I breathe so deep that it crackles. I say: "Now is my joy complete. I must become even less than I am. Don't laugh, Joseph. I can hear you. I know you. It's true that you afflicted me in a prior life, yes, as a brother in God, you did. Admit it, brither.
There were no oceans then on the earth, and yet You were there, true or not? No calendars or crosses or safes, yet You were already reigning and letting the world see Your face full of love, weren't You, my foster father?
Now You turn a book-keeper's face to the world, now that this season is upon us, the season of the caterpillars. For souls have to be saved, like capital earning interest. You shrewdy! Learn about mankind? Sand in everyone's eyes!
Your brother needs you, otherwise you wouldn't be here, you crumb! But you don't see with His eyes. I can sense them, your eyes, they want to console me. Well get your ass out of here, little god, you with the consoling eyes.
And I don't want your charity either. Gratitude wears you down. I

can't concern myself with something as crumby as virtues. No people, no fashions, no names. Except names like scabies, sister snot, sister shit.

But how then? Having no hows.

Why? Having no whys.

So, brother, you want to live forever, do you? A Greek idea. Oh, yes, you want to resurrect and hunt Easter eggs unto eternity. Then do it. Go ahead, believe in so paltry a thing as your soul eternal, and believe in the triumph of your earthly skin. Be born again, you jerk.

My dearest Joseph, how could you resurrect, how could you want to? It's a longing for something else than yourself. It's a longing for death, like the fulfillment of desire. It's disgusting, husband mine.

Do you want to hear about your brother? He is my heart and my guts. He is not good, He is not evil. He claims only everything, judge He, police He. Even Lazarus, once resurrected, died again from misery and despair, all because he took refuge in the desert after the miracle, for Lazarus loved His person as himself. But He is not a self, He is a stranger, syphilitic, toothless, and He laughs, He's crumbling to pieces like a leper, He howls with pleasure at still births, He has no soul, He doesn't know the meaning of the word soul, my bridegroom doesn't, when my soul is ravished and forgets all impressions of the senses He cracks up, my Sweet Heart shoves a stick in my wheel while I'm rolling, He plays with me like a ball, even as He strips my soul naked till I lose every possession, every image, every form, I have Him not, He is but what He is and what I must become, having no why's, having no means, having no distinctions. And His promises, let's not get into that, His lies and masks and effects and contrasts, always running the same strophes by, sing-song, disgusting, and we are but running through a desert, a chasm, and straying we throw ourselves into the cesspool and then must become what we are. But never may we throw ourselves into His special works. Oh no, never that. The Rat! Domine!

He works not, rests not,

He gives off no warmth, He has fish blood,

He exacts cold, hunger, illness, contempt, drought,

How could I ever refuse?

How? Me in my trough?

How could I ever care for the taste of the wafer? He, He, salty as brine, bitter as iodine, stinking like rotten eggs, He is all through my clothes, is in there, snoring there, dancing there, He is thin, He is dead, He is deformed, and with my dumb impatience, I want no more of words, reasons, signs, works, virtues, I want--Domine--deformed as I am in Your image,

dippipult, slinfy,

to Your prophetic snout, washering over Your jaws, help,

with threadbares, bilitated, mells, O Him, Him, Him."

(All down my thighs, the lukewarm stream.)

Him come into mine, singingworm, and cockaroacher, for I am His lesser, the verycutestlittlesest, a bed, a bed in contrarie, that Him is there, but nots for me, and I, dumb shrit, find Him not guiltier of closer by, carabunkles and warty rippers in my budbody, strinking, smelting in my inner castle, I am content because He laughs at me, my sweet poison, my sin. The voice of the Lord is a singing, double-edged sword, and the one sound is of holiness and the other is of blood and guilty substances. Tapeworm, hook Yourself into me by Your head. Please do. Cheat me, keep right on betraying me, O my softness self."

The bishop's name isn't Joseph Malaise at all, but Aloysius de Tremerie. (After Aloysius van Gonzaga who was twenty three when he died and blushed at being alone in a room with his mother.)
The sisters took me away, snivelling with shame, full of feeble excuses.
That it was a weakness of bladder. At my age too. "It is only human," came the answer. The Persian carpet got rolled right up and carried off. That it was probably on account of that one glass of Vouvray. That Sister Bertken ought ot have taken precautions and taken me to the you-know-what. That the carpet would be cleaned and dried. That the stain and the smell would be removed.
"Take her away," said Mother Superior, resigned.
"Where?" Sister Carmen.
"To the you-know-what."
"And where is it, Reverend Mother?" Sister Bertken.
"Ask."
"I wouldn't dare."
"There, down the hall somewhere."
"And what if it's only for men?" Sister Carmen.
"Then say it's an emergency."
"Come. Alley-oop," said the two angels, my sisters, and then they dragged me here.
They're waiting in front of the door.

Time passes. Even for me who said that there was no such thing as time. But what I meant was: TIME PASSES FOR US, NOT FOR HIM.
The sisters are praying in front of the door.
They don't pray to be tormented, but to be released.
And to be released from me too.
And from time to time they drum on the door. It's locked.
I bit Sister Bertken, in her shoulder, I think, when she tried to come in with me in order to wash me.

Tormented by all that is foreign to You, by all that is not entirely You. And as for the peeing: YOU MUST EMPTY OUT THAT YOU MAY BE FILLED ANEW.

Mother Superior comes over to the door by the two sisters.
She bangs and shrieks and burbles.
"It doesn't matter in the least, Sister Mechtild. Nobody noticed anything.
Don't be ashamed. Open up that door.
And the carpet can be cleaned right up with a MacCleaning. With a special foam.
Are you trying to make a scandal, Sister?
I am not angry with you, Sister.
Fine, if you want to be stubborn that way, then just stay in there. Do you hear me? Say 'yes, Reverend Mother.' Come on now."
Sister Hildegarde: "What if she had a heart attack . . . or something like that?"
Mother Superior, dead tired: "Her? She is the last nail in my coffin."
I flush in answer.
Some men are putting their two cents in now. They start to go off to get screwdrivers and axes.
Monte Calvario. The houses were lighted by oil lamps. The warmth like lukewarm water over your face.
A little while later I got shingles.

Somebody. A little boy wriggling through the window.
Oh, how tiny he must be.
I make as though I don't notice him, as if I were sleeping, splayed out on the toilet seat.
"Hey, Sister."
He tugs at my sleeve. Smell of sweet sweat and lemon.
"I'm supposed to check and see if you're alive."
"That's fine, my child."
"I'm not a child."
"Of course not. You're a grown up young man."
"I'm eleven years old."
"When He was eleven, He was talking the socks right off the scribes."
"Who?"
"My husband."
"I'm from the Catholic Youth Movement. I've got an armband on."
"Who sent you?"
"Mother Superior. She thought that you had a heart attack."
The nuns at the door are hooting. I call out: "I'm coming."
The boy lets some water run in the sink, sniffs, and snorts. Says: "This sure is the first time I've been alone in a bathroom with a nun."
"There is somebody else here too."

"Who? Where?"

"In Heaven, on earth, and in all places."

"Oh, him."

"Yes, Him."

"But no one can see Him."

"You can talk to Him."

"Does He talk to you?"

"He'd have to be crazy."

"Shall we go? Hm?"

"No."

"Do you mean to move in here?"

"There are three things. Time, the body, and the plenitude. And I have to chase all three out of me. Wipe them away like dust from a windowsill."

"I don't get it. It's like geometry at school. Hey, they all say you're a martyr."

"Pretty soon they'll be collecting my toe nails. Or they'll be chopping my big toe off for a relic."

He laughs.

Says: "They say that you see saints sometimes."

"It is forbidden for me to talk about it. It would be a mortal sin."

"Forbidden by who?"

"By my father confessor."

"They're saying you just saw Saint Joseph."

"Yes."

"What does he look like?"

(Something with stubble, with lunps all up and down his arms and shoulders, something with a frantic voice, a pawn.)

(Something I don't want to think about now.)

I say: "Joseph holds a flowering staff in his hand. He concerns himself with our good death. And about his feet lay a hammer, a saw, and a plane. He's bending over, looking around for nails, he finds them, and he's going away. And walks towards the one who's lying there in the dust, on the crossed beams."

Keep him away from there! Pull Joseph away!

"Who's the one lying there?"

"I saw His hands and His feet all burned by the sun, because He walked so much, every day, through the sands of Palestine. Joseph is shoving a nail through each hand and is banging them through His hands with a hammer. The soldiers are lifting the gallows up in the air, and He's sagging, for how much does He weigh? A hundred twenty? A hundred? His hands are ripping. They have to start over again, Joseph is banging the nails through His wrists now, and they're hammering together a little bench to put under his feet. His stomach is swollen like five footballs. They're shoving a sponge with vinegar right into His eyes."

"I saw it on t.v. And the soldiers were called centurions."
"Come here."
He comes close, unsuspecting. I grab him by the clothes, pull him up against me, feel his mouth. He has no hair on his upper lip. I let him go, he jumps far away from me.
"You ought to cut your nails."
The nuns are getting impatient. Beating. Moaning.
"Jan Verschoor, is she sick?"
"Sick? She's as strong as a horse. They'll have to bury her alive!"
"Jan Verschoor, what's she doing?"
"She's sitting on the pot and crying."
"Sister Mechtild, get off the pot."
"Sister, think of the reputation of our convent."
"Jan Verschoor, open up."
"She's got the key."
"Take it away."
"I don't dare." The brother of God is everywhere.
"Sister," says the boy, "you're not being fair."
"No," I say.

The veil of the temple splits open. The nuns are yelping, beating on the wood. Gaudete.

THE HAIR OF THE DOG

Translated By
David Willinger and Lucas Truyts

CHARACTERS

MIRA DAVIDS
MIMI, her mother
GEORGE HERREMAN, her friend
FRANS SIMONS
BOB DE SOTER
A SOLDIER

SETTING

The backroom of the Mimosa, a cafe off the highway that runs between Ghent and Kortrijk in Belgium. Downstage, a well tended parking lot covered in gravel with flowertubs. A large tree Stage Left. Most of the scenes take place in the parlor, an expensive, kitschy interior with sofas, an oak sideboard, a t.v., dolls on the sofa, paintings, etc. A door Stage Right leads to the"salon," a door Stage Left to the kitchen. A glass door leads outside.

SCENE ONE

(The living room. George enters wearing a gray suit. He immediately takes off his black tie and tosses it on the table. Mira enters. She is dressed in black, with a black veil. She thrusts back the veil. George plops down into a chair and stretches his foot into the air. Mira undoes his shoelaces and pulls his shoe off. Then she goes and sits down. George looks at her. George turns on t.v. with a remote control gadget, pushes various buttons. Mira doesn't look at the t.v. George turns it off)

MIRA: You want anything?

GEORGE: A shot of gin. *(Mira goes over to the cabinet and pours him a shot of gin.)* After all that champagne. What an idea, champagne at a funeral. And semi-dry to boot!

MIRA: It was Janine's favorite drink. *(Silence.)*

GEORGE: What was Janine's favorite food?

MIRA: Calve's head.

GEORGE: With tomato sauce?

MIRA: Yes.

GEORGE: Hot or cold?

MIRA: Hot of course.

GEORGE: Poor broad! *(Silence.)* We sure were lucky they didn't honor her final wish. Calve's head with semi-dry champagne! Did you catch old Daneels? First one behind the coffin? He never misses a single funeral around here. Sometimes makes three a week. And stands by the grave shaking hands. Shakes his head. "Ah, he was my best friend!" People he didn't know from a hole in the wall. A whole life spent in deepest condolences. Did he really used to go to Janine at the Coocoo?

MIRA: No, he goes to Marietta at the Brooklyn most of the time. *(Silence.)*

GEORGE: Hmph, I thought old Daneels went in more for fat asses. And that that's why he doesn't come here. *(Silence.)* Civil funerals like that are pretty blah. Give me an organ and incense any day. *(Sings)* "Dies irae, dies illa, solvet saeclum in favilla: teste David cum Sybilla . . . ."

MIRA: Cut it out. *(Silence.)*

GEORGE: And holy cards at the funeral saying "May the Lord's blessing be upon his soul." *(Mira pulls the veil down over her face. He sees.)* I had no idea that Janine had so many relatives. Come from the Campine. And that poor slob Piero who wasn't allowed to stay with the family and had to stand off to the side snivelling. He'll have to get a job now, old Piero. Easy life's over. Or else he'll have to find himself another woman. But in a different bar. 'Cause he won't be able to stay at the Coocoo, he says, 'cause he sees blood everywhere, pools of blood. We should probably ask Piero to spend three, four days here with us. But your mother. . . . Anyway, Piero'd rather go to Brussels, by the North Side Railroad Station, where his fellow countrymen hang out. It's better that way. Sorrow should be shared with amici and glasses filled with Lacrima Christi. That goes for you too Mira. Sorrow can tear you up inside more than you think. Especially someone like you. You hungry? *(She shakes her head.)* I am. On account of the fresh air at the graveyard. *(Starts to get up.)* But I can wait. *(Silence.)(Suddenly fiery.)* And all those busybodies who came to gawk at us. The same bloodsuckers that have been driving past the Coocoo for three days now to stand and gape at the front door, all the while imagining how it must have happened, with the knife and the blood. See the photographer from the Courrier of the Lys? Dragging his clodhoppers all over the gravesites? Click, click. I'm going to go have a word with the editor-in-chief on Monday. Just because you're a socialist doesn't mean you can have such bad manners. *(Silence.)* But even worse was who wasn't there. When you consider how all those bastards dripping with money used to batter down Janine's door . . . with their fancy cars driving up behind the Coocoo . . . how they stood there drooling to be turned on with handcuffs, leather, and whips. . . . Where are they now? Vanderijpe, the notary, Professor Christiaens, the industrialists? Sure they'd send her flowers for her birthday or give her a ring now and then, no problem, so long as she was alive and pop went the corks and the semi-dry champagne flowed free, bosom buddies each and every one, and "Aren't we the tightest bunch of shitheads you've ever seen," no problem, but as soon as someone kicks the bucket and gets her head sliced off, and there's a burial right out in the open where you can be seen by everybody, boy oh boy, then they sit home with their wives jacking them off, the rats, the shitlice. Honey, tell me how do we stand living here in this rathole country. *(Silence.)* What do you say to half a chicken? With apple sauce?

MIRA: Dumped.

GEORGE: You're down in the dumps? That's perfectly normal Mira. She was your best friend.

MIRA: She is. They dumped Janine in the ground.

GEORGE: Yeah.

MIRA: And in two weeks time, no one'll mention her name.

GEORGE: Oh yes they will -- if they find the murderer.

MIRA: They'll never find him.*(Silence.)* Did they sew her throat up properly before they buried her?

GEORGE: Yeah, probably.

MIRA: You mean you didn't see?

GEORGE: I didn't pay that much attention.

MIRA: They probably just left it the way it was. They probably didn't think it was worth bothering with. *(Silence.)* If the same thing happens to me, you better make sure they put me back together. Promise?

GEORGE: Promise.

MIRA: Really?

GEORGE *(Raises his hand in the air)* I, George Herreman, known in the art world and the world of journalism as Marnix van Laarne, do solemnly swear on my mother's head that I will have my mistress and love of my life, Mira Davids, put back together prettier than she ever was during her rich and sterile life. *(Silence.)* Mira. *(Silence.)*

MIRA: I want to have cherry-red Lancôme lipstick on and eyeshadow and Payot face cream. It's all lying ready on my dressing table upstairs. And white underwear. My blue Jourdan shoes. And my long Chanel gown. The dark blue one. *(George turns the t.v. on with the remote control. Pop music.)*

MIRA: Turn it off!

GEORGE *(Does so.)* You don't have to get bent out of shape baby. You know what Dr. Minard said. *(Silence.)*

MIRA: You never liked her.

GEORGE: Oh no, that's not true. I always dug Janine. We had our little dissagements now and then, sure, but that's beside the point.

MIRA: You thought she was mean.

GEORGE: Come on, admit it Mira, she was on the mean side.

MIRA: And I'm not, and my mother isn't either.

GEORGE: No, you're not.

MIRA: You even had a fight with her the day before she died. Because she said that you used all those big-sounding words and sentences in the Courrier of the Lys just to show off how smart you are.

GEORGE: Mira, Janine was a dumb twat. *(Irritated.)* And let's change the subject!

MIRA: I can't. *(Silence.)* There was a detective at the graveyard.

GEORGE: There was probably more than one.

MIRA: I recognized him right away from the way he was acting. Like I can recognize plain clothes detectives at the supermarket. He asked "Are you the one from the Mimosa? The Queen of the Road to Kortrijk?" I said, "If you say I am."

GEORGE: Was he by himself? They usually travel in twos.

MIRA: By himself.

GEORGE: The homicide department must think the murderer's going to follow Janine right into her grave. That he'd stick by her side as long as possible. Even after she's dead. That maybe he'd give himself away out of guilt.

MIRA: Like that Russian student we saw on that t.v. show? "Crime and Punishment?"

GEORGE: Yeah. Crime and Punishment. Dumb title.

MIRA: He kept staring at me the whole time.

GEORGE: How come you didn't point him out to me?

MIRA: Well, since you didn't notice him yourself . . . . *(Silence.)*

GEORGE: Shall we open the bar tonight?

MIRA: No.

GEORGE: We can't stay closed forever, Mira. One, two, three days of mourning, that I can understand, but . . . .

MIRA: You have no repect for people, do you?

GEORGE: I'm saying this for your own good. Janine is dead, gone, murdered, pushing up the daisies. These things happen.

MIRA: To our kind they sure do.

GEORGE: There's no proof of that. There's no statistics that show that there's any higher percentage of murders among bar owners than there is for plumbers.

MIRA: I'm not a bar owner. I'm a call-girl. And my mother was a call girl. We attract more murderers than ordinary women do. It's an occupational hazard. *(Silence.)*

GEORGE: *(Goes over to the window.)* It's still overcast.

MIRA: The days are getting shorter.

GEORGE *(Coming back)* Come on, kiddo, pull yourself together. Janine would have wanted . . . .

MIRA: What do you know about what she'd have wanted? In her position there was nothing she could want. The nicest thing she could hope for was for her throat to get sliced with a razor and her head to fall off.

GEORGE: Mira, her head didn't fall off. The razor stopped when it got to the vertebrae. *(Silence.)*

MIRA: Now it's my turn. Everyone has their turn.

GEORGE: Honey, you know you're not supposed to get over-excited. What did Dr. Minard say? That nothing can happen to you so long as you take your pills everyday. *(Silence. He bites into an apple.)* Away. Away. Away from this gray rathole country. Away from this shitty weather. From all the shitheads in the cemetery. Away. Into the bright blue yonder. To a beach with palm trees. Bare feet. Transcendence. Peace and quiet. *(He pushes a button. A neon sign on the side of the house that says MIMOSA flicks on.)*

MIRA: George, I'm going to pick up a hammer and smash that sign to pieces. *(George turns the sign back off. Looks at her.)*

BLACKOUT

SCENE TWO

(Mira sits huddled at one end of the sofa with her knees pulled up to her chest. George is rolling a joint, lights it, and hands it to Mira.)

GEORGE: You can look at it upside down or right side up, but the customers are complaining. Even before the incident with Janine. You're not with the program anymore. Your mind's not on the task at hand.

MIRA: Who's been complaining?

GEORGE: Florent.

MIRA: Oh, him.

GEORGE: And you're losing the customers' trust. What Florent said, "A man comes in in good faith, he whips it out in good faith, and goddamn if she doesn't bite it."

MIRA: I didn't bite hard. My mind was on something else.

GEORGE: I know, but some of 'em go for that and some do not. You've got to be more careful. We're not in the business of circumcising the customers. 'Cause you know how people are. We'll get a bad rep before you can bat an eye. Mira the Guillotine. *(She laughs in spite of herself.)* That's it. That's the way I like you best, with your teeth showing. Bernard from the Horse Shoe said the same thing. "Why is Mira so moody lately? I didn't do anything to her. I like coming to the Mimosa and I got no problem dropping a stack of dough there, but then between us, I want my money's worth George. And what do you get at the Mimosa? You can't have a decent fuck if Mira's in the wrong mood. Then it's Hand-Job Mira. And if you can't even expect to get a little smile along with it, then I'm sorry, but there're lots of other bars on the highway."

MIRA: So why doesn't he go to the Carress, or the Jewel, or the Greenwich Village then?

GEORGE: But then Bernard says, "I know what the problem is, your little Mira's in love." *(Silence.)* And that was before the incident with Janine, mind you. Is that true, are you in love? Well are you? You don't have to answer, you know me, I believe in freedom for my fellow man, but as your pal I'd like to know anyway. Is it a customer? *(She stares him down.)*

Do I know him? 'Cause you've got all the symptoms, honey. Whimpering, nagging, moping, staring. And there's not even a full moon and it's not your time of month. Come on, you can tell your George, who are you in love with?

MIRA: Everybody.

GEORGE: I know that, but anybody in particular?

MIRA: Nobody. And nobody's in love with me.

GEORGE: No shit baby, nobody? No one in the whole wide world? You mean to tell me that at your age there's nobody who sits up and takes notice of you, and you in the prime of your life? *(Silence.)*

MIRA: I've never lied to you.

GEORGE *(After a beat)* I've lied to you.

MIRA: That's not the same thing. You can't *not* lie. You lie because you're scared.

GEORGE: Scared?

MIRA: Scared that everything is no different or better than it seems. So you want to change it. You can't with it the way it is. My father was the same way. Lying and cheating because things were supposed to be different.

GEORGE: You barely knew your father.

MIRA: My mother told me enough.*(Silence.)* But you're right, my father and you. Things ought to be different, like they used to promise us they would be. *(Silence.)* I'm never going to have a guy with a steady job who comes home from work at five o'clock, who I keep house for, who I cook and wash and iron for, who I go to football games with. *(Silence)* Or a kid either.

GEORGE: Well, you have me.

MIRA: A real kid. I don't care if it looks like you or not.

GEORGE: Thanks a lot Mira. *(Silence.)* Well sure, a real kid right there on the sofa. Alongside you. "Mommy, I want to watch Sesame Street!" Wearing thick glasses. With a comic strip in her lap and a walkman in her ears, and she's the only one who can hear it. *(Singing:)* "Yes, my heart belongs to Daddy." Too bad she has a harelip. But we'll have it operated later on, fix it right up, so she can be Miss East

Flanders by and by.

MIRA: Or what if it's a boy. And becomes a murderer.

GEORGE: Everybody has his cross to bear. *(Silence.)*

MIRA: Why couldn't I see Janine?

GEORGE: Because she was too messed up Mira.

MIRA: I'll never have seen a corpse. *(Silence.)* How about a five-month old embryo, is that a person? Does that count as a corpse?

GEORGE: The theologians and all the experts and the Pope have been working on that one for centuries, baby. But person or not, what difference does it make, dead is dead, say amen and forget it. *(Silence.)*

MIRA: I would've loved to go back to Marbella.

GEORGE: Let's do it girl! Let's do it. Through the Sun-Air Travel Agency. 15,000 francs for two weeks, everything included. Okay?

MIRA: It's too late.

GEORGE: Hell no. It's 76 degrees till November.

MIRA: It'll never happen now.

GEORGE: Cut it out Mira, don't talk garbage. *(He rolls a fresh joint.)*

MIRA: If only I'd listened to Janine. "Mira," she said, "get married. You can always get a divorce later. Go to France and wash dishes if you have to. But clear out of the Mimosa. You're still young. I'm stuck with Piero and I don't have the guts anymore. But you.... And I say "I'm making a good living and I can't just leave my mother all alone." "It's gonna kill you" she says, "You don't see it now, but it'll get you all the same, tomorrow or the day after."

GEORGE: Mira, you're talking garbage.

MIRA: George.

GEORGE: Yeah?

MIRA: I'm scared.

(George stands up and comes over to sit by her. He caresses her. She doesn't stop him. He kisses her. She pulls away.)

MIRA: How can you, at a time like this, with Janine barely buried?

GEORGE: It's nature, baby. It bobs up like a cork right in the face of death. *(Suddenly angry.)* Mira, I can't help it that Janine kicked the bucket. That's life, life. And you shouldn't carry everyone's cross for them, goddammit.

MIRA: You're right. My own is enough. *(Silence.)*

GEORGE: Everyone's got their own cross to bear.

BLACKOUT

SCENE THREE

(Mira is dancing to a top-ten song while watching T.V. George is sitting on the sofa. Then she drops down next to him on the sofa, pants.)

GEORGE: You're all out of breath so quick. You better take off at least ten pounds.

MIRA: Practice what you preach. *(Turns down the sound on the t.v.)*

GEORGE: *(feeling his stomach)* I should take off twenty-five. Then the number of pounds I weigh will exactly equal my height in inches over one yard. Then I'll be the ladykiller I used to be. *(Drinks a beer.)* You see! Another 120 calories. Beethoven was fat too. And Rembrandt.

MIRA: Turkey. *(She pulls him back towards her and kisses him. He frees himself.)* Well?

GEORGE: I'm not into it right now.

MIRA: But just a minute ago....

GEORGE: Just a minute ago.... That was a brief moment of arousal, because my glands were over-stimulated by the funeral.

MIRA: You should have been a priest. It's a good thing I go for priests.

GEORGE: Traitors. Cowards.

MIRA: Who? Priests?

GEORGE: The priests that come here. The ones who succumb to the flesh. They don't realize how definitive, how absolute, how lethal copulation is. They can't even stick to their own rules, the rules expressly designed to keep life accidental, indestructable, and unfulfilled. Most Reverend Gentlemen, your Lord has given you the most marvelous gift in the world, a legitimate reason to remain in a perpetual state of sexual longing, a longing that by its very nature mustn't be consummated, that remains undefined and gigantic. But no, they want to penetrate someone like everyone else, have the feeling they're breathing life into something, flaunting life in the face of death. Apostates! Cowards! *(Drinks.)*

MIRA: Too bad you're not a customer.

GEORGE: Why?

MIRA: I'd take you down a peg. Make you see that, even with all your rhetoric, you're not one jot better than all the others.

GEORGE *(Produces a 5,000 franc bill)* Here. A bit of green. Let's see what you can do.

MIRA: *(Giving him a peck)* You turkey. Have you forgotten what I can do?

GEORGE: Yeah.

MIRA: In a minute. Later. After it gets dark. *(She turns off the t.v. Silence.)* Maybe one of my customers this past week was the murderer. Without my knowing it. Maybe he just downed a couple of whiskeys, talked to me about the weather, about women. What did he look like? Blonde with glasses?

GEORGE: Dirty blonde, thin, young, with dark glasses.

MIRA: Dark lenses or a dark-colored frame?

GEORGE: Dark lenses. Mireille from the Moonlight saw him and so did that farmer, Vereecke, who was chopping feed for his rabbits. He was zipping up his fly on the highway, turned to look skittishly first right then left, and took off down a dirt road. That's all we know.

MIRA: Who's going to look after Janine's sheep now? It hasn't stopped bleating.

GEORGE: I guess Piero'll take it down to the slaughterhouse.

MIRA: Can't we bring it here? Rope off a section for it back in the yard? *(She is getting wound up.)*

GEORGE: If you want to, why not?

MIRA: Thanks, George. Go get the sheep. Today. So I can see it one more time. So I can be sure it'll be taken care of. *(Silence.)* We mustn't complain. *(Getting more wound up.)* Mustn't complain. I shouldn't give in to it. I've got to steel myself against it, I know, but I can't help it. I'm so scared, George. *(She stands up feverishly, stammering.)* No, don't say anything. Everything I see and hear is just too much, and it's not going to get any better either, just the opposite, it's like there's someone dancing under my skin, someone who's trying to get out and can't, and won't let up with the dancing and stamping and....

GEORGE: Sit down, Mira honey.

MIRA: *(Going to sit down)* All right, all right. *(Silence.)*   I'm not worried about you. You'll miss me, in the beginning anyway, but you've got so many other things to keep you busy, your articles in the Courrier of the Lys, politics, exhibits, and your books in foreign languages. And Mama's got plenty too with her mind on how things used to be, she won't miss me either, or will she? For a little while. Yeah. Go ahead and laugh at your Mira, George. Say there's a full moon or that it's my time of month. But I have no idea how to still that dancing going on inside me. I'm standing here shivering, kid. Cold. *(Shivers. Gasps for breath.)* George, you know I wouldn't bother you unless it was really necessary, but now ... so cold. *(Shakes her head.)* Help me kid. Please. Cold. *(She stamps her feet.)*

GEORGE: Sit down and be quiet. Sssshh. It'll pass.

MIRA: I have to go to the other side, I'm being dragged there by iron wires. Don't look at me. Go into the parlor and drink your beer. Go on. Go on.

(She rises in an epileptic seizure, spins, and falls forward. George gets up, kneels down next to her, and holds her hand.)

GEORGE: Ssshhh, my sweet. It's all right. It'll be over in no time. *(He looks at his watch and hollers:)* Mimi! Mimi! Come here, Mimi!

(The light changes. Snow falls. Music from "La Traviata" by Verdi. Enter a Soldier in a United States Army winter uniform with a very large coat, covered with snow. He carries a machine gun. He has a huge bloodstain at stomach level. Mira goes over to him.)

MIRA: That I love you. And you ran away without so much as looking at me, me, the one you created. And they came after you and threw you in the klink because you'd been smuggling butter out of Holland, and you ran off to the army in Korea. And you wanted to get away from me who you created. And the Chinese came after you and you got lost in all the ice and snow in the mountains. *(She touches the Soldier.)* Puma. Puma. Should I warm your hands up? On my belly? Come on, it's warm here by me, I'm you're toasty little house, I've got an itsy-bitsy stove inside. Can I snuggle up under your coat? *(She nestles up against him, under his coat.)* You stay here by Mira, Mirabella. And she'll stay with you for the rest of her life. Mira'll take care of you, more and better than for any of her customers, more than for Janine's sheep. Put the gun down. There's no need for it. The Chinese are all gone, far, far away. We don't need anything, you and I. Mira and Puma. You're so gray, so wet, so cold. Do you hear? How refined I talk? Like you. Mama said that you always talked so nice, that you picked it up at the community college. I can do it too, can you tell? I talk real refined. I'm learning it from watching t.v. I learned so much since you went away, at school and later. I'm not the same hick girl you bounced on your knee. I'm still a girl, sure, but now I can converse with the big people. With you, puma, puma.

(The Soldier breaks free and hits her with the butt of his machine gun. She falls backwards onto the sofa. The Soldier leaves. The snow gradually disappears.)

MIRA: I didn't deserve that. I never did anything to you. Or did I? Yes. Sure I did. I forget about you all the time. I can't help it. So much on my mind. Come back. Hit me again. You can, only you. And I want to see you again. Puma. *(Screams unintelligibly. Subsides.)* Puma. You're gone. Where are you, Puma?

BLACKOUT

SCENE FOUR

GEORGE: I'm here. It's George. *(Holds her hand.)* *(Mimi, Mira's mother, enters. She is fat and old and moves with difficulty. She carries a stuffed dog in her arms.)*

MIMI: Are we back to that?

GEORGE: Yeah.

MIMI: I thought as much.

GEORGE: Why? It's been months since the last time.

MIMI: Hold her head a little straighter. *(Watches attentively. Goes and sits down.)* It's starting to let up. *(To her dog:)* You see Zorro, she's pulling out of it. In her own good time as usual. She's a good girl. *(Mira comes to. Rubs her forehead. Smiles.)*

MIRA: I'm back. Did it last long?

GEORGE: No longer than usual. *(Silence. George eats a Mars Bar.)* Mira, you didn't take your pills.

MIMI: Sure she took her pills. I saw her myself. Mind your own business. Take your own reducing pills. Just look at him sitting there with his bloated paunch. Letting himself go like that. Not an ounce of self-discipline.

GEORGE: Have you taken a good look at yourself recently? Hippopotamus non-amphibius.

MIMI: Save your five-dollar words for the Courrier of the Lys.

GEORGE: Mira, did you take your pills today or not?

MIRA: Not.

GEORGE: When was the last time you took them?

MIRA: Oh some time ago.

GEORGE *(Suddenly angry)* But why not? For God's sake, Mira, you have to take them. Scientists the world over are slaving night and day to come up with new medicines in order to help us. You have yours standing right on the table there, and you don't take 'em, goddammit!

MIMI: Hey, no swearing in this house, socialist.

GEORGE: Shut up you!

MIMI: Just look what we've let in here Zorro!

GEORGE: It's for your daughter's own good. Is that so hard? Two pills a day and nothing can happen to her.

MIMI: I take mine every morning. Virasol for my liver, Dispril for my headaches. You've got to give nature a helping hand.

(Silence.)

GEORGE: *(Sullenly)* I'm pulling the hair out of my head, I'm so wired I'm going out of my mind, and all she can do is torment me. How about it? *(To Mira.)* Do you want to get one of those seizures and never come out of it? Just to make my life miserable? Where the hell did you get that silly-ass idea not to take your pills?

MIRA: I don't want to waste time looking after my body anymore.

GEORGE: Bullshit.

MIRA: The body is nothing. I've fussed over it long enough.

MIMI: Idiotic bullshit.

GEORGE: And if you die from it, what then?

MIRA: It'd be better for all concerned.

MIMI: She's the last nail in my coffin, that's what she is.

MIRA *(Giggling)* The nails, the nails!

MIMI: What don't we have to listen to, eh Zorro? As though we didn't have enough problems, with the rent going up again, with the roof the landlord refuses to repair, with the recession, with....

GEORGE: *(To Mira)* Or did Dr. Minard tell you to stop taking the pills? When was the last time you saw him?

MIRA: Last Tuesday, same as always, every week.

MIMI: His fee went up too, Dr. Minard. Now it's twelve hundred francs per week. For a quarter hour. Legs open, a shot, and twelve hundred francs. That's a fine specimen, Dr. Minard. I can still see him the day he came here in '46, a down-at-the-heels family doctor, and now milord's the specialist for all the roadside bars with a B.M.W. and a mansion with swans in the pond. And is he ever horny! Sees all those women in obscene poses, seventy-two years old and he still can't keep his hands to himself. Helluva guy. But he's good. For people and animals alike, right Zorro? That shot, Zorro didn't even know what hit him. He whined a bit, but so what, he's been doing that for years. How was the funeral?

GEORGE: Big crowd.

MIMI: They were crazy about her. And not just because she did special tricks. She had a good heart. You'd better if you're gonna do special tricks. Bert from up at the estate used to tell me often enough: "When I go to Janine I'm dealing with someone who's got her heart in it. With you, on the other hand, Mimi, you know your stuff okay, but it doesn't come from the heart." You've got to have a feel for it, and that Janine had. Not me. Never did. Dressed up in black leather with a whip in my hand I always looked like I was ready for Hallowe'en. *(To Joris)* Did you go to the funeral looking like that? Not so much as a black suit on?

GEORGE: A black tie.

MIMI: That's a disgrace. Didn't even put on a black suit. You see, you can have the best heart in the world, they still won't bother to wear a black suit to your grave. Nowadays....

GEORGE: Janine couldn't see if I had my black tie on or not anyway.

MIMI: *(In earnest)* Oh yes she did. From Heaven.

GEORGE: They're not so quick to let whores into Heaven.

MIMI: Well, if they won't let us in, then we'll go to Hell. At least it's warm there.

MIRA: No.

GEORGE: It isn't warm there?

MIRA: I don't want to die yet.

GEORGE: You better hurry up and change your ways, Mira. Go into a cloister and join the Carmelites, why don't you?

MIRA: I don't have time for that anymore.

MIMI: The crumb thinks it's funny to make fun of nuns. Boy, you're going to get it, both here on earth and in the hereafter.

GEORGE: Janine used to dress up as a nun, sure enough, for special customers.

MIMI: She didn't do it to make fun of them. I know I'm getting conservative, just like all whores when they start getting up there, but I also know that there's a God who exists and that He's going to punish you. If only for your pretention and your high and mighty ways.

(George has gone to the kitchen for a look. He brings back milk and mixes it with some white powder from a box. He rapidly stirs up the mess.)

MIMI: *(sarcastic)* Tasty?

GEORGE: 250 calories.

MIMI: Metrecal. That's supposed to be instead of a meal. Not to take after you've eaten, for desert.

GEORGE: *(To Mira)* Try it? It's vanilla flavored! *(Mira shakes her head.)*

MIRA: Please don't forget to go get Janine's sheep?

GEORGE: No. I'm thinking. Why did she have a sheep? For special sessions?

MIMI: No. I would have heard about it.

GEORGE: Always on top of what the competitors are up to, hunh Mimi?

MIMI: Used to be anyway. You've got to keep up with the Joneses. There's always some new fad. The customers always want something new. It's a tough business. *(Mira picks up a book and reads.)*

GEORGE: Was.

MIMI: Still is. We're scraping the bottom of the barrel now. Everything goes these days -- sex shops, dirty books, nude broads on t.v. What does your ordinary man in the street want with us now? These days middle-class women are grabbing hold of men right on Main Street, doesn't bother them in the least. In the old days, sure, the customers were perfectly happy with wham, bam, thank you ma'am. But these days your normal ordinary customer doesn't exist, you've gotta rack your brains. Back then it was the customer who did the work. He stood there begging, "Please can I stick it in?" Right, Zorro? *(Mira lays down her book.)* Isn't it any good? Which is it? Oh yeah, the one about the carpenter who fell in love with the dancer. I read it twice.

MIRA: I can't see well anymore.

MIMI: You gotta get glasses. Like I did when I was your age. But I couldn't very well sit in the salon wearing glasses on my nose. And you didn't have contact lenses back then either. I could barely see the customers. Pink spots. But it was all for the best. Most customers aren't much to look at anyway. *(Silence.)*

GEORGE *(Suddenly savage)* Why aren't you taking your pills?

MIRA: You can't yell at me like that.

GEORGE: I don't want you having a fit again. Do you understand you dizzy cunt?

MIRA: I understand very well, boy.

MIMI: She can't do anything about what she's got. It's nature.

GEORGE: Your nature, yes.

MIMI: Excuse me, sonny, she gets it from her father.

GEORGE: From the puma.

MIMI: Yes, from Puma. And he got it from his father.

GEORGE: And Shem begot Arphaxad and Arphaxad begot Gelach and Gelach begot Eber and Eber begot Joktan, and they were all fruitful and they proliferated throughout the world, and they were all struck down by Jackson's Epilepsy and whole dynasties and peoples rose up again after the Flood.

MIMI: There he goes again with his smart-ass yacking. Madame Julia said "I read the Courrier of the Lys with pleasure each and every morning, but when Friday rolls around and I hit that column by Marnix Van Laarne, it goes right over my head." I said "Julia, he doesn't have a clue himself, he just copies it out of other books. He's just throwing sand in peoples' eyes to prove he can read and write."

GEORGE: My work has oft been criticized, but that's the first time I've come across that argument.

MIMI: *(roaring with laughter)* He calls that work! Looking at paintings and writing about what's in 'em. As though people were blind. *(Silence.)*

GEORGE: How's about we take a drive to the sea-side, to Knokke? A little game of miniature golf to whet our appetites? And then to a fine seafood restaurant for a gorgeous platter of Dutch oysters and a bottle of blanc de blanc?

MIMI: The oysters are contaminated. They threw some French oysters in with the others for breeding purposes, and some of them were sick. Now all the oyster beds are contaminated. All those lovely oysters down the tubes on account of that French disease. An oyster breeder told me.

GEORGE: The French Disease is the name the English use for

syphilis. And the French call it the English Disease.

MIMI: I've taken good care my whole life. Looked each customer over good and washed up real good first thing. If I saw a little spot, I'd say "Sorry mister, but this won't wash. Better go over to the Brooklyn where they aren't so fussy." That's the first thing I taught Mira. Look real good, watch your step. Zorro, sit up!

GEORGE: Well, Mira? Knokke, the seaside, air, ozone?

MIRA: I'd like to.

GEORGE: Fine, we're off.

MIRA: I can't. Not in these clothes.

GEORGE: Put something else on. Your beige suit.

MIRA: I can't take these clothes off today.

GEORGE: *(Elbows on his knees, head between his hands.)* It's overcast, but the temperature's okay. We're in trouble with the landlord, but we've got a roof over our heads for the time being. My editor-in-chief's a swine, but, still, he accepted my article on Suprematism. The customers are a pain in the ass, but they keep coming back. We can't afford a new car, but we're putting some money aside in any case.

MIMI: You put the money aside and she's got to earn it.

GEORGE: What I mean is that everything's more or less in the bag, but Mira, the Queen of the Road to Kortrijk's got the rag on. She's going to ruin this day, I can feel it, she has to go on being cranky, I can feel it in my bones.

MIMI: She doesn't feel well. And even if she is cranky, that's her right. And if that doesn't suit you, you can go back where you came from, back to your wife and kid, and eat another box of Metrecal there.

GEORGE: Thank you Mimi. You have to put me in my place periodically so that I may learn to be humble and mild.

MIMI: With pleasure. *(Silence.)*

GEORGE: So, we're not going to the ocean, because the fine lady would rather remain in her mourning clothes. But we won't let that upset us. No matter how precarious, pointless and unwelcome our position in this household is. No, we shall withdraw to our castle of the mind, banish our mortification deep inside us, and there strive to be firm in an unstable world, to be great in the face of unpredictability, through both love and death. *(He goes over to a small desk, produces a large art book, and leafs through it.)* Art is illusion. Let's get down to work, au boulot, al trabajo.

MIMI: I had a customer in the old days, his name escapes me now, he owned a candle factory, and he always said, "Does it feel good lying there, Mimi? Tied up tight so you can't move? Good, then we're off and running, let's get down to work, traviata!" Remember Zorro? Traviata?

BLACKOUT

SCENE FIVE

(George sits writing at the little desk. Mira stares straight ahead. Smokes a joint. Yelling upstage causes George to look up. Someone far away is knocking on a window. Mira starts to get up.)

GEORGE: Butt out.

(George goes to have a look through the side door stage right. Comes back. Goes through the glass door stage left and comes into the garden Downstage. Frans, a young man, enters. Dirty blonde, conservatively dressed.)

GEORGE: Hello, sir.

FRANS: Is she home?

GEORGE: Who's that?

FRANS: The younger one, the daughter.

GEORGE: Mira?

FRANS: Yeah, Mira.

GEORGE: Yeah, but we're not open.

FRANS: When are ya going to open?

GEORGE: We're closed all day. Due to personal circumstances.

FRANS: I'd like to have a word with Mira. Won't take long.

GEORGE: It's not the right time. Where's your car?

FRANS: Uh ... there....

GEORGE: I didn't hear you drive up.

FRANS: I was taking a little walk around first.

GEORGE: No kidding. So you've been wandering around here for a while already?

FRANS: I've got money on me. What does she charge?

GEORGE: For what?

FRANS: To sleep with her.

GEORGE: She doesn't do it with people she doesn't know.

FRANS: What does she charge for a little necking?

GEORGE: A thousand francs for a simple hand-job.

FRANS: *(Whistles)* What is she doing, following the Consumer Index?

GEORGE: But there's nothing doing today anyway. She's not in the mood. Later in the week maybe.

FRANS: That won't work for me. *(He shuffles nervously)*

GEORGE: You seem to be in a hurry.

FRANS: I guess.

GEORGE: Why do you keep turning around that way? You looking for somebody?

FRANS: Me? No. No.

GEORGE: You've got the Brooklyn across the road. And a little further down, the Diabolo. Or... if you like, the Coocoo, that's not so far from here. Janine's.

FRANS: *(Starting)* Janine?

GEORGE: Ever been to her place? The Coocoo?

FRANS: No. No. Never.

GEORGE: Well, since you're here, you might as well come in.

FRANS: If it's not too much trouble.

GEORGE: Hell no, just the reverse. You're more than welcome. *(They walk into the living room.)* Mira, there's a gentleman here who insists on seeing you.

MIRA: I'm not working today.

GEORGE: Who's talking about working? Have a seat there, sir, yeah, there.

MIRA: I told you, I'm not open today.

GEORGE: *(Laughing too heartily)* Boy, the way she says that. I'm not open. She doesn't mince words. Either she's open or she's not. Yeah, women can be pretty up-front. We men are more delicate in these matters, more head-in-the-clouds. Women say "We're open or closed." What'll you have? *(He goes over to the cabinet)* A Pernod?

FRANS: If it's not too much trouble.

GEORGE: Just the reverse. *(He pours a Pernod. One for himself as well. Silence.)* The weather doesn't seem to be getting any better, does it.

MIRA: It's the season.

FRANS: Yeah. The season. Cheers.

MIRA: Cheers.

GEORGE: I have a feeling I've seen you before. Here in the neighborhood. On the prowl, shall we say.

FRANS: I pass this way sometimes.

GEORGE: It's a lovely area. The River Lys, "The River Jordan of my heart" as the great poet, Guido Gezelle once said. Do you work around here by any chance?

FRANS: I'm a traveling salesman.

GEORGE: Right. Hmhm. *(Silence.)*

FRANS: *(To Mira)* You look younger than I thought. I mean, I've only seen you from a distance.

GEORGE: Maybe your distance vision's not so hot. You must wear glasses normally. No? They're not in your pocket? Dark glasses for the sun? *(The young man stands. Mimi enters.)* This is Mimi, Consoler to the Afflicted, Mother of Sorrows.

MIMI: Good day sir. Do you write for the Courrier of the Lys too? No? Oh. Good. *(She goes and sits down. Frans likewise.)*

GEORGE: The gentleman's a traveling salesman.

MIMI: Wouldn't the gentleman be more at ease in the salon with a glass of champagne?

GEORGE: A little champagne never hurt anybody.

MIMI: Unless you're stomach's queasy of course.

MIRA: I'm not working today.

GEORGE: *(Jovial)* It's a lucky person who can decide just like that: "Today I'm raring to go," or "I don't feel like it today!" It'd be a fine state of affairs if everyone thought the same way, wouldn't it mister? Because the obligatory work ethic's still deeply rooted in the Flemish people, right mister?

MIMI: *(To Frans's surprised face)* He writes for the paper.

GEORGE: As columnist on the visual arts. In the Courrier of the Lys. A modest little rag, since it's the only real socialist paper in the country. But I judge from looking at you that you're not a socialist. Your traveling salesman's most often pretty conservative. You don't have to answer, of course, everyone's got a right to their opinion.

MIRA: You want another Pernod? *(She's been sitting staring at Frans the whole time.)*

FRANS: Please.

MIMI: Or would you rather have a whiskey? It's the same price.

MIRA: Mama, give the man what he asks for.

MIMI: And you Mira? A Special Cocktail?

MIRA: Yes, Mama.

MIMI: Well, I'll have a Special Cocktail too. *(She pads off toward the parlor)*

GEORGE: *(Calling after her)* And I'll have a brandy.

MIMI: *(Screaming back)* Get it yourself. I only have two hands.

GEORGE: The Special Cocktail's a little too sweet for me. It's more for the ladies, wouldn't you say?

FRANS: What's in the Special Cocktail?

MIRA: *(Smiling)* Sugar water with a couple of drops of crème de menthe. And that costs 250 francs.

GEORGE: *(Shocked)* Mira! Is that any way to talk?

MIRA: I sometimes down fifteen in one night.

FRANS: That must be bad for your teeth. *(Mira shows off her teeth, white and intact.)*

GEORGE: She's laughing. Mira's laughing today? How about putting that in the paper?

MIMI: *(Who is reentering)* Yeah, in your shitty rag. *(The two women click glasses.)*

FRANS: Is it true that they stick stuff in your drink in the bars along the road here? To knock you out?

GEORGE: Young man, this isn't America. We treat our clientele like kings. On a good faith basis. From which we derive our reputation. You ever read the Courrier of the Lys, even once?

FRANS: No, I mostly read "Our People."

GEORGE: I already figured that out. For the sports I bet, right?

FRANS: And for the local news.

GEORGE: And what in fact did they have to say about Janine in "Our People?"

FRANS: Just about the same as the other papers. All the papers sell good when something like that happens. And they dress it up a bit. For sensation's sake.

MIRA: *(to Frans)* Do you want to fuck me?

FRANS: *(Taken aback)* Ahem ... now?

MIMI: Mira, where are your manners? Did I teach you to ask questions that way?

MIRA: I've never once asked a man to fuck me before.

MIMI: You could at least put it a little more properly.

MIRA: *(To Frans)* You come along with me, you handsome fellow, you, and I'll show you what love really is. You'll see stars in broad daylight.

MIMI: That's already somewhat more decent.

GEORGE: *(To Mira)* I thought you didn't want to today.

MIRA: I changed my mind. I don't have much time left.

GEORGE: But the gentleman's in no hurry, are you mister? Oh, by the way, sir, I'm in the market for some sunglasses, because the light here on the Lys is pretty glaring, and I can't decide what kind to choose. Could I take a look at your glasses? *(Frans takes a pair of sunglasses out of his pocket. George puts them on.)* Yeah, the whole world looks different. Warmer, browner. Like a painting by that fine old East Flemish artist, Permeke. Brown warmth. When you see the world through glasses like these, then you're escaping into the warmth. If you take them off *(Takes them off)* then everything becomes cold again, empty, incomprehensible, repugnant. Then something comes over you, a certain kind of toughness with not one shred of compassion. So that you're forced to strike out. Right?

FRANS: I don't get you.

MIRA: What's your name?

FRANS: Frans. Frans Simons.

MIRA: Shall we go into the salon, Frans? It's a bit more intimate in there.

GEORGE: How about that? How often does that happen? This is your lucky day, Frans. It's not every day that she falls so head over heels. She pretends she's in love sometimes, but that's part of her professional function, see? Not that she doesn't mean it, because our Mira's got a capacity for love that knows no bounds. Her affection boils over like warm milk. We have thank you letters from ambassadors, pharmacists, craftsmen, Japanese . . . .

MIRA: George, please.

GEORGE: You know what I think Frans? That she fell for you instantaneously like that because you were a buddy of Janine's.

MIRA: Come Frans, I'll treat you to some champagne.

MIMI: The gentleman'll never go for that, Mira. The gentleman's much too well brought up for that.

MIRA: I've got a headache. An iron band round my head.

GEORGE: Champagne's the best remedy for that. But even better than that'd be a game of choo-choo.

FRANS: A game of choo-choo? *(Gets it)* Oh, that!

GEORGE: Yeah. You see, Frans, now and then a person who's accustomed to being in a field of work considered hermetical and ethereal by the common people, feels the need to express himself in a somewhat cruder fashion. And that's why onomotopeia, imitations of sounds, is the best means. Because no matter how complicated something is, it most often has an absolutely low-level onomotopeic counterpart. And in trying to acheive a certain territorial, syntactical, political, pictorial, and social harmony, you've got to.... I have the impression that you're not following me.

FRANS: No.

(Mira goes over and sits down next to Frans and puts her hand on his knee. They stare at each other.)

GEORGE: There we are. That's what we like to see. Turtle doves. *(Drinks.)* Ah, youth, eh Mimi? I was young once myself, as recently as yesterday. I was even loved, same way, because I was there, because I was me. Who haven't I had running after me -- typists, girl-scouts.... Cats sniffed at my pants everywhere I went. One time I had a turkey so hot on my trail that I had to run for my life.

MIMI: *(Shaking with laughter)* Did you hear that Mr. Frans?

FRANS: And did the turkey catch up to you?

GEORGE: I'd rather not discuss that. But I sometimes wake up nights in a cold sweat. *(Silence.)*

MIMI: Didn't I hear someone mention champagne?

MIRA: Go get a bottle, George.

GEORGE: You go, Mimi.

MIMI: Why should I?

GEORGE: *(Stands up, looks at Frans and Mira, hesitates; then makes up his mind.)* I'll go down to the cellar and get the Laurent Perrier '75. It isn't everyday we have a funeral. I'll be right back. *(Goes out the side door, stage right.)*

MIMI: You have no idea what we have to put up with from that guy, Mr. Simons! You heard him yourself.

FRANS: He seems like a decent person to me. And learnéd.

MIMI: Smarter the man, more like an animal he is.

MIRA: Still, he's good to me, Mama.

MIMI: He'd better be. Well yes, you're right. In any case, he's better to you than Piero was to Janine. *(Mira breaks out champagne glasses.)*

FRANS: Where is he now, Piero the Sicilian?

MIMI: Isn't he home at the Coocoo?

FRANS: No, he's dissappeared.

MIMI: Then Brussels I guess, somewhere near the North Station, with the other Italians. Charming young man, Piero. He sometimes brings me flowers or chocolates. But you know how it is Mr. Simons, horseracing....

FRANS: And breaking into the mansions in Deurle.

MIMI: How do you know about that?

FRANS: Oh you hear all sorts of things in the bars on the road. *(George returns, pops the champagne.)*

GEORGE: There you are. *(He pours the champagne. Mira drinks and rubs a few drops of champagne on her forehead.)*

MIMI: You want a Dispril?

MIRA: It's like an iron band with nails in it. All around my head. *(Frans takes her head between his hands. Kneads it.)*

FRANS: Here?

MIRA: Yeah. *(Frans rubs her neck.)* Oh, yeah, that feels good. A little more. Please.

GEORGE: Aha, so Frans is a masseur. Stong fingers. Strong but sensitive fingers. Round the neck, right Frans? The vertebrae, right? By the way, you got a knife on you?

FRANS: Me? No. What would I want with a knife?

GEORGE: Oh, to clean your nails. Peel potatoes. A knife can always come in handy. And then, a man like you, out on the road late at night, you never know what kind of characters you might run into. And then having a finely sharpened knife on you gives you a nice warm feeling.

MIRA: *(cuddling up to Frans, stroking his crotch)* Oooh, ooh, Mama, he's got a humdinger.

GEORGE: Frans? He's the man of the hour. A real man. Right Frans? *(Mira and Frans kiss. Mira makes little groaning noises. Frans touches her breast. She breaks away and drinks.)* That's right, Fran. *(Mira gets up. George puts his hand on her shoulder, making her sit back down.)* No, you're not going into the salon with him.

MIMI: But George, the guy's raring to go.

GEORGE: I know what I'm doing Mimi.

MIMI: Can't be good for a person's health. Getting him all excited and then . . . .

GEORGE: I haven't heard you mentioning the price yet Mira.

FRANS: I don't have that much on me. Well, travelers' checks.

MIRA: Today it's on the house.

MIMI: Mira! Did a rat bite you?

MIRA: Yes, Mama.

GEORGE: *(Looking at Mira inquiringly)* Complimentary champagne and going into the salon for nothing? I'm telling you, Frans, this woman's a saint. Still, I can't permit it. I'm responsible for her, for her situation. Not that I've got anything against you, you're a pal, through thick and thin. But she's not going into that salon without me.

FRANS: You want to be there?

GEORGE: Why not? A friend of the house -- what am I saying? A house pet, a French poodle in a little corner of the salon. I won't be any trouble. I'll sit by the open hearth and read my book about Michelangelo.

FRANS: I'm not into that. I'm sorry, George, but I'd rather not have any peeping-toms around.

GEORGE: Then it's no go.

FRANS: But still, I wanted to pay a good price. Whatever you think right.

MIMI: George, leave these two kids be. Let Mira do her job, now that she really wants to for once. And maybe it'd make her headache go away.

GEORGE: No I say. Goddammit. I'm not leaving her alone with him.

BLACKOUT

SCENE SIX

(There is now a second bottle of champagne sitting on the table. Mimi, George, and Frans are looking at Mira who is crying silently.)

MIMI: She can't help it. She's been through the ringer.*(Frans goes over to Mira, and wipes away her tears with his handkerchief. She grabs the handkerchief out of his hand.)*

MIRA: Give it here. There's mascara on it. And base. Your wife'll notice it tonight.

FRANS: I'm not married.

MIRA: Your fiancée in that case.

FRANS: Not engaged either.

MIMI: But you will be before you know it. A young man like you with such a nice job. And won't that be better than running after low-life women and dashing off to whores? A nice household's the most beautiful thing in the world. But them that's got one don't appreciate it. People are dumb.

MIRA: Your hands are warm. *(She takes his hands and presses them against her face.)*

FRANS: George, go get us another bottle of the same stuff.

GEORGE *(Saluting)* Yes, sir, colonel. Just a moment colonel. French champagne, colonel. *(He exits by the side door stage left.)*

MIMI: He thinks he's funny. Because he's got it into his head he sounds like my husband who was in the army.

FRANS: The British army?

MIMI: No. With the Americans. In Korea. A volunteer. In Pyong-Yang. A mountain range. He's lying there in his grave on the 38th parallel. December 6, 1951. It was a Sunday.

FRANS: Saint Nicholas Day.

MIMI: Yeah. *(Silence.)* It was the time of the New Look. Still. Skirts were one to five inches shorter than they are now. And tight. And pleated. And a pony tails worn to one side with bangs. *(Silence.)* You've never seen such a handsome guy. A noggin full of hair. And a mouth full of teeth. He brushed 'em three times a day. He was decorated too.

MIRA: They gave him the name Puma in Korea. Because he darted between the bullets, between the grenades, like a puma.

MIMI: I saw him for the first time at a parish dance. We're from the country, Mira and me. "Mimi?" he said. "It's a classic name from the opera. Come on Mimi, let me give you a big smacker." And then we danced the whole night through. Then he said "Let's go to bed." And I say "What are you going to do, park your jalopy in my garage?" And he laughed till his eyes filled with tears. "You're a card," he said, "I'll never let you go." But he did let me go. *(Silence.)* If he hadn't gone off to Korea, the Mimosa would never have existed. A man like that comes along only once in a lifetime. All the others . . . .

GEORGE: *(Burps)* A little champagne never hurt anybody.

MIRA: It hurt Janine alright. There was an open bottle on her night table when they found her.

MIMI: You'd have to be an animal to do a thing like that. First drink champagne and then . . . . They should institute capital punishment for customers like that. And quick too.

GEORGE: What do you think about that, Frans?

FRANS: Capital punishment. That's easy to say. It's not feasible from a political point of view. People aren't ready for it.

GEORGE: But still, you agree in principle? Eye for an eye. What you do to me I do back to you. I can't exactly write that in the Courrier of the Lys, but . . . .

MIMI: *(Fiercely)* Let 'em cut somebody else's throat, their wife, their mother, their daughter! But why one of us? We give 'em their money's worth. They can ask for anything they like, they can order us "Clothes off, legs open, ass in the air, stand on my head, lick my dick, lick my dirty feet," everything they wouldn't dare do at home, we're there ready for them, ready for the whole mess of slop that pours out of that cesspool in their heads, and it's us they do away with because we're too good for 'em . . . .

MIRA: *(Cries silently. Silence.)* They stuck Janine's head back onto her neck. You couldn't see the cut, right George?

GEORGE: No.

MIRA: We used to go swimming together in the good old River Lys. And when I came out of the changing room she just loved splashing water on me, by the handfull. *(Mimi feeds the stuffed dog. She shoves a cookie into the dog's mouth. She makes cooing sounds.)*

GEORGE: Oh no, Mimi, are you going to start in on that again?

MIMI: I'm sorry. I was forgetting. 's my nerves.

GEORGE: That animal's beginning to get on my nerves. Frans, would you believe that she used to feed that stuffed dog cookies and cereal all week long? So one day I'm sitting here reading, I look at the dog, and its mug was moving. It scared the shit out of me. Maggots were crawling out of its maw. All the cookies in its mouth had fermented.

MIRA: *(Laughing hysterically)* Maggots, maggots. Worms.

GEORGE: Mira, calm down. Or else . . . .

MIRA: Or else what? You gonna send me spinning with a punch in my mug?

GEORGE: Mira, you're not supposed to get all hot and bothered.

MIRA: I want to get hot and bothered. My time is drawing near. *(Goes to the side door Stage Right.)* He who wants me may follow.

GEORGE: Sure. Go ahead Frans. But don't make it too long.

MIRA: *(Mock-flirtatious)* However long it takes. *(When Frans tries to go after Mira, George blocks his way.)*

GEORGE: Just a minute. *(George searches Frans from head to toe.)* Okay. Go ahead.

(When they've both gone, George takes a small painting off the wall. He puts his eye to a peephole. Comes back near Mimi. Mimi produces a deck of cards.)

MIMI: A hundred francs a point?

GEORGE: No thanks, I'm not in the mood.

MIMI: *(Picks up the newspaper. Starts to do the crossword puzzle.)* A two-syllable word you hear when two long-ears are conversing. What's that? What do rabbits say?

GEORGE: *(Weary)* Hee-haw.

MIMI: Hee-haw? *(Delighted)* Oh yeah, sure! Hee-haw. Hee-haw.

BLACKOUT

SCENE SEVEN

MIMI: *(At her crossword puzzle)* Ferruginous soil? Three letters.

GEORGE: *(Eating a liverwurst sandwich)* Ore!

MIMI *(Angrily)* What did I do now?

GEORGE: Ore. Ferruginous soil. Ore.

MIMI: Ore. *(She fills in the word looking at him)* You're gonna be up over two hundred pounds pretty soon.

GEORGE: People in glass houses....

MIMI: It's all right for me. At my age it's normal. I've had my life.

GEORGE: I have too. I hate movements that cause a redistribution of lines.

MIMI: I bet you got that out of a book.

GEORGE: Yeah. And Goya was fat. And Thomas Aquinas too.

MIMI: Good-for-nothing layabouts.

GEORGE: *(Rubbing his belly)* We've got to smother the heartless warrior that's lurking deep within this flabby body, choke him to death. Till there's not a peep out of him. And there he is, over two hundred pounds, bald, and blind, in a wheelchair out in the desert. Peace and quiet.

MIMI: Talk about something serious for once. What're we going to have for dinner tonight?

GEORGE: Whatever you like.

MIMI: Lambchops?

GEORGE: *(Kissing her cheek)* What would I ever do without you, my queen of the night? *(He goes over to look through the peephole. Then charges over to the telephone. Dials a number.)* Courrier of the Lys? Marie Claire? George here. George. Marnix van Laarne! Is Mark there? *(Looks at the crossword puzzle, points.)* To eat voraciously. STUFF.

MIMI: Yeah, that you know! *(Fills it in.)* Stuff!

GEORGE: Mark? Stop the presses. I've got a scoop. Scoop. Like that say in America, you jerk. I'm not trying to sound weird. I'm a polyglot. A scoop, asshole, is the standard term for a sensational piece of news that one has unearthed. That business with Janine Fonteyne from the Coocoo, who got murdered. I've got details on it. I'm hot on the trail. Yeah, me, George the Bloodhound. I'll call you right back. Stay glued to the phone. *(Throws the receiver back on the hook.)*

MIMI: What details?

GEORGE: A professional secret.

MIMI: Bladderhead.

GEORGE: Just you wait.

MIMI: You mean that kid? Frans there?

GEORGE: It might very well be. It's a hypothesis. And if he isn't, well, no milk's been spilt. *(He goes over to the cabinet and takes a gun out of a drawer.)*

MIMI: You planning to do something stupid?

GEORGE: Precautions, Mimi, precautions. *(He looks through the peephole.)* They're winding down. She's on her knees.

MIMI: *(Concerned)* Did she fall?

GEORGE: You might say that. A fall from grace. Or the Adoration.

MIMI: Using her mouth?

GEORGE: Her hand.

MIMI: How about him?

GEORGE: A shmuck. Eyes closed. Mouth clenched. Puffing. Like it hurt. *(Turning away from the peephole.)* God, they sure are ugly when they loose their inhibitions and let themselves go. Vulnerable. When people let themselves go, they become ugly my little Mimi.

MIMI: I'm not going to rack my brains over it, but I think you got it wrong. Being vulnerable's not ugly.

GEORGE: *(Peeking again)* She's lousy at it.

MIMI: Mira? Never had any complaints.

GEORGE: She's lost her mind. *(Comes back into the room.)*

MIMI: Now, Janine gave it her all.

GEORGE: You can say that again. *(Goes and sits down.)*

MIMI: But Janine didn't have much of a manual technique either. Heard a lot of complaints about Janine's manual technique. From Vandromme. She used to yank away at it with the one hand and eat salami sandwiches with the other. That's not holding up your end of the bargain, now is it?

GEORGE: *(Burying his head between his hands.)* At night most animals in slumber nest, Most people too, the worst and best. In loving mercy, in quiet rest, But alone go I, and mount the crest. *(Silence.)* I should have been Commissioner of the Arts in Oudenaarde.

MIMI: I wish I'd owned a hardware store.

GEORGE: Sleep. Sleep. And leap for joy when you wake.

BLACKOUT

SCENE EIGHT

GEORGE: I should have become an electrician like my brother. 590 francs an hour. Weekends at the seaside. Crapshooting every night. Going out and visiting people. Watching my favorite t.v. episode on my V.C.R. for the umpteenth time.

MIMI: Well, go to vocational school then.

GEORGE: At my age?

MIMI: Night school then.

GEORGE: I'm all thumbs. And besides, I can't leave Mira all by herself. *(Silence.)* In the beginning, I'd stare at her for ages sometimes without really seeing her, it was more an idea of her that I saw, and I loved her, you can't take that away from me and you can't hold it against me, I loved her, so much that I sometimes had to run out onto the street in pure . . . . I danced for joy . . . in the beginning when I was still with my wife and child and when I could only see Mira from time to time and then only if I paid . . . in the beginning I plopped down half my earnings on her, and that included my salary and money I'd borrowed, true or not? You can't deny that. Because how much did I have to pay Fofo the Frenchman just to be allowed in here, for the honor and pleasure of passing time at the Mimosa, to cohabit with my love and her obnoxious mother here, and how much money don't I still pass on to Fofo to keep him from turning up here with his French friends and switchblades? I should have done it right at the start, in the beginning was when I should have said "George, pull out. It may lead you to glory, but better safe than sorry, so pull out . . . ."

MIMI: Well pull out already.

GEORGE: In the beginning I should have . . . .

MIMI: The beginning, the beginning. It's now that counts. Go and look. How far along are they?

GEORGE: I'm not looking. It cuts me to the quick.

MIMI: You're such a baby.

GEORGE: We're all children, Mimi. There's no comforting us.

MIMI: You disgust me with that talk.

GEORGE: She's going to die.

MIMI: I'm going to die?

GEORGE: You? Not for a long time yet.

MIMI: She is?

GEORGE: Yeah.

MIMI: Oh.

GEORGE: I'm pretending not to notice. But I do see it, by God, I'm not blind. *(Silence. Stands.)* No. I'm not going to look.

MIMI: You used to look every time, every night. In the beginning. . . .

GEORGE: A peeping tom, back then. Yeah, it's true. I couldn't get enough of it, the veins would pop out of my eyes from watching, watching, dying with sadness, but bursting with life at the same time. She's his now, but she's really mine . . . . In the beginning. Now . . . now she's running away from me. From all of us. Altogether. It makes me sick. I'm democratic, and I want to get the most out of life. *(Silence.)*

MIMI: She must still feel something for you. Otherwise she wouldn't stick it out with the likes of you. Come on. Admit it.

GEORGE: She feels nothing for me. Or anyone. Do you want to know what she really does? She serves me. She serves you. She serves anyone. But she doesn't give of herself. I've given up practically nothing, but it's a thousand times more than she has.

MIMI: Giving up. *(Drinks).* Yeah, I know all about giving up. *(Silence)* Giving up to the Americans in '44, yeah, I know all about that too. Giving up to the Resistance Fighters standing there in the street, ready, with a scissor cutting through my hair. *(Silence.)*

GEORGE: And where was the intrepid Puma in '44?

MIMI: He wasn't called Puma back then.

GEORGE: That was only when he was dodging grenades? In Korea?

MIMI: Yeah. In '44 his name was still Joseph. Where was he? At some friends' house. In the cellar. Hiding out. *(Silence. Mimi sticks her nose in the air.)* Giving up. That kind of talk disgusts me.

GEORGE: So the omnipresent father, the sleek, lean Puma wasn't around in time of need?

MIMI: *(Grinning)* No. Never in time of need. *(Silence. Sullenly)* It's all because Mira has no child, no daughter, of her own. *(Drinks.)* Go forth and multiply. It says in the good book that Jesus said that. Multiply. Or else you perish.

GEORGE: And why shouldn't we perish?

MIMI: As far as I'm concerned you can, you and everyone like you. Every last one of 'em. And quick.

GEORGE: And so we are, peg o' my heart. We're going down the tubes, you and me.

MIMI: If it's all the same to you, I'd rather you went first. *(Silence.)*

GEORGE: *(Tears coming suddenly to his eyes)* She's going first. She is. Before all the others who've humiliated her. *(Drinks.)* But what difference does it make who goes first? The whole earth is a grave we're dancing on. Billions of 'em are lying there beneath our feetsies.

MIMI: Give me a break. How can you say feetsies with those clod-hoppers of yours?

GEORGE: *(Drinks, chokes)* And I keep drinking champagne even though I know it's bad for my gastritis.

MIMI: *(Raising her glass in the air)* In that case, just give me the dregs.

GEORGE: *(About to pour it in, trips, and the bottle falls out of his hand.)* Sorry.

MIMI: Jerk, clumsy idiot!

GEORGE: Mimi, you want my hand on your craw?

MIMI: Hear that, Zorro? George is going to actually act a real pimp yet, one that beats up his women. Because like all real pimps he thinks there are no good women.

GEORGE: Did I ever say that there're no good women? Did you ever hear me say that Zorro? *(He takes the dog off the sofa. He dandles Zorro on his knee.)* Do you know how you can tell if a woman's good or not? The great James Joyce has a satisfying answer to this all important question. The great James Joyce said as follows: "You must take the woman in question to an art gallery and put her in front of a number of paintings. In a leisurely fashion patiently and comprehensively reveal the meaning of the paintings to her. Well if she breaks wind, that is not a good woman."

MIMI: You disgust me with that kind of talk. *(Silence. She takes back the dog.)* You're never going to become a good pimp, jerk, because you're too scared and ashamed of us.

GEORGE: Who am I scared of?

MIMI: Of Mira.

GEORGE: Who am I ashamed of?

MIMI: Of Mira.

GEORGE: You don't know me and you don't know your own daughter. No, even if you did feed her from your own breast reeking of all your customers' cigars, you don't know her.

MIMI: My daughter tells me everything. He may talk big, she says, but between the sheets he's a big zero.

GEORGE: She says that? Are those her own words? Unquote? Roger, over and out? *(Holds up a switchblade. Flicks it open. He grabs the dog out of Mimi's hands. She gives a shriek.)* Is what the lady says true, Zorro? Answer me. No? Do you refuse to recognize the authority of the infallible George, who can neither err nor lead another astray?

(He cuts the dog's belly open. Wads of hair fall out. Mimi screams

as though she were being murdered.)

BLACKOUT

SCENE NINE

(George and Mimi are watching t.v. A kiddie show. The dog is lying on the sofa. Mira enters, goes and sits down on the sofa, and watches t.v. Frans enters. George turns off the t.v.)

GEORGE: *(with forced joviality)* So Frans? How was it?

MIRA: He did the best he could.

FRANS: So did she.

GEORGE: Sit down, Frans. Make yourself at home.

FRANS: Yeah, well ... it's about time I....

GEORGE: I don't want to hear it. Sit down. *(Frans goes and sits.)* As a gentleman and traveling salesman you ought to know that at the very least you've got to do some after-sitting, some after-shmoozing, and some after-snoozing. Never overlook the afterplay, Frans! The ladies are very sensitive on that score, right, Mirabella mia? *(Silence.)* A beer, Frans? To wet your whistle? *(Frans nods, George exits out the side door stage left.)*

MIMI: *(To Frans)* And the least you can do Mr. Simons is to zip up your fly.

FRANS: *(Zipping his fly)* Sorry. I don't do this very often.

MIMI: Peasant! *(Softly to Mira)* How ya doin', honey?

MIRA: Fine, Mama, fine. *(She turns the t.v. on, then off again. Frans glances through the novel Mira was reading. She looks at him. He avoids her glance.)* I thought it was going to be different, just this one time. The last time. Dumb cluck that I am. I always think there's something else lying in store for us, for me, but I have no idea what it could be, but it's something else. But when I look around me, all I see is the t.v. *(Frans looks at his watch.)* Time to go?

FRANS: No, oh no. I've still got a couple of minutes.

MIMI: That's a Velona, that watch of yours?

FRANS: *(Surprised)* Yeah....

MIRA: Mama knows all the watches. One of the first tricks of the trade is to check out the customer's watch. See if it's a Rolex or a Cartier.

MIMI: Or a 1200 franc Velona. *(George re-enters with two beers.)*

GEORGE: But then you've got sneaky petes like our Frans here who run and switch their watches when they're taking off for the bars 'long the road, right Frans? Cheers.

FRANS: Cheers.

GEORGE: *(Listening)* Do I hear something? Sshh. Quiet a minute.

FRANS: It's the wind.

GEORGE: I thought I heard something.

FRANS: The wind started up, that's all.

GEORGE: Hey tell us Frans, what do you sell actually?

FRANS: Cars.

GEORGE: What do you know?

FRANS: Better quality cars. *(Silence.)*

GEORGE: I'm just about to buy my Mira a Porsche. 160,000 francs.

FRANS: Then there's got to be something wrong with it.

GEORGE: There's nothing wrong with it. It belonged to the late Janine. Her pimp Piero put it on the market. He can't stand to sit in it anymore. It cracks him up. So he'd rather pass it on to a buddy.

MIRA: I bet that Porsche reeks of Brylcream.

FRANS: Piero has absolutely no right to that car. We're gonna put a stop to that. *(George looks up)*

GEORGE: Right you are. That Porsche belongs to her. Legally. *(Goes to the door.)* Excuse me. I've got to ... er ... like they say in the quaint idiom of the region ... plant my potatoes.

MIMI: Peasant! *(George exits out the side door Stage Right.)*

FRANS: *(To Mira)* Everything'll work itself out. Don't get bent out of shape. Life goes on.

MIRA: *(Smiling)* You really mean "You're still young and healthy in life and limb, you've got a roof over your head and enough to eat, what more do you want?"

FRANS: Yeah. Something like that. *(Suddenly suspicious, looking at the stage right door, then at the stage left door.)* I thought the john was out that way.

MIMI: He went to the upstairs bathroom.

FRANS: Oh yeah?

MIMI: He has strange ways. Look. *(Showing them the wrecked dog.)* The good fellow got over-excited. The gentleman got angry. The good fellow took it out on Zorro. But Zorro's already been through so much in his poor dog's life, he can take it, can't you Zorro?

MIRA: *(Staring at the dog. Screams)* His guts are hanging out, his liver, his kidneys! All his insides! Mama! Why? Tell me, why? *(She gets up, stamps her feet, her eyes roll in their sockets. She falls. Frans jumps to his feet, goes to help her.)*

MIMI: Leave her be! Don't touch her!

FRANS: *(Dazed)* I didn't do anything. It's not my fault. *(He runs to the door, then out.)*

MIMI: Hey. Your bill! There's a bill that needs paying here! *(In front of the house, Frans looks right then left in a panic.)*

FRANS: *(Screaming)* Bob! Bob! I'm heading for the car!

MIMI: *(Holding Mira's wrist. Mira makes little moaning sounds.)* Sshh. Quiet, my child, quiet. Relax. Quiet.

(There is a light change. Music from "La Traviata." A storm wind rises, blows Mira clean off the sofa. She flies upstage, stands up with difficulty, runs to the door, smashes onto the ground. Rolls on the floor. Then she shoots up to a standing position like a marionette with flaccid limbs, and her entire body is convulsed with shaking. An irresistible force drags her backwards till she lands back on the sofa next to Mimi. The storm comes to a sudden stop, the music as well.)

BLACKOUT

SCENE TEN

GEORGE: *(Entering, sees Mira.)* Again?

MIMI: Again.

GEORGE: But there's usually one to four weeks in between.

MIMI: Not this time.

GEORGE: *(Angry)* Then we'll simply have to ram those goddamn pills down her throat. She can't just keep bouncing against the floor. Up and down, like a yo-yo. *(He sits down next to Mira, holds her head, and kisses her gently.)* I turn my back for one minute and boom, it starts in again! I had to ... I had to make a phone call in the bedroom ... to the Courier of the Lys.*(Walks over to the side door Stage Left. Returns with a bottle, pours a drop onto a towel, and holds it under Mira's nose.)*

MIMI: What're you doing now?

GEORGE: Vinegar. *(Angry)* One of these days she'll start in and not come out. Get me, you witch?!

MIMI: Should we call Dr. Minard?

GEORGE: What the hell does he know about it? Bullshit about "the twilight state" and about ... "nothing definite ... an opthalmic migraine...." We'd better get a specialist in.

MIMI: It's all Janine's fault. *(Mira comes to. Her mouth moves. What she is saying is inaudible.)*

GEORGE: I can't hear you, honey. I can't hear you. *(She keeps on speaking inaudibly. George gives her a swig of beer. She chokes on it. He slaps her on the back. He tries to loosen her collar. She defends herself against him, holds her dress collar tight. George tugs nervously at her dress. It tears right down the middle.)*

MIMI: Hey, have you gone crazy? A dress from Dior!

GEORGE: *(Throws the dress down onto the ground)* She's got to get out of those mourning clothes. Black, black, it's evil. There's nothing that needs mourning, the dead are dead. Murdered. Say an amen and forget it.

MIRA: *(Very carefully articulated)* It's time for me to go see my father again.

GEORGE: *(Suddenly looking up and down)* Where's the guy?

MIMI: What guy?

GEORGE: Mimi, how many guys were here just now? Were we

having a party, an orgy? The guy, the killer with the shades, Frans!

MIMI: He's gone. Without so much as by or leave. Like a peasant when he's finished eating.

GEORGE: Which way?

MIMI: Out into the open air.

GEORGE: And you just let him go?

MIMI: Without paying. *(George runs to the door. Goes out into the garden, searches.)*

GEORGE: Frans? I know you're out there somewhere, spying on us. That you're prowling around here like before. Come inside. We're not going to hold you responsible for anything, Frans. Won't say a word about the bill. Frans? We won't do you any harm. Not the least. We've got some stuff to talk over together, lots of stuff. Frans?

BLACKOUT

SCENE ELEVEN

GEORGE: *(Now softer)* Frans? *(The sun suddenly breaks through. Birds. A man, Bob, suddenly becomes visible in the tree by the front of the Mimosa. He sits, in his well-cut suit, quite at ease, on a branch.)*

BOB: He's gone back to his car.

GEORGE *(Takes fright as he sees the man in the tree)* Where?

BOB: On the highway.

GEORGE: Why?

BOB: He probably didn't like your place. *(Bob climbs lithely down from the tree. Jumps to the ground. Puts binoculars away. Comes up to George.)*

GEORGE: What are you doing here? Hold it right there. *(George takes out his gun and takes aim.)*

BOB: Do you have a license for that?

GEORGE: There's no need. It's tear-gas.

BOB: Oh, but there is. That falls into Category N.T.38 as a dangerous weapon. This one here *(Takes out a pistol as well)* falls into category W.G., article 40, dangerous weapons. "Dum-dum bullets." *(He brushes the dust off his pants. Puts his gun into a holster, brushes off his jacket.)* It may look uncomfortable, but a good tailor can fix that. Ya see? You can barely see it. Unless you know it's there. Then . . . .

(He makes for the Mimosa with decision. George follows him, confused. Bob's entrance provokes a certain amount of stir from the two women. Mira stares at him.)

BOB: Hello one and all!

MIMI: Hello, sir. *(Mira puts her torn dress to rights as best she can.)*

GEORGE: *(Comes inside as well. Looks inquiringly at Bob. Then, to Mimi:)* He was sitting up the tree. *(Bright light floods the room)*

BOB: I learned that when I was a para-commando. You've got to select the highest possible point for an observation post. *(Silence.)*

MIMI: You brought good weather with you, sir.

BOB: Yeah, but it's gonna rain anyway. Weather report says changeable. *(He goes and sits.)* It's nice here. Stylish. *(Points.)* Those hydrangea should get some more water though.

MIMI: It's like Grand Central Station here. The one runs off without paying and the other pops right in.

BOB: Come, come Mimi. Don't tell me you're not used to a little traffic in your establishment.

MIMI: It's not my establishment. Hasn't been for years.

MIRA: *(To Bob)* You were at Janine's funeral.

BOB: I asked you if you were the Queen of the Road to Kortrijk.

MIRA: Oh yeah, that's right.

BOB: That was a real funeral. All the right people. Atmosphere. Tears. Janine would have been pleased. *(He picks up a champagne bottle and looks at the label.)* '76.

GEORGE: May we offer you something?

BOB: I won't say no.

GEORGE: Cause I take it that you, considering your function ... since you're on duty ..., that you'd like to question us.

BOB: You're a sharp little devil, aren't you?

MIMI: What do you want to know?

BOB: Cool it, Mimi, cool it. Easy does it. Let me catch my breath. *(Silence.)* Do you have a digestive? Grand Marnier?

GEORGE: Sure enough. *(Goes Stage Right.)* How about an ice cube.

BOB: Ice? In Grand Marnier? Never.

MIMI: We don't get much call for Grand Marnier. The mayor of Schoonbeke used to drink it all the time, but he's been pushing up the daisies quite a while too. His Peugeot hit a powdered milk truck in a tunnel. He wasn't injured, but he suffocated under all the powdered milk.

BOB: *(Examining the butts in the ashtray. To Mira:)* Are you the one who smokes?

MIRA: Yeah.

MIMI: But never in the salon. That's a private room. There's nothing you can do about it.

BOB: But that's not my department, Mimi. As far as I'm concerned, you can smoke till you drop. Go ahead, smoke. Laugh yourself silly for all I care. That's up to you. Keep up the act as long as you can. *(George returns with a glass of Grand Marnier and the bottle. Bob sips.)* Not bad. I've always had a sweet tooth. By the way, I'm Bob. Easy to remember. B.O.B. from the B.O.I., Bureau of Investigation.

MIRA: I've heard of you. By name. But I didn't know it was you.

GEORGE: And your last name?

BOB: De Soter.

GEORGE: May I see your badge? It's our right.

BOB: *(Smiles)* You're not only a sharp little devil, but you're a nervy one at that. *(Faster than the eye can see he whips out a card, flashes it, and puts it back in his pocket.)* Seen it? Satisfied? Reassured? *(He looks at Mira. And she at him. The torn dress has fallen wide open.)* You certainly look relaxed sitting there, in your underwear. And you're right. You're easy on the eyes. Gorgeous flesh. *(Silence. Mira turns her back on Bob.)*

GEORGE: An interesting little piece of information regarding Grand Marnier is the story of how it got its name. The drink was invented by someone who was actually called Marnier, a real neurotic. Mainly because he was very short. And at the very moment when he wanted to bottle his invention and was looking for a name for it, his doctor told him "Mr. Marnier, you should call your brainchild Grand Marnier. You're small, but your art is great." And for the rest of his life...

MIMI: . . . he was happy.

GEORGE: Delirious even. So they say.

BOB: You learn something new every day. *(Silence.)* Why aren't you looking at me Mira?

MIRA: I can't.

BOB: *(Laughs)* There are three things you can't look square in the face: the sun, death, and me. Right?

MIRA: *(Muffled)* Right. *(Bob picks the mourning veil off of the sofa and shines his shoes with it.)*

GEORGE: You've gotta let us see a search warrant.

BOB: Correct. We've got to show one. Those are the rules.

GEORGE: And there're supposed to be two of you.

BOB: That is indeed the case. The rules.

(He brushes dust from the shoulder of his jacket.)

MIMI *(Gets up and and takes a small clothes brush out of a drawer in the cabinet and brushes off Bob's jacket.)* A little green from the tree rubbed off on it.

BOB: Many thanks, Mimi.

MIMI: My customers have never had anything to complain about when it came to cleanliness. I've always been on top of that. Everything clean.

BOB: Everything clean, except you, right? *(He laughs. He holds his glass out in front of him. George pours some Grand Marnier into it.)* Mira. Mira. A beautiful name for a beautiful broad.

MIMI: It comes from a book by the famous writer Stijn Streuvels. I got it as a present from Stijn Streuvels himself. Whenever he went out sailing with his pals, industrialists and so on, he always paid a visit to my father's farm, and then he'd drink fresh buttermilk. It was always summer in those days. It got real hot as early as April. Butterflies by the hundreds, clouds of butterflies. And evenings all the frogs in the area gave a concert. And when there was no smell from the flax, there was the smell from the smoke of the boats on the Lys. They used to sail the Lys with Queen Elizabeth sometimes. And Queen Elizabeth played the violin, you could hear it over water and over land. Seppe Coen, the furniture maker from Kortrijk was there, and Mr. Saverijs, the landscape painter of stuff that brings in half a million these days, and Stijn Strevels! They always drank fresh buttermilk at my father's. Streuvels most of all. Sometimes a whole quart. A handsome man, Stijn Streuvels, he never said much and he was a little grumpy, but he was a man of his time. He wore a light gray suit, a straw hat, and a walking stick, and that big bushy moustache with drops of buttermilk hanging off it. When he wrote the book about Mira, he got into a lot of trouble with the Catholics, because it was about a pretty girl that all the men stopped dead in their tracks for, and her name was Mira. And Puma said, "If it's a girl, then we'll call her Mira." *(Silence.)*

BOB: And you do get on your back for all the men, don't you Mira?

MIRA: That's what they really want.

BOB: *(To George)* And you're in charge of the cash register?

GEORGE: Never, never. I never take a cent. I have a legitimate profession at a reputable newspaper. I pay my taxes, I pay into my insurance and my retirement.

BOB: *(Smiling)* Then everything is surely in order. But you do live here. In a house, beg your pardon, of ill repute.

GEORGE: But really, a man can't leave these two women alone at night. Not these days.

BOB: That is noble. A fearless knight.

MIRA: *(To Bob)* Why did you come to the funeral?

BOB: To see you.

MIMI: Oh Mira, an admirer! It's been a long time.

MIRA: Then I shall have to admire him. *(Silence.)*

BOB: The thing is, I've got a little problem.

MIMI: Problems are our business. For each of our customer's problems we have a remedy.

BOB: *(Sharply)* Listen up good, Mrs. Whore, I'm no customer of yours. If you're able to retain that bit of information, then we might just get somewhere. All right?

MIMI: All right. *(Silence.)*

MIRA: What's your problem?

BOB: While working on Janine's case, we uncovered a whole slew of things. But we're under the impression that many things occur in the bars in the vicinity of the Coocoo -- like the Mimosa here -- which bear looking into. Which is why I've come to have a little sniff around here.

MIMI: Well, if you want to sniff, we've got some good stuff. From Rotterdam.

BOB: Mimi, do you think you can keep playing me for a fool? I've got a book full of information about you. I could bust you right here and now.

MIMI: Just try.

BOB: Oh, I know every well that a number of investigators from the Bureau come here for a free fuck, and that our chief's a customer and that he's into . . . um . . . we'd better not get into that.

MIMI: Every customer's entitled to his own little specialties.

BOB: Mimi, from here on out, either you keep your mouth shut or I shut it for you. *(Mimi laughs; a hoarse chuckle.)*

GEORGE: Hey, how about a little decorum if you don't mind, hm?

BOB: George.

GEORGE: What is it?

BOB: I have no use for you. I eat pimps of your stripe for breakfast. *(Silence.)*

GEORGE: Just for starters, there've got to be two of you.

BOB: There are two of us. Just not together. Mr. Simons, my right-hand man was here just now, and now I'm here. *(Silence.)*

GEORGE: I thought he might have been the murderer. He's dirty blonde and he was wearing sunglasses.

BOB: Our very own Frans a murderer? We're going to have a good laugh up at headquarters when I tell 'em that.

MIMI: I saw right away that there was something wrong with that guy. Policeman's eyes. A policeman's mouth.

MIRA: I didn't see that.

BOB: Did the fella at least have a good time?

MIRA: I know my trade.

BOB: So it seems. You've got a good reputation in the area.

MIRA: What do you want from me? Of all the women you have chosen me. Have you come to take me away. Must I go with you?

BOB: That'll depend.

GEORGE: On what?

BOB: On the evidence.

GEORGE: Regarding?

BOB: Potential aiding and abetting.

GEORGE: Who?

BOB: The killer.

GEORGE: Then you know who the killer is.

BOB: We have strong suspicions. *(He raises his glass. George pours him some Grand Marnier.)* I'm not going to question you. Because you're a quick, smart-assed devil. You've taken your precautions, you've got an alibi, witnesses. *(Drinks)* No. What interests me personally, is the why, the motive. Why does a person do a thing like that with a switchblade?

MIMI: I thought it was a razor.

BOB: No. A switchblade.

GEORGE: Yeah, why does a person do a thing like that?

BOB: My feeling is that we're dealing with a malcontent. You know the type. Someone who's not satisfied being who he is and having what he's got, someone who wants something else, something more, who's seeking sensation outside his own little circle.

MIRA: The killer was dirty blonde, a skinny young guy wearing dark glasses.

BOB: Young? Thin? Where did you get that? Who told you that? *(Mira looks at George.)*

MIRA: That's what I thought.

BOB: *(Looks in his notebook)* Mireille Martens from the Moonlight Café and Jules Vereecke, farmer, mention a dirty blonde man with sunglasses, that's all. No, Mireille Martens says a man about forty.

GEORGE: I hear ... that it was a young man.

BOB: Who from?

GEORGE: Oh, here and there.

BOB: Oh yeah? Well, just right now it doesn't matter what you may have heard. *(He looks at Mira. Silence.)* Didn't you think Frans was a handsome fella?

MIRA: I didn't pay any attention. A customer like any other.

BOB: *(Sharp)* Frans is no customer of yours. How much did you bilk him for?

MIRA: Not a penny.

BOB: And rightly so. The boy's about to get married. And he's my right-hand man. Whoever goes against him, goes against me. Why did he run off like that so suddenly?

MIMI: So he wouldn't have to pay, like all the other cowards in the B.O.I. *(Bob goes over to her and gives her a vicious kick in the breasts. She falls back onto the sofa.)*

BOB: I warned you.

MIMI: *(Yells)* Go ahead, hit me. Come on. Right here. Hit me why don't you? You're not a man anyway, you're a customer!

GEORGE: Now, sir, you're going too far. I'm going to report this to your superiors immediately. And that'll be just the beginning. If you think you can get away with anything just because....

BOB: *(Putting on black leather gloves)* I can do anything.

GEORGE: We may not be a nice Flemish family, as you've already indicated, but we've got our rights too.

BOB: My heart breaks to hear you talk about rights. It gives me a foul taste in my mouth. Rights, you? Dirty scumbags, pissbags, pieces of shit! *(Goes over to George.)* And that includes you. *(He strikes George on the behind.)* Is this where you earn your living sweety? Are those the Mimosa house rules? She takes it up the front and you take it from behind. Spreading illnesses throughout the region, so that anyone who sets foot in here and gets a whiff of your sewer breath rots right where he stands.

MIRA: That's not true. I'm clean.

MIMI: The doctor examines her twice a week.

BOB: Which doctor is that? The fine whore doctor Minard. He's well-known back at headquarters. Doctor Abortion! Isn't he the one who fixed you up after that business with the five-month old fetus a couple of years back? The file's right on my desk baby. Read it just this morning.

MIRA: I was cleared.

BOB: Not by me you weren't! In the eyes of the law maybe, but not by me! *(Goes over to Mira)* Don't you have the least little shred of self-respect? Never even heard of it? You let all the scum on the street dick with you, guys from the racetracks, Turks ... "Come one and all, fire away into my target..." with degenerates, with sick men with their diseased minds....

MIMI: Our Lord cares for the sick. We care for the sick.

BOB: Just as long as they pay, right?

MIRA: That's the arrangement. They're glad to pay.

BOB: What do you charge nowadays? For how long? The time it takes to smoke one cigarette? Light a cigarette, set it down on the night table, and when it's burned down, it's over, ready or not. And don't tell me I'm lying because I've been through it at Les Halles in Paris! And what else is in the rule book? Never kiss a customer on the mouth, right? Up the asshole as much as you like, and all kinds of fuckery, but no kissing on the mouth, oh no, that's reserved. *(He grabs her by the face, bites and kisses her on the mouth.)*

MIRA: *(Wipes her mouth. Smiles.)* Happy now?

GEORGE: Even if my report to your superiors gets thrown in the wastebasket up at the station, Mr. B.O.B. from the B.O.I., I'll get you just the same. I won't stand for this. I'll write about you in my paper if I have to. Last name and first.

BOB: *(Approaches him)* The gentleman's going to write, is he? He can write letters and get 'em published. Paper's cheap, bub. *(He grabs George by the neck and forces him down until he drops to his knees.)* Mercy. Say "mercy."

GEORGE: Mercy. *(Mira comes over and stands by George.)*

BOB: *(Lets go of him, but barks in his face)* We're going to make short shrift of your kind. This country's been far too patient with your brand of scum. We're going to take measures.

(He pours himself a glass of Grand Marnier and drinks.)

MIRA: Why do you do such things? For what reason?

BOB: I'm the reason.

MIRA: You aren't good after all. They uttered your name and said "He is cruel, but he is good." It isn't true.

BOB: *(Chuckling)* Me, Bob De Soter, good? *(He goes and sprawls out on the sofa. Looks inquiringly at Mira.)* What's wrong? You're laughing at me.

MIRA: *(Points)* You're sitting on Zorro.

BOB: Zorro? *(He jumps to his feet. The dog's hair is sticking to his suit. He grabs the hairbrush from the table and starts brushing the hair off.)* This dirty rotten crap. All over my suit. I pay twelve thousand francs for this suit, have it specially made in England, and the fucking hair from a dead dog in a whorehouse sticks to it. *(Mira smiles. George too. Mimi makes cackling sounds. Bob looks himself over thoroughly. Then goes over to Mira.)* I'm gonna nail you for this girly. *(He gives her a punch in the ear. She doesn't move. To George who is about to step in:)* Don't take another step you. Or you won't have one tooth left. Give me the coke Mimi. The stuff from Rotterdam you were chatting about.

MIMI: That was a joke. We can kid around, can't we?

BOB: Do you want to wind up in the hospital for a couple of months, Mimi? *(He sticks out his hand, she goes over to the cupboard, and hands him a little mother-of-pearl box. He looks inside, takes a lick of the powder. Sticks the box in his pocket.)*

GEORGE: You're strong. Okay. What you'd really like to do is to throw everybody like us in jail. Okay. You're the boss. If you like, we'll go down on our knees. Okay. Leave us in peace.

BOB: Never. I'm going to nail you, I'm telling you.

MIRA: *(Utters a plaintive sound. They all look at her.)* I'm frightened.

BLACKOUT

SCENE TWELVE

MIRA: *(Utters the plaintive sound once more)* I'm frightened.

BOB: Why is she meowing like that? *(Mira stands still and stiff as a rod with her mouth open.)*

MIMI: Baby! You're sweating so much.

MIRA *(Comes over to Bob, a professional grin on her contorted face. The words are emitted mechanically.)* Take your coat off. Is it that cold out? Your ears are all red. Hey, come here quick. By the open fire, by the flames. What'll it be? Whiskey? With soda? I'll have a Mirabelle. Sit back and relax, handsome. I'm gonna take real good care of you. What a gorgeous tie you have on. Take your jacket off. And your shoes. Make yourself at home. And tell Mira the one thing in the whole wide world you'd like the best. *(A thick stream of blood pours out of her ear.)*

GEORGE: The pills. Mimi, get those pills this instant.

MIMI: It's something else.

GEORGE: Mira. *(Mira takes a few steps, wobbles.)*

BOB: She's drunk.

MIRA: I'm so thirsty. *(Mimi brings over a glass of beer. She drinks, then spews it out.)* Pu-ma!

BOB: Oh, you know me! Boom-Bam Bob!

MIRA: Why did you run off, Boom-Bam?

BOB: I never ran off.

MIRA: You said that I ... I remember it so well .. never forget ... that I was your little queen. I sat on your knee, and you bounced

me up and down and said "Hop, hop, there's my little
queen." *(Blood starts to pour out of her other ear as well.)*

BOB: She's bleeding. *(George takes her carefully by the arm, makes
her sit, and wipes away the blood.)*

GEORGE: Goddammit Mira, you're doing it on purpose. Just to hurt
me!

BOB: Does this happen often?

GEORGE: *(Desperate)* Mimi, get the pills I'm telling you!

MIMI: It's too late.*(Mira emits a death rattle. Blood streams out of
her mouth.)*

BLACKOUT

SCENE THIRTEEN

*(The light changes. Music from La Traviata. The Soldier
enters, this time without snow on his coat or helmet.
Mira goes over to him. Snuggles up against him.)*

MIRA: You're so warm. It took so long. Thirty years. Come into my
arms, come. Am I your little baby? Or are you my little baby?
(Sings) "Me and Johnny sat on a pony. Johnny said see, it's
not me!" My angel. My angel with a peepee. Angels don't
have any peepee. But you do. I'll take good care of it. For as
long as I can. Till I can't anymore. *(Silence.)* I can't anymore,
my dear one. *(The Soldier takes her back to the sofa.)* Don't
leave. Please. *(The Soldier exits.)* No. Don't leave me alone
again. Just for once, no. Not now. Especially not now.

BLACKOUT

SCENE FOURTEEN

BOB: *(Goes over to the lifeless Mira, feels her wrist. Listens to her
heart. Gets up and makes the sign of the cross, murmurs
something. Then, to the others:)* Listen. It's just your bad
luck. She fell off the staircase, and the two of you brought
her over here from the stairs and laid her down on the sofa in
the hope that there was something still to be done. She bled
steadily. She kept falling down.

GEORGE *(Frantically eating a hot dog)* No. *(Mimi sits frozen.)*

BOB: We'll order an investigation. We'd better call Doctor Minard this instant. He'll be able to confirm the diagnosis. Fell. Brain hemorrhage. Weak blood vessels.

GEORGE: No. The real story.

BOB: If you prefer. It'll cost you a lot of money, a lot of bother, it'll go on for ages, lawyers, trouble. *(He goes to the door, goes outside, whistles through his finger. George goes over to sit by Mira, arranges her black dress.)*

MIMI: She already had her black clothes on. In mourning for herself.

GEORGE: You've got to put her blue Chanel dress on her, with the plunging neckline. And her blue satin Jourdan shoes. *(Silence.)* And white underwear.

(Footsteps. Outside Frans comes on the run. He goes over to Bob.)

BOB: We've got a problem here.

FRANS: I had a feeling. *(They come inside together. Frans sees the dead Mira.)* Is he the one who did it?

BOB: Yeah. He said "A mattress has gotta be shaken out good from time to time." Pimp talk.

FRANS: Okay. I'll go call headquarters.

GEORGE: Wait. *(Silence. George looks at Mimi who is staring straight in front of her.)*

FRANS: What do we do? *(Silence. A strong wind suddenly rises up. A door slams against the wall. Tinkle of breaking glass.)*

BOB: He says that she fell down the stairs. That could've happened too of course.

FRANS: We'll figure it out at headquarters.

BOB *(To GEORGE)* We might question you for twelve hours. We're sworn to. We can ask you about anything. About Janine for example.

(The telephone rings. George picks up the receiver.)

GEORGE: Mark? I was wrong. No, a false scent. No, I've got nothing to say. No. *(Lays the receiver back down.)*

MIMI: Do we have to go with you to the station?

BOB: You could make your statement here instead.

MIMI: That she fell down the stairs?

GEORGE: Yeah.

BOB: Yeah. *(Silence. Bob takes off his gloves.)*

FRANS *(Holds a notebook high in the air)* She had a criminal record, didn't she? *(To Bob)* What was it for again? An abortion a couple of years ago.

GEORGE: *(Furious)* No, no. No. She told you. The charges were dropped. She never had any children. Not one! She was Nullipare. Atokos, no child and no son. Atokos is the opposite of Theotokos, who gave birth to a god, goddammit! She fell down the stairs, say amen and forget it. Amen and forget it!

FRANS: Yes, but we've got to go according to the rules . . . .

GEORGE: She knew the rules. Humiliation, that's the rule!

BOB: Calm down.

(Silence. The two B.O.I. agents look at each other. Frans puts his notebook away.)

MIMI: She donated her heart to the university hospital. Her eyes too. The heart and the eyes. It's in a letter. She wrote it herself. It's upstairs.

FRANS: It'll all be taken care of, madam.

MIMI: "Madam" he says. Just say "whore."

FRANS: What's that?

MIMI: Ore, ferruginous earth. Whore, from the word "amour, amour." *(Silence)* Whore, that's what they called me in '44. When they cut my hair off in the street. And the wind howled and blew all my hair right in their faces!

(She grins.)

BLACKOUT

FRIDAY

Translated By
David Willinger and Lucas Truyts

CHARACTERS

GEORGE VERMEERSCH
JANE VERMEERSCH, His Wife
CHRISTINE VERMEERSCH, His Daughter
ERIC, A man from the neighborhood

(The action takes place in present-day Marke, a community in West Flanders.)

SCENE ONE

(Seven o'clock in the evening. It isn't totally dark out yet. The living room of the Vermeersch family, which up to one year ago, served as a beauty parlor. A few pieces of cheap furniture together with some imitation Malines furniture. Stage Left, there is a dressing table with a large mirror, onto which publicity posters are pasted. A few bottles and spraycans. A hairdryer. Upstage: A brown-stained staircase, leading to the top floor. Behind it: A sideboard on top of which are family portraits and a statuette of Our Lady, which can be illuminated from the inside by an electric light. Stage Right: The door leading to the hallway. A tartan sofa is positioned against the right wall, covered with a plastic zebra skin. Alongside it is a small table with a rather large transistor radio. Between the upstage wall and the sofa, almost out of sight, a crib. The Stage Right wall has a window that looks out onto the street. The Stage Left wall by the staircase has a door that leads to the kitchen. A t.v. on a low table. We hear a key turn in the front door.)

MAN'S VOICE: *(Outside)* Ah, so you're home again George.

VOICE OF GEORGE: Yes, Jerry, I'm home again.

MAN'S VOICE: Isn't it ahead of time George, hm?

VOICE OF GEORGE: Right Jerry, you can say that again.

MAN'S VOICE: Will you be coming over to the Zanzi tonight George?

VOICE OF GEORGE: I just might Jerry.

MAN'S VOICE: She's probably not home yet George. I don't think she is anyway.

VOICE OF GEORGE: Thanks Jerry.

MAN'S VOICE: All righty, take care George.

VOICE OF GEORGE: *(Closer.)* Thanks Jerry.

(The front door slams shut. The door to the hallway opens. George enters. He is 40 years old, powerfully built, with a pale, puffy face. He wears a light gray trenchcoat, a blue cap, a brown wash-and-wear suit, and a blue shirt with no tie. He carries an imitation leather

suitcase. He closes the door to the hallway behind him. Walks into the room, slightly ill at ease, looking around. He walks around the table and carefully opens the kitchen door.)

GEORGE: Jane! *(Briefly glances into the kitchen, goes over to the staircase.)* Jane! *(Waits. He sets the suitcase down on the sofa. Louder:)* Jane!

(Waits. A children's choir, singing a capella: "In Lourdes, in the mountains, appeared in a grotto, all shining, a-glow, the Mother of God." The song ends abruptly. GEORGE goes toward the sofa, picks up the suitcase, and sets it down next to the sideboard. He looks into the crib, picks a tiny light pink sock out of it, puts his hand in the sock and moves it around. Suddenly he listens tensely to the sounds outside and throws the sock back into the crib. Turns the light on. Waits, turns it off. He goes over to the sideboard, pulls the top drawer out and feels around in the empty space, pulls out a jack-knife, and puts it into his pocket. Closes the drawer; takes the jackknife back out. Pops the blade. Puts it back in his raincoat pocket. All of a sudden dashes to the window, looks out, and comes back. Sits down on a chair. Looks in front of him. With decision, he suddenly heads for the kitchen door. A door opens. Offstage, he shouts very loudly:)

GEORGE: It can't be. Goddammit!

(The kitchen door slams hard. He comes back. Grumbles under his breath. He holds a rhubarb stem in his hand. He bites into it and spits on the floor. Hits the stem violently against the table a couple of times. Sits down. Gazes at the crib. He gets up and stands with his back against the hallway door. Goes over to the sideboard, pulls out a bottle of gin, and drinks from the bottle. Puts the bottle back and sits down again. He rocks in his chair a bit, leans forward, and lays his head on his forearm. He lets out a loud shriek. Stares in front of him, his eyes wide open.)

BLACKOUT

SCENE TWO

(The front door. George jumps up. Adjusts his clothes. Assumes a rigid waiting posture, as Jane enters. Jane is an ample woman, 38 years old, attractive, neat; every now and them, when her guard is down, a touch of resignation and fatigue comes over her; but she is usually lively, even playful.)

JANE: Ah, there you are! So it's true!

GEORGE: Yes.

JANE: *(Uncertainly, quickly)* I thought it was a joke. Jerry said, "Your husband's home," but he's always talking and he's always pulling somebody's leg. "It's true," he says, "just go and see for yourself" I say, "If this is a joke, I'll pull all your hair out you creep." "I'm bald anyway," he says. Are you sitting here in the dark? *(She turns on the electric light. The statuette of Our Lady turns on too.)* It's really true.

GEORGE: I got here on the seven o'clock bus.

JANE: You're not out on leave, are you? You don't have to go back, do you?

GEORGE: No, it's for good.

JANE: Oh, George, George. *(She goes over to him. She tries to embrace him. He backs off a little.)*

GEORGE: Get away.

JANE: *(Pretending that she hardly noticed it. Suddenly fighting back the tears.)* If I knew, I'd have put on another dress, done my hair. How come you didn't even write me a postcard? Didn't call once? *(Wipes away her tears.)* It's true. So unexpected. You were supposed to be in for another two months. A person gets used to the idea of two months. And here you are, right in front of my nose. *(She goes very quickly up the stairs, looks in through the open door and comes back.)* Take off your coat.

GEORGE: How long were you out?

JANE: What do you mean?

GEORGE: Now, this afternoon.

JANE: Fifteen minutes.

GEORGE: I've been here for an hour.

JANE: (*Smiling*) Liar.

GEORGE: Yes. Really. . . . Half an hour anyway.

JANE: Why? (*Silence.*)

GEORGE: And you leave the baby all alone?

JANE: Did you see it?

GEORGE: No, I heard it. At first I thought it was rats.

JANE: (*She tries to smile; trying to keep it light.*) Rats on the roof, hunh? Didn't you even get a look at her?

GEORGE: No.

JANE: Don't you want to see her?

GEORGE: Not me.

JANE: You don't care. Is that it? You're right. You have a right not to want see her. But you're not going to have any choice in the matter. You'll have to see her sooner or later, tomorrow or the day after.

GEORGE: Tomorrow.

JANE: Yeah. You've got all the time in the world now.

GEORGE: I had plenty of time while I was there too.

JANE: It was rough, wasn't it?

GEORGE: You have no idea.

JANE: Jerry told me you'd lost weight, but I don't think so. Older, yes. You look like a different person.

GEORGE: They can really let you have it, you have no idea.

JANE: (*After a silence.*) How was the food in there? Beet soup they say. And rotten potatoes. A dog wouldn't go near it they say.

GEORGE: Yeah, but a hungry dog sure would. Besides, you don't notice it after a while, that there're black spots on the potatoes. Down they go. Just the opposite, you focus on the food while you're eating and keep yourself busy and you're almost satisfied.

JANE: Come on, sit down. Take your coat off. You look like you were stopping in for a visit!

GEORGE: It's been such a long time.

JANE: Wait a second. (*Sits down*.) Everything's spinning in front of my eyes. You could have knocked me over with a feather. They told me "Have a drop to drink first," but I said "If he gets a whiff of my breath first thing after such a long time, he might get the idea that . . ."

GEORGE: (*Goes to sit down too*.) I forgot this place was so big.

JANE: Weren't you even curious? (*Listens for sound upstairs*.) You didn't want to go take a peek at the baby? Really.

GEORGE: Really.

JANE: Men are strange customers.

(*Silence*.)

GEORGE: And women aren't? Goddammit Jane! (*Jumps up, throws the door open, and points*.) What about my garden? Take a look at that. The leeks, the winter celery. And take a look at that pear tree! And that rhubarb. And those weeds. Goddammit Jane, is weeding too much to ask?

JANE: (*Almost in the same vehement tone*:) And who was supposed to do it? I'm too pooped to pop when I get home at night from Filatex.

GEORGE: Oh come on Jane! So the garden's gone to shit. Look at it. (*Waves the rhubarb stem; his voice is softer now, almost threatening*.) It's like a rubber club. . . .

JANE: I meant to make jam out of it. And I started to too, but when you've been standing on your feet at Filatex all day. . . .

GEORGE: You had other things to worry about, didn't you?

JANE: (*Pulls at his raincoat*) Take that off. (*She helps him out of his rain coat and hangs it up in the hallway*.) What's in the pockets that's so heavy?

GEORGE: Just some stuff I couldn't fit into my suitcase. Keep off it.

JANE: (*As she comes back*.) You're stuffed into your shirt like a link sausage. You're fatter around the middle.

GEORGE: Didn't you hear what I said? I said that maybe you had other things to worry about.

JANE: Maybe so.

GEORGE: Were you coming back from his place just now? Was it with him you were spending those "fifteen minutes?"

JANE: Yes. His mother isn't feeling all that well. In her stomach. The doctor says she can't drink coffee anymore.

GEORGE: How about him? Was he there too?

JANE: Damn straight. He gets off work at five. And he always comes right home.

GEORGE: You mean here? Isn't this his house?

JANE: He's not the same man anymore George. You wouldn't recognize him. He works, he brings home his paycheck. He's like a different man.

GEORGE: He's like a different man, I'm like a different man. I don't recognize myself here in Marke anymore. And he really doesn't play cards anymore?

JANE: Oh sure. But that's his only hobby.

GEORGE: His only one. And you, what do you call yourself?

JANE: Yes, he gets pleasure from me too. You going to make something of it George?

GEORGE: (*Takes the bottle of gin out of the sideboard. He puts small glasses down, takes the bottle out of his hands and pours the drinks.*) Cheers.

JANE: To true love, like they say.

GEORGE: You can say that again.

JANE: (*She gets up and strokes her hips.*) Notice anything? I've put on some weight, but not too much, hm? What d'you say? If you didn't know about it would you say I'd just delivered a baby three months ago?

GEORGE: Yes, if I didn't know. . . .

(*Silence.*)

JANE: It's nice having you sitting right here George.

GEORGE: Good behavior. You have no idea.

JANE: Don't dwell on it anymore. Seriously, don't you want to see it?

GEORGE: Son of a bitching Christ, do you have cotton stuffed in your ears? It's got nothing to do with me, I don't have to see that animal.

JANE: It's a girl.

GEORGE: I knew that all along.

JANE: It's not an animal.

(*Silence.*)

GEORGE: And is she healthy?

JANE: (*Stubbornly.*) She weighed almost six pounds. Now almost nine.

GEORGE: Almost double. Is that normal?

JANE: So they say. At the day-care center they can't take their eyes off of her.

GEORGE: I can imagine. My God, everybody wants to get a look at her, that's for sure. Some of them probably think we conceived the kid in the space between the bars!

(*Silence.*)

JANE: What do we do about that whole mess George? It's up to you. Eric and I will go along with whatever you say. Divorce? It costs a whole load of money, it takes forever, and -- I don't know -- we're not that kind of people. It's not like it is in the city.

GEORGE: And where would you have to go?

JANE: To his place. He says it's okay. So does his mother.

GEORGE: (*Nodding his head in the direction of the sideboard behind him.*) Where's the picture?

JANE: What picture?

GEORGE: You know damned well. The one of Christine. Of her Holy Communion.

JANE: I put it away. In the attic.

GEORGE: Why?

JANE: Because.

GEORGE: Put it back where it belongs. PUT THAT PICTURE BACK THIS INSTANT!!

JANE: Now?

GEORGE: Now! And make it snappy!

JANE: Stop shouting like that! You'll wake the baby. (*She goes to the dressing table, takes a photos in a silver frame out of a drawer, and puts it down on the sideboard, next to the other family portraits. George stands up and places the picture at an angle.*) Now are you happy?

GEORGE: Yes.

JANE: Another one? (*She immediately pours a drink.*)

GEORGE: (*Smacking his lips.*) Is that Filliers?

JANE: Yes, the special kind.

GEORGE: It's bitter. I forgot how bitter it tasted.

JANE: It's all chemicals now. How about a glass of beer to chase it?

GEORGE: Sure, okay. (*She heads for the kitchen.*)

JANE: (*Off.*) But if they watch themselves and stay on "good behavior," does that mean all prisoners can go home, even the killers?

GEORGE: The warden, I mean the assistant warden, called me into his office. Vermeersch, George, he says, we haven't had any complaints about you, you've done your time all right and -- due to circumstances back at your house -- he says, it's all right for you to go home.

JANE: (*Who has come back in the meantime.*) Well, you see that at least there's one good thing about it.

GEORGE: What?

JANE: What he was talking about I mean. The circumstances at home.

GEORGE: That's for sure.

JANE: Oh, you have no idea how many times I got ready to come on Tuesdays with a bag full of tobacco and oranges and newspapers. Every Tuesday I stood here raring to go. But, hm . . . you didn't want to see me. Your mother, yes, and the lawyer, them yes! How could you George, to your own wife?

GEORGE: That's exactly what the assistant warden said. Vermeersch, George, he says, she has visiting rights, same as you. Stubborn as a mule, he says. "I've been unjustly locked up in here," I said, "Well, why don't you go ahead and lock me up altogether? I don't want to see anybody." "Well, work it out for yourself," he said. (*Silence.*)

JANE: Aren't you hungry?

GEORGE: Not now. A little later. Not yet.

JANE: You gotta get used to it first, hm?

GEORGE: I'll never get used to it.

JANE: Never ever?

GEORGE: Not me.

JANE: That's too bad. (*Silence.*)

GEORGE: How about you?

JANE: I don't know. You know me. If I'm not sick and I've got a sandwich, a glass of beer, and a bed, then nothing can really get to me.

GEORGE: Well, you've got a bed now all right. And nicely warmed up too, right?

JANE: (*Very angry.*) He's been here half an hour and he's already pestering me again, and hitting below the belt, and nagging just like in the old days, as though nothing ever happened. If you don't like it here go back to where you came from. Why don't you stay there if you like it so much?

GEORGE: (*Grimly*) If I ever go back to jail, sweetie, I'll get you good, you'll get what you deserve all right. (*Silence.*) What are you thinking? (*Long silence.*) That I belong in jail?

JANE: I didn't say that.

GEORGE: But you were thinking it.

JANE: There's freedom of thought. (*Silence.*) I wanted to have your garden cleaned out and weeded before you got out, but you came back too soon.

GEORGE: Who would have done my garden?

JANE: Him, Eric.

GEORGE: He's all thumbs.

JANE: (*A tiny triumphant laugh*:) That's what you think!

GEORGE: (*No pause*.) Oh, they stand up straight for fucking around, do they? I've got to hand it to him, then, straight as a nail.

JANE: He wants to marry me and adopt the baby. He doesn't care what the neighbors say. They can all go to hell as far as he's concerned.

GEORGE: But he sure cared what they said during the trial. Your fine Eric with the handkerchief over his mouth. "Yes, Your Honor, I know George very well, but that business with his daughter, Your Honor, well I wasn't there and I can't say anything about it."

JANE: What should he have said? "I was standing there with my nose sticking out?"

GEORGE: He could have testified the way he was supposed to. "Your Honor, George would never have done such a thing with his daughter. He had too much respect for her."

JANE: But I said it 20 times over. George would never do a thing like that. He's got too much sense of honor. And did they believe me?

GEORGE: (*Suddenly laughs very loud; stops abruptly. Then clumsily imitates the judge*:) A sense of honor is entirely alien to the defendant as is the most human feeling on earth, that of a father towards his underage child.

JANE: Child! Are you putting me on Your Honor? Don't say that where people down the block can hear it. Our Christine, a child! They'd pee in their pants laughing if they heard that.

GEORGE: Another outburst of that sort, Mrs. Vermeersch, and you'll be convicted same as your husband, maximum of three years for contempt of court . . . . (*Trails off; listens*.)

JANE: Yup, he almost threw me out. (*A sudden gust of wind. Hail. Rain. Jane doesn't hear it*.) But anyway, it's all over. You're free.

GEORGE: Not really. I'm on parole for two years still. (*Silence*.) Sometimes when I think about this neighborhood here, of this house, and you and that other one, it almost seems to make no difference if I'm here or there.

JANE: Fine. That's gratitude for you, after all I've been through.

GEORGE: (*Taken aback*) What did you do for me?

JANE: Didn't I go see the warden? Didn't I get down on my hands and knees in front of him?

GEORGE: To the Warden?

JANE: Yeah, that gray-haired man with glasses.

GEORGE: What did you say to him?

JANE: "Let him go. George didn't do it. He didn't lift a finger against our daughter. She's a whore. The whole city of Kortrijk's been to bed with her. And she's the biggest liar you'll ever see. It's a disgrace that the court would believe that slut before her own father." And I howled like a dog; right into his coat. Every time I saw him. He got drenched with tears every time. He had to push me away.

(*Silence. Jane goes over to the t.v. and turns it on.*)

GEORGE: Turn it off.

JANE: But it's "Bonanza."

GEORGE: Off I said. (*She turns it off.*) There's more noise in prison, doors slamming, inmates walking around. I didn't realize that our street was so quiet.

JANE: They're all watching "Bonanza." (*Silence.*) It's as though there were a stranger in my house. (*Silence.*) Why wouldn't you let me come to the jail? You can tell me now.

GEORGE: Everyone lied to me and cheated me. You too. You did your best during the trial. But not enough. You did shout "He's innocent" to the judge, but it didn't ring true, the judge could hear it in your voice. And when a man sees that going on in front of his very eyes, when a man knows that no one believes him, not even the Lord, then he shuts the doors, all the doors.

JANE: But you yourself sat there on that bench, acting like you didn't even believe it. That's what the lawyer said. Madam, he says, tell your husband he's got to answer the judge. I'd rather he were lying through his teeth, he says, but he has to give an answer when he's spoken to. He's digging his own grave.

GEORGE: If I'd had some money I'd have gotten a real lawyer, a rich one. Not a snot-nose assigned by the court.

JANE: That fucking bitch Christine!

GEORGE: She had me by the balls, didn't she?

JANE: And she laughed as if to say: You threw me out of the house and now I'm paying you back. There. Ha! And she laughed.

GEORGE: You and your daughter, two peas in a pod.

JANE: I'd never do things like that.

GEORGE: (*Not missing a beat.*) What things?

JANE: Well telling lies like that. My heart's still in the right place.

GEORGE: Watch what you say.

(*Silence.*)

JANE: She stood there shaking and wriggling in her mini skirt and lying right to your face. And you, you hardly dared to look at her.

GEORGE: Because I'd be ashamed if I were her. Dragging her own father through the shit while everyone's right there watching.

(*Silence. The phone rings.*)

JANE: It's ringing.

GEORGE: (*Rough.*) Pick it up.

JANE: Hello. Oh, it's you Mom! (*George makes vehement gestures that he's not there.*) Yeah, yeah, it's a long time ago. Asthma? Last night! Oh we've all got problems with our nerves Mama. Yes, I made jam. Apricot. With that stuff. Thursday night? Is that all right? Okay, I'll be expecting you. A permanent? All right. George? Well he's okay, absolutely fine apparently. No it won't be long now. He'll be here before you know it. Good behavior. You don't have to cry on account of that Mom. Of course he was innocent. I know. Okay now, blow your nose once real good. Yup, see you Thursday. Don't let it get to you so much, Mommy. Okay, goodbye Mommy.

GEORGE: (*Rolling a cigarette; almost casually:*) What was that she said about "being innocent?"

JANE: She started crying.

GEORGE: What did she want?

JANE: It was as though she sensed you were home.

GEORGE: She did her best at the trial. Even though she raised too much hell with Christine. The judge caught on that she was trying to save me.

JANE: I've got to give her a permanent Thursday. For when you come home, she said.

GEORGE: She's getting old.

JANE: In the beginning she didn't want to talk to me when she'd just found out about Eric and me. The neighbors rushed over to tell her about it. At first I denied it of course, you know how your mother is with her priests and her Saint Anthony and all. And then, well, I couldn't hide it anymore. She saw it in a flash. I wasn't even three months along. She peered at my belly. Jane, she said, is that what I think it is? Yes Mama, it is. Oh, she said, and you haven't been to see George in jail either? Not me, I said. So it isn't George's, she said. No, I said. But when the baby was born she did come to the maternity ward. She said something about "forgiveness," but they'd given me a shot and I only half understood it. I was so alone there George. And then after the whole neighborhood turned against me even more than before. Nobody wanted me to do their hair. I had to do hair-dos for forty-francs a piece. That didn't even cover expenses, and then even the forty-franc ones stayed away.

GEORGE: And then you went to work at Filatex.

JANE: It's not so high-paying there either. 35 francs an hour.

GEORGE: Doesn't that guy give you any money?

JANE: He paid for the shots and the iron pills the insurance didn't cover. And for the day care center.

GEORGE: He should have paid for just one pill a lot sooner.

(*Silence*.)

JANE: (*Worried*.) And he's been losing at cards lately.

GEORGE: That means he's in love.

JANE: (*Smiling*.) You numbskull. He wanted to sell the dressing table and the hairdryer, but I said, "Wait until they let George out. It's from his money just as much as mine." What should I do? Sell the works or not?

GEORGE: Whatever you want. If people don't want to have their hair done anymore, so what?

JANE: We could move. (*Silence. She goes and sits.*) What do you say?

GEORGE: Who? Us together?

JANE: I'm just saying it to say something.

GEORGE: Do I really have to hammer it into your stupid fucking head that it's over and done with and thank God between us? You've got yourself a new guy, a young guy, a guy that takes good care of you in bed and who pays for the day care center -- well grab him and bag him, you and the brat together and leave me out of it!

JANE: All right, all right! Don't get upset.

GEORGE: (*Stands.*) Get up. (*Fiercely; she, frightened, stands hesitantly.*) Stand up straight when I come in. Vermeersch, you've been standing at the window. The guard saw your face and your right hand holding on to the bars. Are you trying to say that the guard is lying Vermeersch? Who slipped that little note to Jules the customs inspector when you were taking your walk? Answer me Vermeersch. Was it you Vermeersch? No. No who? No Sir. Three days no canteen Vermeersch. We'll teach you. You haven't shaved. You were lying on your bed, see for yourself. I can see the dent in your mattress. The dent in your mattress. (*During this outburst George has grabbed Jane's wrist and twisted it. She screams.*)

JANE: You're breaking my hand!

GEORGE: (*Lets go at once. Sits at the table. Pours himself a drink. Then fills her glass.*) Here.

JANE: (*Rubbing her wrist.*) I don't want anymore.

GEORGE: (*Drinks.*) Is this really Filliers Special?

JANE: (*Yells.*) Yes! (*Silence.*) Have you forgotten everything?

GEORGE: (*Softly.*) I haven't forgotten anything, anything.

JANE: You've got a mind like a steel trap. Whatever goes in never comes out again. Is that right?

GEORGE: Yeah, that's right.

(*Silence.*)

JANE: Christine even said it. Ma, she said, that's the kind of man my father is -- thinking and scratching his head till it bleeds.

GEORGE: When did she say that?

JANE: Two weeks ago.

GEORGE: She came here? You're lying. Does she come here?

JANE: (*Contemptuously.*) She came here to have her hair done. It's cheaper than in the city. It's for free. Mother'll use the stuff left over from when she was a hairdresser.

GEORGE: How's she doing?

JANE: I don't ask her. Okay I guess. She sold me that transistor radio -- 1000 francs. It was Freddie's. He left it behind when he had to join the army. He decided to be a paratrooper just like all the scum do. She's got a new boyfriend now, Rickie. He's got long hair and wears a woman's blouse.

GEORGE: Does she still hang around that same café all the time?

JANE: No, the police won't let her anymore. But now she practically lives at the Tropicana with Rickie. She wears a mini skirt that comes up to here. I told her, you can do anything you like in the city, run around with your ass bare, but see to it that you're decent when you come back to Marke. Of course it goes in one ear and out the other. Anyway I don't really care, it's in now and if the neighbors don't want to see it they can just look the other way.

GEORGE: And . . . and how does she look?

JANE: Good, she turns plenty of heads.

GEORGE: Yeah, she takes after you.

JANE: Yeah, when I was younger. But she can be so tough. I don't understand her. She's so smart and educated and some-times, when you hear her talk it's as though she wanted to destroy herself. Men smell it and they come after her.

GEORGE: On top of her.

JANE: Yes.

GEORGE: I better not see her or else. . . .

JANE: Or else. . . .?

GEORGE: I'll beat the shit out of her. (*Silence. The frontdoor bell* rings, very loud and shrill. George cringes.) I'm not home. Don't open the door. It's the police. From parole.

JANE: (Looks out the window.) It's Jeff. He's got a bottle under his arm.

GEORGE: I don't want to see anyone.

JANE: (Parts the curtain a bit, taps on the window, and mimes as she talks.) No, he's tired. He's already asleep. Bye. Tomorrow. (She comes back over to George.) He says he'll come by tomorrow. (He doesn't answer. She goes to the t.v. and turns it on. There is a program about the port of Antwerp; senators are debating each other.)

GEORGE: Turn it off.

JANE: It's just about over. "The Van Outrijve Family"'s on next.

GEORGE: Off.

JANE: But it's about that family, rich families from the Campine that have it in for each other. From the nineteen hundreds. I've seen all four installments. This is the fifth. That one, Juliette, wants to marry her friend's father, a manufacturer, but he's about to go bankrupt. You'll like it. It's terrific.

(George gets up, turns it off. Silence.)

JANE: And now? What are we supposed to do now? Listen to the sparrows?

GEORGE: Yes, to the sparrows.

JANE: (Is about to go over to the t.v., doesn't, circles about quickly and nervously.) I understand we can't live together anymore. A blindman can see that. We're not cut out -- not cut out to be together anymore. . . . Right? Hm? You agree? You're a worry-wort and I know that it takes all kinds to make up the world, worry-worts included, but now, after all this time being alone, I'm not going to put up with it anymore, George, I can't handle it like before. We're much too different, you and me, you're more like. . . .

GEORGE: How do you know what I'm like? I don't even know myself and --besides-- you yourself said I'd turned into a different man.

JANE: What I mean, George, is that you're not satisfied, you never were. Christine's the same way. . . .

GEORGE: (*Cutting her off.*) You can move. In with him.

JANE: Fine. (*Silence.*) That's settled then. You here and me there.

GEORGE: It's not that I've got anything against Eric, you know that, but it would be best for all concerned, a clean sweep. You here and me there.

JANE: Anhanhanh!

GEORGE: (*Noticing the mix-up. They both laugh.*) Aaah, I meant . . . Christ Almighty, that'd be some pretty picture, you here and me there.

JANE: Yeah, you there with his mother! She's always got something wrong with her, with her stomach, with her heart; and she keeps harping on about it for days on end. She goes to a quack near Lille; a real saint she thinks. She brings him a urine sample and he swings a silver cross over it. Last week she got some little coin and when there's a sour taste in her mouth she's supposed to suck the coin.

GEORGE: Why didn't his mother come to testify?

JANE: Well. . . .

GEORGE: I never did anything to her, did I?

JANE: No, no, but she's like all those other people in the neighbor-hood. You've got to kick their asses to let 'em know you exist and even that they exist. But at the same time, you can't kick too hard. And the whole neighborhood testified against you. And why? Because you acted like they didn't exist. People think you think you're too good for them, that you're too high and mighty, that you look down on them. And then when things go wrong, when you're in trouble, they all gang up on you at the same time.

GEORGE: But that the court should let itself be taken in by that! What kind of testimony could they possibly give? The butcher who came and said that Christine sat on my lap, is that a witness? Is there one, one who saw what happened, or what's supposed to have happened? And how about the psychiatrist, a man who studied all his life getting one diploma after the other said it was nothing but suppositions. But the court doesn't listen to that, oh no, the scum from off the street can come explain it all and come lie and that's what judges listen to, because that's what they want to believe, because they want man to be a beast, act just like a beast! Suppositions! I told my pals in jail, I told Jules the customs inspector who sat next to me in the cell for three months (*Falters.*) and they all said the same thing, that a person who's not in jail wants just one thing: to stick his neighbor in as soon as possible for as long as possible.

(*Silence. Hail, wind rattle the tiles.*)

JANE: When do you want me to move?

GEORGE: Whenever you want to.

JANE: Me? You've got to decide. I don't have the law on my side. You do.

GEORGE: (*Drinks slowly.*) There's no rush.

JANE: What am I supposed to tell him?

GEORGE: Your sweet little Eric? Tell him that George understands it, understands very well that people lie and that they live off other peoples' misery, that Vermeersch, George is no better either . . . (*Suddenly very angry.*) but that he could have taken care of my garden, goddamnit! That lazy bum. My wife, yeah, her he could water, but my beautiful garden?!

JANE: (*Goes over to the t.v. and turns it on.*) If that's the way it has to be.

GEORGE: Listen to me when I talk to you!

JANE: I'd rather listen to "The Van Outrijve Family."

GEORGE: The problem's with the Vermeersch Family.

(*He jumps up; in one leap he's next to the t.v. and turns it off.*)

JANE: (*She is over by the t.v., tries to get to it. They push each other out of the way.*) It's my t.v. set as much as it is yours. I've been keeping up with the installments on it all those months. And I want to see the fifth episode, otherwise I won't be able to follow next week's.

GEORGE: (*Heading for the hall door.*) I'm going to Zanzi's.

JANE: Get out. And don't come back until you've come to your senses. (*She tries to turn the t.v. back on but the knob is stuck.*) The knob is stuck! It's broken! You were so violent. You turned it way too far. You were so rough with it. My t.v. is broken!

GEORGE: (*Turns the knob.*) Wait. Here. Shit. It won't go. (*He tries something else.*)

JANE: Not that, numbskull! That's for sound.

GEORGE: (*Turns. A very loud noise.*) It was already broken. (*He smacks the set hard with the palm of his hand. His anger rises.*) Goddamn shitting . . . lousy box!

JANE: (*Pulls him off.*) Keep your paws off of it!

GEORGE: (*Pushes her off.*) There. Watch this. (*He gives the set a kick right in the middle of the screen. Kicks it onto the floor and stamps on it.*)

JANE: You're out of your mind. My t.v.! There's still 6,000 francs to go on the payments. (*Shouts louder.*) Now what am I sup- posed to do tonight? I wanted to watch "The Van Outrijve Family." That's all I asked. Look at it now. You filthy animal. (*She flies at George, claws out-stretched. He fends her off. A heavy tousle follows. He holds her by both wrists.*)

GEORGE: An animal? What do you mean by that? That I'm to blame? Well is that it? (*He bends her over backwards.*) That that was where I belonged, behind bars? You're nothing there, in the dark, and when you breathe too loud there's no one can hear you. And when you drop dead there's no one to help you in that darkest of dark pits. (*Wind. Rain. Clicking of keys.*) Go ahead and scream. Shriek all you want. Concrete walls and a hole in the ground and you're lying there naked as a worm, screaming until the Dear Lord comes with His hammer and nails and hammers the nails right into your belly.

JANE: (*Yells.*) George! (*He lets her go. Silence. Softly.*) You can't hold your booze anymore kid.

GEORGE: I know what you're thinking. Oh don't think I can't read what's in your eyes after all this time. I can see right into 'em. I'm not scared of you. Of nobody. All those days, all those bags I put together, all those books I read, all the stench from the other men. No one can make up to me what I went through. You, you stupid bitch, you're not dancing on my grave yet. You with your small-time con-artist and your stupid brat upstairs! (*He tries to strangle her.*)

JANE: Kill me. If that's what you want, go ahead.

GEORGE: (*Lets go of her.*) You'd like that too much.

JANE: Yes, I'd like for it to be over! Do it. Please! And fly on back to the clink. You shouldn't be allowed to walk around loose, you wild dog. (*He grabs her again, but this time the violence is more subdued. He pulls her hair, feels her breasts, slips his hand under her skirt. She suddenly stops resisting.*) No. (*But she lets herself be dragged over to the sofa. He kisses her on the neck.*) Oh George, please. Come, George, come. (*She embraces him.*) You're it George, you and no one else. (*He swings his leg over her.*) No. Lie still. No George, not now. It wouldn't work now.

GEORGE: (*Who hasn't been listening to her, but to something else nearby.*) No. (*He crawls further on top of her. He backs off a little.*) I don't feel like it anyway.

JANE: (*Staring. She gets up, straightens her clothes.*) You don't feel like it?

GEORGE: No.

JANE: Why not?

GEORGE: My head is spinning.

JANE: It's been too long.

GEORGE: It's the booze.

(*Silence.*)

JANE: What are you thinking about?

GEORGE: Of nothing, nothing at all.

JANE: Are you sure?

GEORGE: (*Looks at her in a new way. What does she mean? Doesn't answer. Then says, almost tenderly.*) It won't work Jane.

(*Silence.*)

JANE: (*Softly.*) You said my name. Jane.

GEORGE: It's too big a change. Man wasn't meant to be thrown from one thing to another like an egg in a frying pan. (*He sits down. She starts to clear away the debris of the t.v. set.*) From jail straight back here just like that, it's too much all at one time. They should let you out every now and then on a

> Sunday for a day or two. That way you'd know that the
> world's still spinning 'round on the outside.

JANE: It's my fault.

GEORGE: Jules the customs inspector said, "It's always, everywhere,
at each and every moment, our own fault."

(*Silence.*)

JANE: You've kicked that t.v. to pieces just because we bought it
from Eric.

GEORGE: I hadn't thought of that.

JANE: Sure enough. Go on and say it.

GEORGE: I won't say it because it isn't true.

JANE: As though you always told the truth. (*George looks up.
Silence. Jane puts the t.v. back on top of the low table.*)
We'll have to make payments for another six months now.

GEORGE: Maybe he'll forget about it.

JANE: (*Laughs.*) Who? Eric?

GEORGE: Why not? He paid for the doctor and the day care center,
but that's for his baby. But what's he paying for you?

JANE: He doesn't have to pay anything for me. He gets me for free.

GEORGE: Everything everywhere has to be paid for. Anytime you
want something, cash. On the table.

JANE: Then I should be paying him because I was interested in him.

GEORGE: And how about him? (*After a silence. They are attempt-
ing to explore this terrain nonchalantly.*)

JANE: He did too.

GEORGE: And does he do it good?

JANE: He's young.

GEORGE: Younger than me you mean.

JANE: Well he is younger. What are you driving at?

GEORGE: Well you're so happy.

JANE: He hasn't known me all that long. It's still pretty new.

GEORGE: Is it because he's good at it? And does it a lot? More than me in the old days?

JANE: Worry-wort! (*She goes to the kitchen, comes back with a dustpan and brush. She cleans up the mess and takes it back to the kitchen.*) He wants us to go and live in Kortrijk, all new and modern-like, with a Bolinex hairdryer. Nobody knows us in Kortrijk and there are a lot more women that get their hair done. He'd be closer to where he works and it would be easier for the baby too.

GEORGE: Why not? You could have Christine come and live with you. You get along so well, the two of you.

JANE: Over my dead body. She may be smarter and more modern than me, but she's rotten to the core.

GEORGE: (*Sharply.*) Do you mean she's sick?

JANE: No. I asked her one time. I said, "One day with all those bums you shack up with, one of these days. . . ." "I'm careful Mom, I'm careful," she said. Even though she'd been having an affair with a Turk there for a while, some kind of Algerian.

GEORGE: An Algerian?

JANE: The idea that they let that kind into the country!

GEORGE: And that's who she gets it on with?

JANE: I told her, "Christine," I said, "did you ever count how many of those guys there've been one after the other?" "Fewer than you think," she said.

GEORGE: There were six of them at the trial.

JANE: Yeah, but two of them were liars. (*She laughs briefly.*) Do you remember that young guy with the curly hair and the short leather jacket that couldn't understand the judge? Have you had intercourse with Vermeersch, Christine? Excuse me Your Honor, he said. I beg your pardon. What is intercourse? (*George can't help but laughing too.*) And then it came out that they were lying, those two, so they could brag about it at the Tropicana.

GEORGE: That makes four.

JANE: For those young squirts nowadays four isn't that much. She's young and she does what she wants with her body. Right George? Right? (*She is insisting too strongly.*)

GEORGE: (*Grimly.*) Anyway it's better that she's doing it now than later, after she's married.

JANE: (*Fiercely, angrily*.) One time, one guy beside you the whole time we've been married, that's all. And what was I supposed to do? You didn't want to see me during visiting hours, even the murderers got to see their wives. And here with the whole neighborhood turning against me, a stargazer in jail and nobody to say one word to, I'm still young, am I supposed to bury myself like you maybe? You've got to admit that you're lucky that I didn't go running around before this. Sometimes with you it was like being married to a sailor away at sea or a priest. You were already in jail before you were actually in jail. (*The kettle whistles in the kitchen. She goes for it.*)

GEORGE: You can have him, your young guy, hair and all.

JANE: (*Offstage.*) You're jealous of his hair, aren't you? It's so thick you could make a brush out of it.

GEORGE: Against your belly.

JANE: Yes anywhere!

GEORGE: Drop dead. And him too.

JANE: (*Comes back carrying two cups of steaming coffee.*) Here.

GEORGE: (*Drinks. Burns his mouth.*) Goddammit. (*Blows and tastes.*) Is that coffee?

JANE: Yes it is. Was the coffee in jail better? It's instant. Moccona.

GEORGE: (*Drinks the coffee. Grumbles.*) It's too much to ask her to make real coffee. It's too much to ask her to weed the garden.

JANE: Yes it is too much if you want to know the truth, it's all too much for me. Just try going to Filatex and standing up all day long until your legs start swelling, in the dust, till your throat cracks it's so dry, with all that racket and shouting, till when night comes and you're in bed, you're still shaking as though you were riding on a machine? Christine's absolutely right to sit on her butt in the sun or at the swimming pool everday with a long-haired sucker to screw her every now and then. If I could do it over, I'd do the same thing and pronto. Just like that.

GEORGE: But you are doing it, my dear wife!

JANE: (*Fiercely.*) The thing with Eric and me is different. We love each other and you can go stand on your head with shaving cream all over your filthy puss, that's the way it is.

GEORGE: But just a minute ago on the sofa you said, "It's you George, you and no one else."

JANE: (*Softly.*) That's what I was thinking. (*George reacts to that. Drinks coffee.*)

GEORGE: Instant.

JANE: Put some sugar in so you won't taste it.

GEORGE: When I go back to work I don't want to have this lousy tasting dishwater. You're going to make me some real coffee then. (*Silence.*) I mean I'm going to make sure I have real coffee when I go to work.

JANE: Are you going back to Honeywell?

GEORGE: Where else can I go?

JANE: If they still want you there.

GEORGE: I'll have to. Otherwise parole will be at the door.

JANE: If you go ask Mr. Hendricks and you're polite and you say that the whole thing was based on suppositions. . . .

GEORGE: Yeah. I'll go there hat in hand. You mustn't be scared Mr. Hendricks. Yes Mr. Hendricks, I'll do my best. No Mr. Hendricks, I'll never do it again. No Mr. Hendricks, I won't look at young girls again, I won't sit next to them in the canteen, I'll sew my pants shut Mr. Hendricks, I'll cut it off Mr. Hendricks, and I'll throw my little dick into the River Lys Mr. Hendricks.

JANE: (*Can't help laughing.*) You asshole.

GEORGE: The trouble is that there are so many people out of work as it is. And that they'd rather have young squirts.

JANE: What did you do with your little dick while you were in jail?

GEORGE: (*Silence.*) I'd rather not talk about that.

JANE: I was only asking. (*Silence.*) I was only asking, no one's forcing you to answer.

GEORGE: It's only when you're in jail that you realize how stupid we all are, how we never really think, how we only think about our normal everyday lives.

JANE: What else is there but our everyday lives? You'll wind up in a monastery, you.

GEORGE: Jules the customs inspector told us that jail wasn't so bad, we're getting ready for the next life.

JANE: But your customs inspector was put away too, wasn't he?

GEORGE: Yeah. Two years.

JANE: For smuggling?

GEORGE: No, for his dick. (*Silence.*) Like me. Hm, exactly like me. Exact same dick, hm? Jesus, the same one Jane.

JANE: I didn't say anything.

GEORGE: (*Gazing at the cup.*) Is that a new cup?

JANE: Yeah. From the margerine coupons. (*Silence.*) Do you want to see Eric?

GEORGE: How many times in a row can he do it?

JANE: I'm not going to talk about that. It's none of your business.

GEORGE: You're right. Not that I'd be angry if I saw him.

JANE: If you saw him would you behave yourself and not lose your temper?

GEORGE: But I've always liked Eric. He's a guy with a lot of common sense. And whatever happened between you, well, these things happen. There's really not much he could do about it. It's his blood type, his make-up. (*Jane goes to the hallway after having picked up a red hand towel from the dressing table.*) What are you doing? Keep out of my pockets.

JANE: Why?

GEORGE: Because.

JANE: I never looked in your pockets before. (*Comes back.*)

GEORGE: (*Holding the empty bottle up in the air.*) We'd have done better to let Jeff come in with his bottle.

JANE: Jeff's another fine feathered friend. He spun around my house like he had to lay an egg or something. You hadn't been in jail two weeks when here he stood, ready for attack. It's been fourteen days already he said. So what I said. I won some money, he said. So what, I said. Well, he said, I might just want to split it with you, he said. I can see you coming you prick, I said. Right, he said, you can see my prick coming, he said. I said, hey come on now, please Jeff, please. He said, I thought you were such a hot bitch and that fourteen days without a man would be more than enough, that's why I waited so long. I told him this: Jeff, you'll have to wait till your teeth fall out and you're dead and buried. Well thanks a lot, he says. Well if at first you don't succeed... One month later he was standing here again. I've got one great big bill here for the asking. You're not going to spit on that are you? I said, Jeff I won't spit on the money, just on you, right in your eye. You're not listening.

GEORGE: Are you trying to tell me that you've still got a chance with the men? I know that Jane, I know. You don't have to rub my face in it.

JANE: Oh brother, his lordship got up on the wrong side of the bed this morning. (*Silence.*) Aren't you hungry?

GEORGE: A little. My stomach's still going by prison time. It's routinized down to the minute. In the beginning I wouldn't eat. Well Vermeersch, George, are we on a hunger strike like in India? Do you want to make trouble for me with the inspector? So then I started to eat. At first it tasted like cardboard. Even the pie, and you know what a sweet tooth I got.

JANE: I used to call you Sweet Tooth when we got engaged George.

GEORGE: It's a long time ago already.

JANE: Twenty years this winter.

GEORGE: (*Gets up, goes into the hall, comes back with a package, and hands it to her.*) This is for you.

JANE: For me? (*She opens it. He sits down, watches uncomfortably as she digs out a small bottle of perfume.*) Soir de Paris!

GEORGE: (*Quickly.*) I bought it with the money I made from putting the bags together. Other inmates buy sardines and canned peaches and chocolate, but I thought it was a sin to waste valuable money that way. Twenty, twenty five francs a day adds up.

JANE: Thank you very much George! (*She approaches him as*

though she wanted to embrace him. He gets up and goes toward the t.v.) Soir de Paris, you remembered. *(She puts some perfume behind her ears. He looks at her.)*

GEORGE: Put some in your armpits too. *(She does.)* You can let him smell it.

JANE: You can too George, you can too. *(He goes in her direction. All at once there is hail and heavy rain. Doors banging. He sits down.)*

GEORGE: May a landslide rush all through the whole town, may the whole hill come tumbling down in one fell swoop, may it slide right off and all of Marke and the whole street under mud and clay and foam, in through all the windows and doors, one huge heap of mud, and all of them scratching and rummaging in the swamp, five minutes, no more, no less, and then, all of a sudden there's no more screaming left to hear, no breathing, nothing.

JANE: Only the sparrows.

GEORGE: Yes exactly. Only sparrows and thrushes. *(The bell rings just like the last time, very loud and shrill.)*

JANE: *(Before George can say anything, he's already making a gesture of defending himself.)* It's Eric. *(She goes to the hall.)* I asked him to come over.

BLACKOUT

SCENE THREE

(Jane comes in with Eric behind her. He is about 30 years old, dressed in fashionable country-wear -- striped suit with polo shirt. A cheerful aggressive expression. Thinner than George, yet strong.)

JANE: It's Eric. I asked him to come over. *(George sits up in his chair, then sits down again.)*

ERIC: Well?

GEORGE: *(Smiling.)* Well?

ERIC: Goddammit, it's none too soon you know, none too soon. *(Comes toward George and gives him a pat on the* shoulder.)

JANE: Have a seat Eric. (*Eric sits down. Silence.*)

GEORGE: I heard you're back to work again.

ERIC: No more card games. I lost the pants off my butt. They started to plan out their strategy against me at the Zanzi. Lucky I figured it out in time.

GEORGE: And how about business? The t.v.'s?

ERIC: Don't like it anymore. Every house on the street has a t.v. set all its own, and to go begging in Kortrijk? Oh no, I'm happy at Northern Textiles. There are six of us warehouse clerks. I do play cards sometimes, sure, but not for the big bucks anymore.

GEORGE: Is that right?

ERIC: Sure is.

(*Silence.*)

JANE: Would you like a drink?

GEORGE: There's no gin left.

ERIC: I don't drink that anyway. Give me a glass of wine Jane.

GEORGE: Wine? Is there wine in the house? That's new too.

JANE: He can't take hard liquor. (*She takes a bottle of wine from the sideboard.*)

ERIC: Yeah, it makes me scratch. One drink and I itch all over. Which doesn't happen with wine.

GEORGE: Give me a glass of that wine too. (*They drink.*) It's not bad.

JANE: I bought 12 bottles at one time. It saves you ten francs a bottle.

GEORGE: Especially for him?

JANE: And for me.

GEORGE: Is that so?

ERIC: If you don't like it George, all you have to do is speak up and I'll go back home.

GEORGE: Why? She asked you over, didn't she?

ERIC: Yes.

GEORGE: And you waited a while for me to settle down a little after all this time. What went through your head? I'll give him an hour to get used to things and then I'll show up?

JANE: I signalled to him with a towel. I have a red towel by that window

GEORGE: And that means the coast is clear? Congratulations, it's a good idea.

JANE: It saves you the four francs for the phone.

ERIC: (*Spotting the t.v.*) Holy shit. Look at that! (*Goes toward the set.*) Well have you ever in your life? Smashed to bits. That's beyond repairing.

JANE: He did it.

ERIC: Out of anger?

GEORGE: Out of anger.

ERIC: At us?

GEORGE: At you.

ERIC: I understand George, I do, but -- Jesus -- George, a brand new set . . . . (*Assesses the damage.*) It's totally fucked up. Terrific. Well done.

GEORGE: I could have done the same thing to your face.

ERIC: Think so? (*He smiles. Silence.*) You can throw it in the garbage bin. Maybe a couple of spare parts can be salvaged, but it won't be much. Hey, you won't be able to see Eddy Merckx tomorrow night at the Milan Racetrack. He sure is something, ain't he? They say he takes pills, but they all do and he comes in first anyway, right? You can come over and watch it at our place tomorrow if your want.

GEORGE: (*Pouring himself another glass of wine.*) I'll be working in my garden tomorrow Eric. You dirty rotten son of a bitch, did you look at my garden even once? All my vegetables in the mud and covered over with weeds!

JANE: (*Laughing nervously*) He said, he sure can water my wife, but not my garden.

ERIC: Didn't I say, 20 times over, Jane, we've got to clean up his garden by the time he comes home? It's not my fault you came back too soon George.

GEORGE: I can go right back this minute if you want, on the first streetcar that comes along and stay there if you want me to. I can even give the police a real good reason to put me behind bars again, for life even if that's what you want.

ERIC: (*Grinning.*) Then go ahead and do it George. (*George gets up, gives Eric a hard blow in his face before he can stand all the way up. He then pulls Eric up to his feet, kicks his legs out from under him, causing Eric to fall over backwards. This happens very rapidly and efficiently. George holds up his jackknife, flicks it open, and holds the knife one inch from Eric's eyes.*)

JANE: George! Honey! Please!

GEORGE: (*Hissing.*) The madman's back home again. You can't hide anymore. There'll be no more laughing. You've hung out your last red towel.

ERIC: George, don't!

GEORGE: (*Pushes the blade back in. Backs away from Eric, who is getting up with difficulty.*) You see, I could have done it easy. And I wouldn't have gotten a life sentence either. They would have been forced to let me go. I was in my legal rights. A man can protect his wife when she brings a pimp into his house.

ERIC: I thought I was done for.

GEORGE: Sit down. Have another glass of your wine. Our wine.

ERIC: You really had me scared.

GEORGE: What were you thinking about? What passed before your eyes?

ERIC: I almost wet my pants. (*They laugh together.*)

JANE: Now are you happy? You showed us all that you're the boss.
. . .

GEORGE: (*Interrupting her:*) I'm nobody's boss. Not me. People who think they're boss are a different breed. People like me never get to be boss. People like me need a knife to make people think we're the boss. (*Silence.*) Well, where are my parakeets? You promised you'd take care of them.

JANE: But we told the lawyer that we had to get rid of the parakeets, that there was nobody to take care of them since we both go to work.

ERIC: We ate them up. Jane, Mother, and me.

GEORGE: Were they tough?

ERIC: Like seagulls.

GEORGE: Have you ever eaten seagulls?

ERIC: No I haven't. Thrushes, yes.

GEORGE: Then what are you talking about?

(*Silence.*)

ERIC: Cheers. To your coming home.

JANE: Cheers.

GEORGE: Cheers.

(*They drink.*)

GEORGE: You've been here 15 minutes and you haven't even asked how your baby is.

ERIC: (*To Jane.*) Is she sleeping?

JANE: Like a rose.

ERIC: She weighs almost nine pounds.

ERIC: She's such a beauty.

GEORGE: They're all beautiful when they're small.

ERIC: We named her Elizabeth, after Elizabeth Taylor. But we call her Lillie. Get another bottle Jane. It's not Sunday every day of the week.

GEORGE: Friday. (*Jane goes to the cupboard, takes out a bottle, and pours the wine. Hail. Clinking of keys. Metal doors slamming shut.*)

ERIC: And five pounds've gotta come out. That's quite a load for such a tiny passage. The Good Lord could have made it a little easier.

JANE: Still it came like a letter in the box. I gave one or two shrieks and there she lay.

GEORGE: It was the same thing when Christine was born. They

called Honeywell and I was stuck with my bike on the road by the bridge. I raced like a speed demon but . . . by the time I got here she was already lying in the crib. Christine.

ERIC: Was it this same crib? (*Nods to Upstage.*)

GEORGE: No. Another one.

JANE: Who's hungry?

GEORGE: I've been hungry for a long time already.

ERIC: What you got to eat?

JANE: Hamburgers, rare just the way you like them. (*Jane goes to the kitchen. She walks in and out with plates, etc.*)

ERIC: Let's have it. They say if a hamburger's rare, it's supposed to be eaten right after it's made. Three minutes later, it's already full of worms. And every minute it sits there, more come. It seems like they just keep multiplying. . . .

GEORGE: You haven't shut your mouth from the minute you walked in here.

ERIC: (*Not missing a beat.*) This isn't a jail you know! It's nerves. It's seeing you again George. (*Silence. Eric can't take the silence.*) What do you think about the Darings? Anderlecht's going to make mincemeat out of 'em. Did they let you watch t.v. in there?

GEORGE: No. Why are you so nervous?

ERIC: I'm scared of your knife.

GEORGE: You never know when it might come in handy.

ERIC: Not on account of her I hope.

GEORGE: Not anymore I guess. (*Casually.*) Who's going to wind up in the number two spot this season do ya think?

ERIC: Assa from Ostend they say, or Beerschot. (*Jane has now finished setting the table. She starts to sit down, but George points to the sideboard.*)

GEORGE: Take out another bottle, just in case. (*They eat. George eats only bread with cheese.*)

JANE: (*Putting some meat on his plate.*) Here, take it before that slob devours it all.

GEORGE: I don't eat meat.

JANE: Why not?

ERIC: I grossed him out talking about the worms.

GEORGE: No, today is Friday.

JANE: (*After an amazed stare.*) I've still got some tuna salad left.

GEORGE: Okay

(*She goes to the kitchen*)

ERIC: Eating fish on Friday's not so fashionable anymore, is it?

GEORGE: To me it is.

(*Jane brings the tuna and sits right down weary.*)

ERIC: (*To Jane.*) Isn't there any ketchup?

GEORGE: (*Seeing that Jane is about to get up again.*) No. (*To Eric.*) You're over-heated enough as it is.

ERIC: All right, all right. They didn't give you hamburgers in there, did they?

GEORGE: Mainly head-cheese. Sausage . . . . Gives you tape-worm real easy.

JANE: How's the tuna?

GEORGE: Not bad.

(*They eat in silence.*)

JANE: The two of you are going to have a serious talk together.

GEORGE: Well, Eric, we going to have a serious talk for once?

ERIC: You start.

GEORGE: No, you gotta start. 'Cause you were the first to start in with Jane.

ERIC: Me? Me?

JANE: I started first.

ERIC: No, George was the first to start with Christine.

GEORGE: (*Stops chewing. Holds his sandwich up in the air.*) What do you mean by that? Hanh?

ERIC: That if that case between you and Christine hadn't happened, if there'd never been any trial, things would've taken a whole different direction, and I wouldn't have set foot in this house more than necessary. So there.

JANE: He came to see if there was something I needed.

GEORGE: (*With heavy irony.*) And you did need something, it turns out.

ERIC: You let your mother and your lawyer visit you in prison and she was sitting here eating her heart out.

GEORGE: Which means that she was the one who started.

ERIC: Both together.

GEORGE: Which day was it? What time was it?

ERIC: Yes, what time. . . .

JANE: A quarter to five. We were coming back from the burial of Charlie, the fishseller.

GEORGE: Is Charlie dead?

ERIC: Cancer of the liver.

JANE: But I wrote you about it in a letter, didn't I? George, don't tell me that you didn't read any of the letters I wrote. It's your own business if you didn't want to answer them, but please George, you did at least read them? I sat here all bent over. You know how hard it is for me to write letters. (*She is crying.*)

GEORGE: I read them, but I forgot about Charlie.

ERIC: We'd just come back from the funeral and you know what that's like. . . .

GEORGE: No I don't.

ERIC: Well, we were talking about Charlie of course.

GEORGE: Not about me?

ERIC: About you too, but mostly about Charlie, about how quick it happened. They cut him open and had a good look and sewed him back up again in a flash. And fourteen days later, his liver gave out.

GEORGE: And you were here all alone.

JANE: Yes.

ERIC: She says, it's hot.

GEORGE: And in order to give her some air you pull her skirt up over her face.

JANE: Cut it out George.

ERIC: It's too hot in here, she says. And I open the window and she stands behind me, like she wanted people passing by on the street to be able to see it real good. And she kisses me on the neck.

JANE: But that was after you said, "It's too bad the women on the block don't want to have their hair done anymore, because George is locked up." "But," you said, "I'm not going to let that keep me away." And then, laughing, I said, "Well, I'll wash your hair." And I washed his hair.

GEORGE: And then?

ERIC: We stayed here till I went to the Zanzi to see the Tour de France on t.v. Van Springel won that day, eight minutes ahead of everyone else.

JANE: Goddamn it George! It was simple. We could see that we loved each other.

GEORGE: How could you see it? How can someone see it?

JANE: I'd finished washing his hair and it must have been because of the steam rising up, because of my nerves. My head started spinning when he touched me.

ERIC: And then I laid her on that couch there.

GEORGE: On the couch.

ERIC: With her head to the door.

GEORGE: (*In an artificial voice.*) Was the electric light on at the moment of intercourse and is it possible that persons on the public road noticed you, saw or heard you? Yes or no? (*Screams.*) You're lying through your teeth. (*George rubs his fists in his eyes. Silence. Fragments of pop music.*)

ERIC: Did the jailers treat you decently anyway?

GEORGE: You're supposed to say guards. They were called jailers before the First World War. Well yes, they did. The warden, I mean the assistant warden, was a serious guy. You're all my children, he said, so long as you abide by the rules. Otherwise you're in trouble. "Vermeersch, George," he said, "what kind of music would you rather hear?" I said, "Any kind, warden." "That can't be," he said. "Every man has a kind of music he prefers, which matches up with his blood type." And he checked my file card. "You see," he said, "you're bloodtype AB. So you need to have soothing background music."

JANE: Where did they get that?

GEORGE: "And I myself," he said, "I really must have rousing music." He was type O. Do you know why they let me out so soon? (*Leaning back, drinking, liking the attention.*) It was Christmas day and they'd baked a cake with whip cream and jam, especially for the occasion. And the officer said, "Boys, cake for everyone tonight, including the ones in solitary." And the chaplain said, "All right, so long as it's after midnight mass." Okay, so everyone gladly ate the cake, two, three pieces, me too. And guess what happens? The cake was made from flour that was six to eight years old, delivered by Bellegem Mills. They always get the contract because they have the lowest prices and because the manager of Bellegem Mills is the brother-in-law of the commissioner for tourism. Anyway, the flour had fermented or something, you see what I'm getting at? Everyone, all the inmates, got sick in the guts. Poisoned. I've never heard such a racket in my life, everyone screaming and shitting till their guts were hanging out. Jules the customs inspector was blue and green and did nothing but spit up and moan. It just so happened that the warden was away on a skiing trip in Switzerland. The doctor was at a party and a bunch of jailers were home for Christmas at their mothers'. The assistant warden stood there all on his own, and he couldn't remember where the doctor's party was and there we stood, the inmates out of their cells, lying in the hallway, screaming, howling, and throwing up. The assistant warden was pulling his hair out. They were dropping before his very eyes. "Vermeersch, George," he said, "my whole career, all those years of service, down the drain." So me and him and a few nurses and two or three other inmates like me, tough guys, we worked all night like stretcher carriers, giving them shots and pills one by one. Anyway, it all worked out all right in the end and only three of them had to be sent to the hospital. "Vermeersch, George," the warden said, "You're better than any nurse from the Red Cross." Yup.

ERIC: And that's why he let you go early.

GEORGE: When my case came up before the commission, he put in a good word for me. Against the officer's better judgement. (*Silence.*) And the day after I had to sweep and scrub out the corridors.

JANE: And you were able to handle the cake. You could even down cobblestones.

GEORGE: Yes, but not your instant coffee. Have you seen her new cups? (*Shows a cup.*)

ERIC: Yes, they look like they come from India or China or somewhere over there.

JANE: Yes, the design's the tree of life they say. A hundred fifty margerine coupons for the whole set.

GEORGE: New cups, twelve bottles of wine, things are going good here.

ERIC: And soon, a new t.v.!

GEORGE: My ass, buddie!

ERIC: I can take it off your hands, if you want, but first you'll have to finish making the payments.

GEORGE: Take it and take her. Go ahead and take her right now, clothes and the whole kit and kaboodle. Take the works and that'll be an end to this yapping about it.

(*Silence.*)

JANE: And who would take care of you here?

GEORGE: I can pull my own weight just fine.

(*Jane laughs too loud.*)

GEORGE: (*Tough.*) Pull down the blinds. Now. (*She does.*) Let's not let the people in the street see how I'm entertaining a whore sitting there laughing and her pimp here in my house.

ERIC: (*Fiercely.*) It's your own fault and nobody else's. You shouldn't have left us alone.

JANE: You would maybe have preferred Jeff here in his place. Or Jerry?

ERIC: If it hadn't been me it would've been somebody else, someone who might've sold the furniture out from under her and neglected her.

GEORGE: I really hadn't expected it Eric, I didn't think you would. Especially since you like HEAVY women. (*He draws breasts in the air.*) I can still hear you say, she's gotta be thin around the waist, but on top you've gotta have something to hold onto. And Jane's just the opposite.

ERIC: Oh I don't know.

JANE: I'm not that skinny am I? It's gotten better since the baby.

ERIC: And isn't a man allowed to change his mind?

GEORGE: His mind yes, but not his preferences. No sir, you did it just to get at me. I'd never have imagined it. No sooner do I turn my back, but you swipe one of my balls.

(*Silence.*)

ERIC: (*Low.*) And you, you didn't do nothing. You're white as a lamb. I can hear you saying a few things too. "Look," you said, "I don't understand why people should stick so tight, that I don't get, why they should hang on to each other like that. If someone wants to fuck my wife and she's interested in him, well why should I get bent out of shape over that?"

JANE: Did you say that George?

GEORGE: Just to have something to say! To sound off. It was before the trial. At the Zanzi.

ERIC: Well, I didn't forget and she was interested! (*Fiercely, to George, who had taken his knife out.*) And put that knife away. You're not a cowboy.

GEORGE: (*Gets up. Pacing up and down, taking even steps. Comes to a stop near the sofa.*) It was here? (*Sits on the sofa.*) Pretty soft. (*Paces again, like prisoners on their daily walk do.*)

JANE: Sit down George.

ERIC: Were you alone in the cell?

GEORGE: (*Stops pacing.*) Yes, but when it got too crowded they stuck three prisoners in together. Never two, always three.

ERIC: (*Laughing.*) But whatever two can do, you can always do with three.

JANE: Don't talk about that Eric.

GEORGE: Why not? Our section, cells nine to seventeen, was the prick section. I was in one cell with Jules the customs inspector for nearly three months. With him and Johnny Bosschaerts, the football player.

ERIC: The frontman for the Eendracht Merelbeke team you mean?

GEORGE: That's right.

ERIC: Now that you mention it, he hasn't been in the game at all this year. They beat Waregem, 6 to 3.

GEORGE: He was a good buddy, let's call it that. And Nachtergaele too, the manager for the Nachtergaele Laundry. The president was on Van Eendracht. But Nachtergaele felt like getting another player, a much younger one. Johnny realized that the good life was over so he ran off with four hundred thousand francs he stole from Nachtergaele. And they caught him at Zaventem Airport. Yup. (*George drinks.*)

ERIC: So that's what he was up to. Did he leave you alone?

GEORGE: Oh Johnnie only did it for money. Otherwise he was just like you and me. He was no Algerian.

ERIC: And what do people do there by themselves or in threes, George, when it gets dark?

GEORGE: Some of them tried to do it into a keyhole.

ERIC: Goddamn.

JANE: The poor slobs.

GEORGE: What would you do?

ERIC: Me? I wouldn't care if it were a woman, a man, or a cauliflower.

JANE: Well thanks a lot kiddo.

ERIC: I mean at a time like that when you don't know if you're coming or going.

GEORGE: Still, it's not you at your best, saying something like that in front of Jane.

ERIC: (*Angry.*) Wrong again! I can't say a word without you getting on my case. What's got into you?

GEORGE: In prison no one ever thought I was getting on their case. People liked me there. The warden said so. "Vermeersch, George," he said, "you're from the country, you come from good stock, you've got common sense." (*A voice outside:*

"Vermeersch, you son of a bitch." The sound of about ten people near the window: "Vermeersch come out." Only George hears this and he is scared.) Who's there?

ERIC: Where?

(The noise stops abruptly.)

GEORGE: Nothing.

JANE: The baby? *(She tip-toes up the staircase. Listens, comes back down, and clears the table. Disappears into the kitchen. She stays there and does the dishes. Now and then she can be heard doing things.)*

GEORGE: No. *(When she is gone.)* Well?

ERIC: Well what?

GEORGE: Why are you staring at me like that?

ERIC: No reason.

GEORGE: Am I black or something? *(Fiercely.)* Hanh?

ERIC: No.

GEORGE: You didn't even go and take a look at your baby. It might be lying there dead in its bed, and you, you keep sitting here. And you call yourself a father?

ERIC: More than you are.

GEORGE: That's going too far, Mac. Way too far. *(Silence.)* Have you seen Christine lately?

ERIC: A couple of times. When she was here. She's getting finer every day. She may turn into one fine woman some day, but so far she's still a little girl. She's not our kind of people anymore, running around with those guitar players and those long-haired good-for-nothings. I told her, Christine, sometimes you'd think Jesus Christ himself was there with you, with all that hair and those beards. We talked about it some more. Jesus, she said was a serious man, he set an example, but nothing else. He was a good man, from something B.C., but not anymore. God is everywhere, she says, in the house, in the meadow, in a pear tree, in a Japanese beetle. And if only we'd love each other, there'd be no more wars and no more misery. I said, is that why you all get together so much and stick your legs up in the air? Is that the new religion? You should see her with her mini-skirt on. When the wind blows it's a technicolor spectacular.

GEORGE: She say anything about me?

ERIC: I said, Christine, how could you bring such disgrace down on your father? It was the plain truth, she said. You fucking liar, I said. And even if it was true, why did the police have to know about it? Otherwise they'd have kept Freddie locked up, she said. It was either him or my father. And Freddie got a suspended sentence because he swore he'd marry her.

GEORGE: (*Ponderously; the alchol starting to take hold.*) And Freddie ran off to join the marines. He left her alone, all alone. (*The voice outside: "Vermeersch, get a move on. Come on, we're waiting!"*) All right! All right! (*He listens. Nothing more is heard. Silence.*) Isn't it amazing, Eric, that there aren't more murderers in the world than there are?

ERIC: Weren't there enough murderers in there?

GEORGE: The pharmacist from High Street was there, the one who'd taken too many of his own pills and burned his wife with an iron. And the secret agent who'd shot that kid in a bar. And then of course there was Célestin, who committed a murder in France, and they'd almost got hold of him when he quickly fled to Belgium, and he hid out at his old schoolteacher's place in Roeselaere. He asked if he could spend the night. The schoolteacher said it was okay and Célestin cut his throat while he was sleeping, in order to get convicted here in Belgium, you see, since they don't have the death penalty here. A man is worth less than a worm.

ERIC: For those guys it is I guess.

GEORGE: For everyone. Less even, less. (*There is some heavy thumping on the door. George jumps up. Voices bawling outside. George alone is able to hear this.*) I'm not home. I've got my rights.

ERIC: Jane! Come here.

GEORGE: Leave me alone.

JANE: (*Comes onstage.*) What's going on?

(*The voices become clearer. Someone is kicking against the door. Voice: "Yoohoo! George -- I dare you to come out. Dirty overheated dog. We'll teach you.*

We're gonna let you have it you cocksucker! We'll cut
your little pecker off with a razor, you scum! You're not
gonna live on our street anymore you asshole. There'll
be no more daughter-fucking here.")

GEORGE: The first one in here loses both his eyes. (*He slices the air
with his jackknife.*)

JANE: Who? What?

ERIC: He's just being silly. (*Horns honking. Voices.* "Jane, we're
gonna tar and feather you too. Takes one to know one,
we're gonna plaster you up with tar, Jane, so no one can get
inside you anymore.")

GEORGE: (*Beside himself.*) Where's my shotgun?

JANE: Come on guy. . . .

GEORGE: I'll shoot 'em down like sparrows. (*The noise stops
abruptly. He sits down. Rubs the heels of his hands in his
eyes.*) Give me a glass of water. (*Jane goes to get it from
the kitchen. To Eric:*) Don't look at me. Look somewhere
else. Over there. (*Pointing to the kitchen.*) No! Over there.
(*Pointing to the hall. Eric does so. Jane gives him the glass
of water. George drinks greedily.*) My wife working at
Filatex and you at Northern Textiles. That's settled, right?
Fourteen, fifteen thousand francs a month between you,
living it up behind my back. Did I confess even when they
were pounding me like a punching bag? Do you want her,
dear sweet Eric? Here. (*Grabs Jane and pushes her
towards Eric.*) Give her another baby. She was scared
when she was with me. Watch it buster. It's her time of
month, so hold it in.

ERIC: Let her go.

GEORGE: Here, I say, Vermeersch, George, Cell Number Nine, here
she is -- a present for you. Or is she already more than you
can handle? You already on the lookout for another one, a
heavier one? Is she good enough for me?

JANE: (*Breaks free.*) I'm not a slut you can just throw from one to the
next.

GEORGE: (*Suddenly dazed. Drinking more.*) Oh yes you are, a
fucking slut.

JANE: Go home Eric.

GEORGE: Yes and call the police. "He just confessed. Put him away again in   the six by nine pigpen!" *(Long silence. Eric sits down on the sofa. Fragments of pop music.)*

JANE: *(Wearily.)* Eric, ask your mother what happened on "The Van Outrijve Family." How did it work out for Miss Juliette? Will she finally get her antique dealer?

GEORGE: *(Walks toward the t.v. Kicks it in some more.)*   Miss Juliette was fucking everything but the kitchen sink.

ERIC: George, cut it out. You're going crazy.

GEORGE: *(Threatening, raging.)* Off the sofa! Off it!

ERIC: *(Getting up.)* There's no more reasoning with him.

GEORGE: *(Sitting at the table, drinking wine.)* They hurt me, one with a truncheon and the other with his shoes. One of them said, I've got two daughters too." *(He is drunk. His eyes are bleary.)*

ERIC: *(Softer.)* Listen George.

GEORGE: I'm listening.

ERIC: I was so sad when they put you away I couldn't even eat, I swear.

GEORGE: Jane loves you. And you?

ERIC: I think I do too. I mean it. *(Silence.)* 'ts really something, hunh?

GEORGE: Wait a minute. The booze is going to my head but I can see things clear, so clear it's giving me goosebumps. *(The baby suddenly starts crying.)*

JANE: Right on time. She's like an alarm clock.

GEORGE: Are you breast-feeding her?

JANE: No, not anymore. *(She goes up the stairs.)*

ERIC: The first four days she had crossed eyes. My heart was in my mouth, but then they straightened out.

GEORGE: Eric, you're my friend for life. We understand each other, right pal? Like in a card game. If you play clubs, I'll follow suit, always. Eric, murderers are people who say, that's enough, this far and no further. One more step and you'll be sitting on my knife. Eric, please go away. Get your nose out of our business. It's been in it long enough already. (*A mean little laugh.*) It's somebody else's turn now. The one that had the marrow sucked out of his bones and the juice squeezed out of his balls, Eric.

ERIC: Okay. I understand. (*Calls upstairs.*) Jane!

JANE: (*Offstage.*) I'm busy.

ERIC: I got to go. Lock your door.

GEORGE: (*Vaguely afraid*) What door? Where?

ERIC: The bedroom door.

GEORGE: (*Ponderously.*) All right, lock it. Don't let any horse-flies or ladybugs get in.

ERIC: Okay. All the best then, right?

GEORGE: Yeah. And a stiff wind in the rear.

(*Eric exits.*)

BLACKOUT

SCENE FOUR

(*A scarcely noticable change in the lighting indicates that this scene is imaginary. The fade-outs into darkness are extremely short. Each time there is a moment of darkness George and Christine change their posture, their way of sitting or standing, facial expression, and so on.*)

CHRISTINE: (*Has come onstage in the dark from off-right. Her back is turned to the audience. A nineteen year old girl. Fashionably but not too expensively dressed. She's gotten her introversion from her father, but flirtatious and sensual side from her mother as well. Her movements are fluid. A provocative and cheerful laugh. She is eating a sandwich and speaking with her mouth full.*) Turn the radio on.

GEORGE: (*Sitting on the sofa. A newspaper on his knees.*) Why?

CHRISTINE: Just to hear something. It's so quiet here. A car, a horse-fly. When you cough it's like in a church. Don't you watch the t.v. when you sit here all alone like this?

GEORGE: I don't sit here alone that often. When your mother's not home I don't watch. Except if there's a soccer game on.

CHRISTINE: Or "The Untouchables?" (*She drinks a bottle of beer.*)

GEORGE: It's so stupid. Eliot Ness always wins.

CHRISTINE: (*Imitating the t.v. commentator:*) The smugglers crossed the border, but the police shot them down like sparrows. Mortally wounded, he made it to Elliot Ness's office. (*She drops onto the sofa.*) He pulled out his gun. (*She points the beer bottle at George.*) Hands up, you squealer, or I'll blow your brains out.

GEORGE: You nut. (*She sticks her bottle in his ribs. He puts his arms up.*)

CHRISTINE: (*Frisks him, tickling as she does so.*) Where is your gun Elliot Ness? Where're ya hiding it?

GEORGE: (*Hits her hand very hard.*) Cut it out Christine!

BLACKOUT

CHRISTINE: (*Sitting at the table on a chair.*) Of course Freddie isn't your idea of the kind of man for me. He thinks different, how could it be otherwise? He's so much younger. He doesn't take everything so seriously.

GEORGE: (*Now on a chair.*) But why does he have to wear his hair down to his back like a woman?

CHRISTINE: In the old days all men wore their hair that long.

GEORGE: How do you know?

CHRISTINE: All you have to do is open an art book on the Middle Ages and look at the prints from back then.

GEORGE: Yeah right. I've got time to look at prints. Is that how you spend your time in Kortrijk, looking at prints?

CHRISTINE: You'd rather look at Honeywell machines all day.

GEORGE: Just so long as he's serious about you.

CHRISTINE: He isn't. But I don't ask him for anything. If he's there, that's fine. If he's not there, that's fine too.

GEORGE: (*Playfully.*) There's a little crucifix on your forehead Christine.

CHRISTINE: You're right. When he's not there I could just scream like a baby.

GEORGE: You are still a baby.

CHRISTINE: Me? (*Cooing.*) Me, Daddy?

BLACKOUT

GEORGE: (*Drunk, as in the end of the last scene. She is sitting stationary. Muffled singing:*) Christine, jellybean's got a cross on her forehead, God said. Unto eternity. Amen. (*Silence.*) Don't you have to wash my hair in front of the mirror there? I won't do you any harm sweety-pie, my angel. Why did your mother let that child be born? Is this how she re-pays me? Is it? Watch out Christine, watch out. Your father is watching over you! How do you support yourself now? Do you do it for money like Johnny the soccer player? No. You do it out of compassion. To wipe out misery. You're the light of my eye and you don't even know it. I'd rather let 'em chop my head off. . . .

BLACKOUT

CHRISTINE: (*Walking up and down.*) It's stifling in here.

GEORGE: (*No longer drunk.*) You mustn't open the window because they're working on the sewer.

CHRISTINE: I can smell it.

GEORGE: Go sit in back, in the garden by the pear tree.

CHRISTINE: No, I'd rather stay here. With you. You don't like me to say that, do you? You're ashamed. You're not supposed to say things like that, right? You and me, we never see each other anymore and we used to be such good pals. Weren't we? Today's the third time since you threw me out. The first time was at a department store. You were buying two cans of green latex paint and I was eating a sandwich with Freddie, a couple of yards away from you. And then you saw us and turned as white as a turnip. I said, Daddy sit down with us for a second. But you said, go to hell.

GEORGE: You want to do whatever you feel like, live like Algerians, not work, sitting in the sun on your ass. Well go to hell.

CHRISTINE: Bitch.

GEORGE: Yeah, bitch, that's what I said. And your Freddie tried to hide under the table.

CHRISTINE: (*Laughing.*) The scaredy-cat thought you were going to sock him in the face. He was already starting to grab his fork to stick in your eyes.

GEORGE: He's not a man.

CHRISTINE: How do you know?

GEORGE: He's not the man for you's what I mean.

CHRISTINE: (*Seriously, pressing.*) We're never going to find a man who's the right man for me, will we Dad?

BLACKOUT

CHRISTINE: It's quiet here. You cough like you were in church.

GEORGE: Well then, sing a song.

CHRISTINE: (*Climbs up on the table. She dances like a stripper, tinkers with the zipper of her dress, lifts up her dress for an instant. Sings:*) In Marke's leafy bower, Appeared beneath a cave's cover, To our little Georgie sour, God's very own mother. (*Voices outside. The letterbox rattles. Heavy pounding on the door. Meanwhile George pulls Christine down off the table and throws her onto the sofa.*)

BLACKOUT

CHRISTINE: (*Walking coolly up and down, just like before.*) And the second time was at my aunt's burial--you know, the nun. You were paralyzed with fear again. I didn't wear a black dress on purpose.

GEORGE: That's right. It was a green one with those funny colors that run together, like it had been left in the wash too long.

CHRISTINE: It's called psychedelic Dad.

GEORGE: You might just as well call it scratchmyassky.

CHRISTINE: (*Laughing, childlike.*) It's a long time since I heard that. When I was little. Anytime there was a strange word or someone was talking about a Russian or some other foreigner, he was invariably called Mr. Scratchmyassky. And anytime there was an Englishman talking on the radio it went "Aaoow dyew yew dyew?" And when it was a German it was-- what was that word again? Oh come on, the word for pig. . . .

GEORGE: Schweinhund meat!

(Silence.)

CHRISTINE: My aunt was my friend, eben if she was a nun. So old, so quiet, so good. And she was always laughing there with her false teeth clacking. They were too big for her mouth. Often when I was at the Tropicana and feeling lousy, I'd think I'm gonna leave all this behind, I'll leave all the customers far behind me, and I'll rush to her side, to that woman before she dies, and she'll tell me what I ought to do. We'd always sit together in the cloister garden among the grapes and she'd say, There's only one thing in the whole world that means anything, and that's loving, loving others Christine, I don't understand Christine how you don't want to love our Lord, but it'll come back, just wait.

GEORGE: You didn't take communion at the funeral.

CHRISTINE: Not me.

GEORGE: The whole family noticed. Everyone went up but not you.

CHRISTINE: I was in a state of mortal sin. I've never been any different. *(Silence. She sprawls out on the sofa.)* And this is the third time. And the third time, you've got to pay the piper.

BLACKOUT

CHRISTINE: *(At the hairdresser's table. Inspecting the bottles near the mirror. Smells them.)* All those women in the street smell the same. Well what have we here? Aha! Sortilege. *(She puts some on. Goes over to George.)* Smell this.

GEORGE: *(Cryptically.)* It was smuggled out of France.

CHRISTINE: *(At the table. Finds a huge bottle.)* And here, like always, we have the perfume of the lady of the house, our mother, Soir de Paris. From before the First World War, always the same. Why don't you say something about it to her? Tell her to try something new. When is she coming home?

GEORGE: Tomorrow afternoon.

CHRISTINE: Well then. You have the house to yourself till tomorrow afternoon.

GEORGE: Yup.

CHRISTINE: Aren't you scared to be alone with me? You're turning your eyes away. Did you throw me out because you were scared of me? Or of yourself? *(Silence.)* Have you thought of me since I've been gone? What? What's she doing there in town with those good-for-nothings? What? I feel like giving her a good slap across the face for all the anxiety she's caused me. I'll go get her out of the Tropicana and drag her back to Marke and make her kneel at my feet and beg forgiveness. (*Kneels.*) Forgive me Daddy.

BLACKOUT

CHRISTINE: Do you remember how mad you were when I found that magazine with those naked women in it in your garden work-shop? That's when you hit me and you never hit me. That night I kissed the black and blue marks on my arms. Poor Daddy. (*Goes over to him.*)

GEORGE: Why do you say that?

CHRISTINE: Poor boy. With a magazine. You'll never have a young woman again. You're letting the young ones pass you by. You stare after them and bite your nails. (*Grabs his hand. Spins around.*) You see? (*She sits on his lap.*) You smell like the oil at the factory. You better clean your ears out for once. You'll never understand that all I want is to be a thing. A thing anyone can do anything they want to. That's the God's honest truth.

GEORGE: But tomorrow. . . .

CHRISTINE: Tomorrow, tomorrow. Now.

BLACKOUT

(*Suddenly, violently, we hear the pop music from before. George and Christine are dancing. She, loose and exuberant. He, rather clumsy.*)

CHRISTINE: And one and two. See, you can do it. You've gotta let yourself go, loosen up. Closer. Together now.

GEORGE: (*Breaks free.*) It won't work. (*He sits down. The music stops abruptly.*)

CHRISTINE: You're eating yourself up alive. I can see you shriveling before my eyes. Going to Honeywell and coming home, fall-ing asleep in front of the t.v. Once in a blue moon with my mother. And pretty soon you'll have grass growing on your belly Dad. (*She kisses him on the mouth. He pushes her off.*) I was still only thirteen and you got embarrassed when I kissed you before going to bed. You mustn't be scared of anyone George. You'll always think of me. Your whole life long. I'll be holding onto you tight as a vise. (*He has backed off. His back is against the wall next to the hall door. She suddenly laughs very loud. Stops.*) You made me. Without you I wouldn't be walking on the earth. I'm yours. (*One long phrase of pop music.*) I could have been made by somebody else. Who knows for sure? Do rabbits know, do ladybugs? There's nothing I can do about it George. You neither. We're things George, and they're pulling and tearing at us from all sides, but if we're nothing but things, let's hold on tight like nobody else in the whole world. No one's above it, not even you. (*She is right up against him now. Unbuttons his shirt.*)

BLACKOUT

CHRISTINE: (*At the kitchen door.*) It's quiet here. Only every now and then a car. And what's that buzzing. A horse-fly? (*She looks for the insect. Finds it.*)

GEORGE: It's a ladybug.

CHRISTINE: No it's not. (*She opens the window. The horse-fly flies out. She follows it with her eyes.*) It's gone. The sparrows'll get it. (*She goes over to George, takes him by the hand and leads him towards the sofa.*) Pretend I'm Jane before she was married. Jane Vandale. Or pretend that you're married to her and I've been in her belly for three months. One big net made of threads George, and we're all hanging onto each other, and we're scratching at one another with our nails. But not us George, you and me, not tonight. (*She kisses him passionately. He kisses her back.*) It's either this or you've got to kill me. I'd rather you did that. (*She slips between his knees. The phone rings. She doesn't hear it, but George does. He listens. The phone keeps on ringing.*)

JANE: (*Shouting from upstairs.*) Answer it George.

CHRISTINE: We'll never be together again like we are now. It'll never be the same again, no matter what. (*The phone keeps on ringing. He looks at it. Christine takes George's hand and puts it against her cheek.*) You have my eyes George.

JANE: (*Coming down the stairs and going over to the telephone.*) Can't you answer the phone? Did you forget how it works or what? I'm washing the baby and . . . .

GEORGE: (*In a thick voice.*) A gnawed-off old dick won't perk up too quick.

CHRISTINE: Touch me. Don't leave me here.

JANE: (*On the phone. Every now and then she looks at George who is sitting bolt upright with Christine on his knees.*) Hello. Oh, it's you. No, no. He doesn't anymore. He sits on the sofa. No, he's not asleep, but he's quiet. (*Gives George a wink.*) Yes, quiet as a corpse. He can't hold his liquor anymore. The baby's finished eating. I'm going back upstairs. She's still got to be burped. Maybe tonight. I'll tell him. (*Puts the receiver back down.*) Eric says you'd better hit the sack as soon as possible.

GEORGE: Tomorrow, tomorrow.

JANE: What about tomorrow?

GEORGE: I'm staying here for a while. You go ahead. Go to your baby. (*She goes up the stairs, gives him one more inquiring stare. George stretches out his arms. Christine flies into them and starts passionately hugging and kissing him. George stops her and holds her tight until she can no longer move. He utters a loud shriek, just as in the first scene.*)

BLACKOUT

SCENE FIVE

(*A half hour later. George is asleep with his mouth half open. Snores every now and then. The sound of the front door slamming shut makes him wake in fright. He jumps woozily up, rearranges his clothes. Jane comes in. She is wearing a different dress and has put on make-up. She hangs up her coat*)

GEORGE: Well?

JANE: I took a little walk. I didn't want to wake you up. I needed a little fresh air.

GEORGE: And that's why you're all painted like for an opera?

JANE: Well yes. If you must know, I went to see him. So there, so there, so there! (*She cries and clears things away.*)

GEORGE: Was he mean to you?

JANE: What do you care?

GEORGE: Or was it his mother?

JANE: Oh her. If she ever bit into her own tongue it would poison her to death.

GEORGE: What did she say?

JANE: (*Shrugs her shoulders.*) Always the same stuff.

GEORGE: She'd better watch it, they'd all better lay off, they'd better keep out of my business.

JANE: Eric wants me to tell you. . . .

GEORGE: Well?

JANE: He called Mike, the foreman from Northern Textiles on the phone to say that he wasn't going to work tomorrow and wouldn't be coming for the rest of the month, well, that he wouldn't be coming to work anymore and he wants me to say that you can go in his place.

GEORGE: And what about him? Is he going back to living off of card games?

JANE: He says that things got out of hand between us and that this affair with me and him is going to turn out bad in the end anyway, that he feels that he doesn't matter to me when you're around and that I'm not even aware of it, but that I've swallowed you whole, that it's for life.

(*Silence.*)

GEORGE: And he isn't going to work anymore?

JANE: He'd . . . (*Sobs*) he'd go to France, to Rouen. He was offered a job there at the casino as a doorman. His French is good, he's a man of the world, he puts up a good front.

GEORGE: That filthy con-man.

JANE: It's only for a while, he says, but I know what "for a while" means.

GEORGE: He's lost his mind.

JANE: His mother started to screech that I destroyed him. That since he's known me she can't get him to do anything anymore.

GEORGE: And him?

JANE: Well. What did I just tell you? That he's arranged things for you, you're getting his job on a silver platter. All you have to do is go present yourself to Mike tomorrow.

GEORGE: What did Mike say on the phone?

JANE: He said, whether or not George has been in jail, he can come whenever he wants to. He'll earn 40 francs, just like anybody else. And even if he's lost his civic rights. He'll get a pension and paid vacations and health insurance like anybody else.

GEORGE: He's doing it because then I'll have to thank him. Thank you Eric dear. Over my dead body. (*Silence.*) But tomorrow is Saturday.

JANE: You can work in shifts. From four o'clock to one o'clock.

GEORGE: Should I go? (*Sits down.*)

JANE: In a minute! And say thank you.

GEORGE: (*Nervous and angry.*) And he says this to you just like that? Right to your face? So long Jane, take it easy. I'm off to France. I'm leaving you out in the cold. Au revoir, the ball's in your court now. (*Building in intensity.*) You're not good enough for me anymore, I've had you, legs opened, legs closed, and I'm off, fare thee well, you can just pine away for me now. But that is not how it's going to turn out goddamn it.

JANE: He's doing this for you as much as for me.

GEORGE: Is that what he says?

JANE: No he didn't, but I know it.

GEORGE: You know him, hm?

JANE: Inside and out.

GEORGE: He just flies here and back again, outside and in like it was a bird-feeder. He plays around with peoples' legs and with their hearts as though he was the Good Lord himself.

(*Long silence.*)

JANE: (*Muffled.*) I'm going to throw myself into the water.

GEORGE: (*Jumps up.*) I'm going over there! I'll teach him some manners!

JANE: He's gone.

GEORGE: Where to?

JANE: Er . . . to the Zanzi, I guess.

GEORGE: Then I'll go to the Zanzi.

JANE: He's home. Leave him alone. Let him sleep on it. He'll change his mind. He loves me. He doesn't want to hurt me. He says things like that because that bitch of a mother of his is putting him up to it. He doesn't mean it.

GEORGE: (*Clears his throat. He goes to the kitchen. We hear water running. He comes back with a glass of water and drinks.*)

JANE: Are you drinking water again? Well that's a new one. And you always used to say, water is for frogs.

GEORGE: The jail's full of frogs. That's all there is there.

JANE: (*Faint smile.*) Well, you're turning water into wine.

GEORGE: You can say that again Jane. (*Fists in his eyes.*) What I feel like doing is taking a bath.

JANE: A bath? Where?

GEORGE: Or a shower.

JANE: You'll have to go to the swimming pool for that.

GEORGE: When I was in jail I sometimes had a bath two, three times a week. Well after a while you get to like it. If I had money I'd install one here, that's for sure.

JANE: Where? Attached to the kitchen? Out through the garden?

GEORGE: Just forget it.

JANE: There's no reason why not. You break through that little wall. . . .

GEORGE: (*Laughing uncomfortably.*) We could take a bath together.

JANE: That would be nice and tidy! (*They both laugh silently. Jane suddenly starts to cry.*) What's going to become of us George? It's as though they were pulling on our guts with a rope, in one side and out the other!

GEORGE: Sit down Jane. (*Jane keeps pacing up and down. Silence.*) One day in jail I had a drop of jam on my sleeve after dinner, when all of a sudden a ladybug came down to sit on it. It took a walk up my sleeve with its little dinger--

what am I saying?--with its little puss licking up the jam.
Every now and then it'd fly away, but it kept coming back
until it got dark and very late. I didn't dare budge and Jules
the customs inspector said. . . .

JANE: Was it in May?

GEORGE: Yeah.

JANE: Our little daughter was already six months along by then.
(*Sits down at the table.*)

GEORGE: Yeah, that's right.

JANE: And it got so hot all of a sudden that I thought I was going to
burst open, that she'd pop out on account of the heat. She
was so pretty George. When she wakes up I'll bring her out
here.

GEORGE: (*This makes him uneasy.*) There's something I still didn't
tell you about that customs inspector. When he came along
to our cell he looked as though he was coming to the fair.
Well guys, he said, how about the fun side of life here? Are
you in here on account of your pricks too? asked Johnnie.
Johnnie, he said, you're prick's all that matters. The cock in
the box, that and some good money. But no French fries.
'Cause he was a customs inspector at the French border,
y'know? Are you listening?

JANE: Of course I am. I'm sitting here. Why was he in jail?

GEORGE: (*Drinks water.*) One night he was doing his rounds with
the Peugeot from customs. In the middle of a cornfield he
spotted a Volvo. He went over to it with his flashlight.
Nothing moved. He pulls the door open and flashes the
light. What does he see? Adam and Eve. In the back seat.
Well, he says, what have we here, and in the middle of the
corn besides? And he recognizes the girl. Well Solange, he
says, is that any way to behave? She starts to scream. Her
lover, she says, is French (but he looks more like a Turk) and
she says, my father is is mean, please Jules, let me go or
else my father'll chop me into French fries if he finds out.
And Jules says, all right, it's the young people today, it's not
hurting me any. Go ahead and get lost, he says. But he told
the story at his office and one of 'em told it to some others
and anyway his boss called him in. Well, Jules, he says,
what's this I hear? You were doing your rounds and don't

report a serious matter like that to your superiors? And he was severely reprimanded! Well, man dozes, God disposes. Three days later he runs into Solange on the street and says, girl that's gotta go on my report, I got no choice in the matter. The law's the law. She was about to cry again and he felt sorry for her and his crotch was getting a little itchy I have a feeling, and he said, you know what? Come over to my house and we'll discuss the matter. That's fine with me, she said, I'll come over and discuss the matter. But of course she understood right away what kind of discussion it was going to be. And without so much as a by or leave she went into the bedroom, and there she stayed, she lay there stark naked. Hey, said Jules, first one into the bathtub. And then they had a hootenanny all night long. But two days later the police were on his doorstep. The Turk must've squealed. And Jules had to explain the whole thing. (*Quick blackouts as in Scene Four.*) You've put your hands in certain places I'd rather not name. No, Commissioner. Do you have any physical or mental defects? No, Commissioner. (*Rapidly.*) Hands up. Bend over. How old are you? How old is your father? And your mother? What time did you get in? Did you turn on the electric light? (*Louder.*) Who started, you or her? Neither did, Commissioner. You turned her over on the sofa! Yes Commissioner! (*Stops abruptly. Silence. Wearily, the story starts to peter out.*) And Jules was out of a job of course. And got two years. They're tough on government workers.

JANE: A customs inspector is like a policeman. They're supposed to set an example.

GEORGE: Jane.

JANE: Yes George.

GEORGE: (*After a silence. Coughs. Softly.*) I've been telling you filthy lies Jane, the whole time, all those months. Filthy, Jane. About Christine.

JANE: I know.

GEORGE: How?

JANE: Do you think I'm totally blind, after all the time I've known you? I was so furious that my blood was boiling. And I noticed it the day after Christine was here. You turned your eyes away, you blinked. You were glowing. You were hot as hell. And I couldn't tell a soul, not even myself. I was this far from going to the police myself. I aged. I aged twenty years in one week, twenty years of Christine's. And you saw nothing, nothing!

GEORGE: And you said nothing about it, nothing.

JANE: What could I say? "George, I'm going through change of life. And you're still on the prowl." And she's cut from the same cloth -- hunting, grabbing, star-gazing.

GEORGE: And all through the trial you stood there lying and screaming and deceiving the court. Why? For me?

JANE: No I did it for the Pope. (*Silence.*) There's one thing I can't understand. Why did she do it? How much did you pay her?

GEORGE: No, no.

JANE: Then why did she do it? Just to get her rocks off?

GEORGE: (*With difficulty.*) I think, I think . . . she did it out of pity.

JANE: (*Sly laugh.*) Out of pity! That's the first I hear of that. She sure was born on a Friday.

GEORGE: Our Christine? Well, now that you mention it.

JANE: A girl born on a Friday is either unhappy or a witch. And on Friday strange things happen.

GEORGE: Today's Friday too.

JANE: All day long.

GEORGE: (*Silence.*) Get him.

JANE: Eric?

GEORGE: No, the Pope.

JANE: Now? Why?

GEORGE: Call him. Tell him to come over.

JANE: His mother must be sleeping now, and the phone is in her room.

GEORGE: Go get him then.

JANE: What will the neighbors think? (*She is already making for the hall.*)

GEORGE: That it's just like a birdfeeder here!

(*Jane exits. George rubs his knuckles in his eyes. Drinks a glass of water. Suddenly goes up the stairs but stops halfway up, comes back down, paces off the room like a prisoner. With terse movements he opens his suitcase, digs out a framed crayon drawing. Then he takes the three publicity posters of seductive women off the wall and, in the center, hangs the crayon drawing on a nail. It is the image of Jesus Christ with the crown of thorns, very clumsily painted in bright colors. He inspects the drawing and hangs it straight. Shuts his suitcase. He walks around. Listens. Jumps over to the window. There is nothing to be heard. He kneels in front of the sofa and buries his face in it. His voice is audibly choked. He sings, "In Lourdes, up the mountains. . . ." Stands back up. Goes into the kitchen. Sound of splashing water. He comes back, his face soaking wet. Dries it with a the red towel that's on the dressing table. He sits down in the barber chair. Noise from the front door that is being opened. He gets up and sits down on a chair at the table.*)

JANE: (*Comes onstage followed by Eric, wearing a sweater and slippers.*) Here he is.

GEORGE: Ah, it's you. Don't be scared. I won't carry on again.

ERIC: I was already in bed.

JANE: His mother doesn't get it at all. Either it's off or it's on, she says. That woman is really bent out of shape over this.

ERIC: Yes. Well I don't feel so good about it either.

GEORGE: You were already in bed. At ten thirty. That's funny.

ERIC: I just finished watching "The Van Outrijve Family."

JANE: So?

ERIC: Well the manufacturer who we thought was going to go bankrupt is saved in the nick of time by an old schoolmate he meets unexpectedly at a private club, and it's a count from Limburg, and he'll lend him money, no question about it.

JANE: And Miss Juliette, did she finally get married?

ERIC: They did say something about it, but I wasn't paying too much attention to it. Well, next week the manufacturer and that count'll go hunting together and Juliette is invited along too. That'll be exciting. It's well put-together.

JANE: Oh well, we'll find out next week.

ERIC: Will you have your t.v. fixed by then?

GEORGE: But you said it was beyond repair!

ERIC: Yes that's right. (*Silence.*) What do you want from me George?

GEORGE: Sit down.

ERIC: Thanks. (*Sits.*)

GEORGE: (*To Jane, who is about to go into the kitchen.*) You too. Did you tell him?

ERIC: About what?

JANE: No.

GEORGE: About Christine.

JANE: There's nothing to tell. It's strictly a family matter. Let sleeping dogs lie. It's all over.

GEORGE: It's not over. I want to tell . . .

JANE: Well go to confession then.

GEORGE: Eric, the thing between Christine and me, have you thought about it?

ERIC: What about it? Spit it out man.

GEORGE: Well at the trial and at the commissioner's office, I denied it and yelled that it wasn't true, but it was.

ERIC: Like Christine said?

GEORGE: Like she said.

ERIC: Well I'll be a monkey's uncle! (*Silence.*) That's a weight off my mind. Of course I didn't believe it at the time, but even so George, there was always a worm somewhere in the apple. I didn't dare believe it was true. And now . . . well it doesn't speak too well of you George.

GEORGE: No.

ERIC: Of course you're not the only one. Far from it. But it's more something the lower classes do. Workers, metal workers. There's none of 'em but do it to their daughters first, but someone like you George, I'd never have guessed it. At first Christine said you were drunk and her too . . . (*It is a question.*)

GEORGE: We weren't drunk. We were in our right minds.

ERIC: Well don't make a novel out of it. It's none of my business and besides, it's all over and done with. Come on George, come on! You always were a little weird. (*Looks at him in amazement and then smacks his lips a couple of times.*) I don't know. I'd like a glass of beer Jane.

GEORGE: Don't you feel like having any more wine?

JANE: (*Getting up.*) Whatever you want Eric.

ERIC: (*To George.*) You'd rather have a beer, right?

JANE: It's bad to drink beer right after wine.

GEORGE: Well then give us wine Jane. (*Jane looks in the cupboard, then heads for the kitchen.*)

ERIC: But why did that stupid bitch have to go tell the commissioner, the whole neighborhood, the newspapers, and the judge? What was the point in all that?

GEORGE: My daughter Christine gets it from me. How can I explain it? When she gets an idea into her head . . .

ERIC: . . . she doesn't let go of it, does she? That's true.

GEORGE: Right. She broods over it, she doesn't hide it away like most people. It's like an egg going rotten. It can't stay a secret. Most people say, just so long as it bends, why break it? But she'd rather it broke. I asked her, Why? Why? Dad, she said, did it actually happen? Yes, I said. Well then it's been happening forever, everywhere. And she said, When the cops raided the place, looking for dope and questioning all those teenage kids, I saw them all grovel and squeal in front of the cops, and she says, I couldn't stand it and if there's   only one person who's gonna tell the truth, it'll be me. And when her turn came she told them who she'd made it with -- Freddie, Billy, Bobbie, and all the other guys whose names I don't remember, it was the fashion to use names ending with "y" and then she couldn't stop telling her God's honest truth and she confessed everything and I got nailed. (*Jane has filled the glasses. They drink.*)

ERIC: What if we were all like that? Things in Belgium would be very nice indeed.

JANE: (*Laughing a little.*) We'd all be in the clink. Together. That would be just lovely!

GEORGE: (*This possible frivolity irritates him.*) But she didn't tell all.

It was true all right, but after you keep telling a story in broad daylight and in front of the judge and his assistants, it starts changing really.

JANE: (*Sharply.*) What was different?

GEORGE: It started sounding different.

JANE: It only happened that one time, right?

GEORGE: Only that one time. But she didn't say -- for instance -- that we were amazed by what we'd done, when it was over, that we could hardly speak, that we fell down on our knees, that we promised never to do it again, that we said a short prayer, "As true as Our Lord stood in the River Jordan, so the blood of these two will still remain."

ERIC: You don't hear that one too often anymore.

JANE: (*Fiercely.*) Talk about something else. (*Silence.*) That whole affair with Christine is over now. Let's close the book on it please.

ERIC: Is this what you got me out of bed for? (*Silence.*)

GEORGE: How come you'd hit the sack so early? That's not your usual time.

ERIC: I was tired. I had all this crap turning and spinning 'round in my head.

GEORGE: After you told my wife she'd have to make it on her own.

ERIC: I said I'd take care of the baby. For the rest of my life. I'll send a check every month. And I crept into bed -- if you must know -- since I wanted to get up early tomorrow and catch the first train to Rouen.

JANE: (*Pacing up and down.*) And he's not coming back!

ERIC: The four forty-five. And I intended to send you a postcard explaining everything, all the where's and why's. But she rang my bell and told me that you wanted to talk to me. And she said something about you desperately needing to take a bath. And I thought, I hope he doesn't jump into the River Lys. I'd better go have a look. (*Silence.*) What was all that about a bath?

GEORGE: Listen. I'd rather you didn't say another word about a check. I don't even want to see any toys you'd buy for the kid in my house. Tomorrow I'm going to the Town Hall and having the kid registered under my name.

JANE: But it is registered in your name.

GEORGE: Oh yeah? Well sure, of course.

ERIC: But I'd like to see it some time in the future George. It is mine.

GEORGE: Is it really yours?

ERIC: Well it's not the Holy Ghost's, is it?

JANE: (*Rushes over to George, gives him a slap in the face. Pulls his hair.*) It's somebody else's! It's somebody else's! (*George lets her hit him.*) Is that what they taught you in jail, talking about people like that, thinking about (*Hitting him again.*) . . . people like that?

ERIC: His brains've gone all rotten inside. Leave him be Jane.

GEORGE: (*When Jane goes off.*) I'm sorry. I'm truly sorry. I didn't mean to say that. It popped out before I knew what I was saying. You must pardon me. I didn't say it. It's that prison! My thoughts are all screwed up, like spoiled milk.

ERIC: Okay, it's forgotten. Jane . . .

JANE: You can pin a whole lot of things on jail.

GEORGE: It's jail I said. Eric, don't go. Don't put the pressure on. I wanted to tell you something.

ERIC: I know that, but what is it? Will you be finished before the night's out?

GEORGE: You're in such a rush, you're so high-strung. I'm not used to it. All day long, listening for the bell, from wake-up to the evening meal, and in between I've got all the time in the world. So I've got to get used to your running around and shoving.

JANE: (*Has all of a sudden spotted the painting on the wall.*) Hey, what have we here? (*Eric goes to have a look at it too.*)

GEORGE: That's a present from Jules the customs inspector. He painted it in prison.

ERIC: He's a real artist.

JANE: He's not bad. But how's about my posters?

GEORGE: Here they are. (*Points to behind the dressing table where he had put them.*) I thought that, so long as you weren't doing hair anymore, that I'd rather see that as a souvenir. Because Jules, the one that painted it's shut up in an institution now. The prison psychiatrist told me he had to paint. They thought it'd help him get better, that otherwise he'd run the risk of losing his soul. And before they took him away, he gave me that. He said (*Short laugh.*), it'll deliver you from all bodily and spiritual ills. So he said.

ERIC: You can see that he's suffering.

JANE: Did he paint it from a photo?

GEORGE: No. Lately he'd been seeing Jesus in person.

ERIC: You can put a candle in front of it Jane. (*They both laugh as though in collusion. George notices that Eric is getting ready to leave again and hands him a glass and pours a drink.*)

GEORGE: What I was trying to say is . . . (*Drinks*) the warden liked me . . .

JANE: You already said that.

GEORGE: (*Taken aback.*) Oh yeah? When?

JANE: Tonight, if you said it once you said it three times already. It's as though only one person in the whole world liked you.

GEORGE: Yes but . . . (*Impatiently.*) Just listen, hunh? It concerns you. The warden called me in to his office. "Vermeersch, George," he said, "how long have you been here now?" "One year, Sir," I said, "one year and six weeks." "And you haven't seen or talked to your wife all this time?" "You know that as well as I do Sir." "Why do you refuse to see your wife Vermeersch, George?" "Because I'm ashamed Sir." "This shame's lasting a long time," he said. "At first it was more anger," I said, "because she believed all that about Christine and me. Oh, she said just the opposite at the trial all right, but I could tell by the way she acted. And the worst of all, Sir, is that she was right. It's true, it's true, it's the God's honest truth. And so I didn't want to see her anymore, since I was ashamed. I wanted to beg her forgiveness, Jane's forgiveness, but I didn't dare face her anymore." "Vermeersch, George," he said, "do you know why I called you here?" "She's not sick, is she Sir? She's not lying in the hospital?" And he started to laugh. His belly was shaking against his desk from laughing. "She sure is," he said. (*George laughs.*) "She sure is lying in the hospital. Vermeersch, George," he said, "I have the pleasure and honor of informing you that your wife has had a baby." I stood there like a jerk. "What's wrong?" he said, "Don't you feel well?" I said, "A   child? Has she had a child by Eric?" And I gave him a hug. He got scared and was about to call the guards. "Come on, come on," he said, "mind your manners!?" But I grabbed his hand and kissed it, the water spurted out of my eyes and nostrils. "Thank you," I shouted, "thank you Warden, this is the most beautiful day of my life. Don't you understand? I did something wrong and I'm doing penance for it now, but she did something wrong too, we're quits, we're even."

JANE: So why didn't you have me come then?

GEORGE: But you were lying in the hospital.

JANE: Not for two months I wasn't.

GEORGE: I said to myself, I've got to let her rest. This isn't the right moment. Now that she's happy with the child and that other guy, why should I be the one to put a damper on everything? Now that they're happy together. I wanted to write you, but I couldn't manage it. "My dear wife," I wrote, but I couldn't get any further with it. I thought it'd hit them like a cannonball, the two of them, the three of them. They'd probably already started to forget me. I'll wait till I can see them with my own eyes.

JANE: Eric and I didn't feel like writing to you either. Eric said it couldn't do any good to someone locked up like that. It'd drive him crazy with anger.

ERIC: You've got to admit, it was a de-li-cate matter George.

GEORGE: That was the same time they took away -- dragged is more like it -- Jules the customs inspector, and that was another hard blow to me. I thought, all is well, everything's been seen to by Our Lord. I won't move an inch, I'll stay right here, it is good so.

ERIC: That's too deep for me pal. You talk like one of them Jehovahs.

GEORGE: The warden called me in. "Vermeersch, George," he said, "I have the pleasure to inform you that the committee has responded positively. The adjutant was the only one who voted against your release, since he believes you're one of those closed-off guys who, boom, could cause a scandal. But even though this is a vice case, we'll apply the LeJeune Act. You can go home in just a little while. But I'm the one who's responsible for it, bear that in mind and . . . I'm here . . . and . . ." (*He pours his glass full, then Eric's, then Jane's.*)

ERIC: Hey buddy, you trying to get me drunk?

GEORGE: Oh no, God forbid!

JANE: George you're beating around the bush. There's something nagging your craw.

ERIC: Yeah. Spit it out, fella, what do you really want?

GEORGE: What I want is for Eric not to run away like he decided to early tomorrow morning on the first train to France like a murderer. It's not right, don't you see? Don't you feel it deep down inside? There's something not right about the whole thing.

JANE: Yeah.

GEORGE: Of course there is. I did wrong Eric, she did wrong. We're even. But you Eric, you and Jane aren't. That hasn't been evened out. We can't just leave it like that. We've got to round things off.

ERIC: But you don't want her to stay with me anyway!

GEORGE: No. That part's settled. She stays here at home and me with her. But before you go off, it's simple, you better not laugh at it . . .

JANE: George!

GEORGE: . . . I'd like you to go upstairs with her.

(*Silence.*)

ERIC: You got me there.

JANE: Well thanks a lot.

GEORGE: You know what I'm talking about!

JANE: Is that all they taught you in jail? And with the warden telling me, "Madam," he said, "the men get re-educated here."

ERIC: George you can't be serious.

JANE: I've heard a lot of things in my time and I've lived through a lot more yet, but that I should hear my own husband saying things like this in my own house and I've got to listen.

ERIC: They really fucked you up in jail. They wound your watch all wrong George.

GEORGE: (*Desperately.*) But what I want is best for us all, you guys, we'll all three of us get something out of it. I'm asking you nice on my hands and knees.

ERIC: Back down on his knees again!

GEORGE: (*Sharply. Has he just been found out?*) What do you mean "again?"

ERIC: Didn't you say that you and Christine, over by the sofa . . . ?

GEORGE: Yeah. Hem. Yes, that's how I'm asking both of you.

ERIC: But can't we work this out some other time?

GEORGE: No! Tonight. Before you leave. Can't you get that into that thick skull of yours? Otherwise we'll be lost, all three of us, each in his own way, with those thorns in our skin. If only I'd, if only he'd, if only George hadn't come home, we'd be holding each other tonight in bed just one more time, if only I could hold my Jane, if only I could hold my Eric just one more time! I say we'll keep dragging the stuff with us, and it's got to be over and done with. It can't keep bending, it's got to rip open! Enough of those bites, that belly's got to heal! Or is it that you want to go on itching, to go on longing and nipping at something that isn't there anymore, and chasing after each other in your minds? Eric, here with her and you, Jane, your thoughts with him in France there, thinking, we'll talk on the phone, with the same itch on our skin, is that it? But it can't be, my children, you're going to burn your wings, you'll have problems with your gall bladder!

JANE: Eric?

ERIC: Yes.

JANE: Come on!

(*She goes to the stairs. Eric gets up, looking at George.*)

GEORGE: You're going?

JANE: Oh brother . . is it yes or no?

GEORGE: Yes! (*To Eric.*) Do you want to take that wine bottle along?

ERIC: Oh, we'll manage without it.

JANE: Eric, why don't you take that blue bottle there? Soir de Paris. (*Eric takes the bottle and walks past George who scrutinizes him.*)

GEORGE: Why are you laughing?

ERIC: Am I supposed to say my rosary maybe?

GEORGE: No. (*Grabs hold of Eric's sleeve.*) You're laughing as though you didn't mean it. Say (*To Jane as well.*), you're not going to make believe, are you? Don't do that to me. Don't pretend. It's your last time. Don't screw me around, okay Eric? Jane? Not tonight!

JANE: And what're you gonna do? Meanwhile?

GEORGE: I'll wait.

JANE: Here?

GEORGE: Yes.

JANE: It may take a while.

ERIC: (*Laughing.*) You never know.

JANE: Go over to the Zanzi George. Say hello to everybody. They'll be happy to see you. And by the time you're back it'll be over.

GEORGE: No. No, I'll go into the garden.

JANE: (*Loudly.*) 'Cause you'll hear it better from there. Climb up in the pear tree. That way you can see it too.

GEORGE: Er, I'll stay here. I'll turn on the t.v. . . . I mean, I can turn on the radio. (*Turns the radio on. Someone doing a reading. He turns the dial until he finds some dance music.*)

ERIC: That's Malando singing "Porque te lo Quieres." It's number three on the charts.

GEORGE: (*Desperately.*) You're taking this far too lightly, both of you. It's like going to -- goddammit -- an amusement park, riding the merry-go-round! The merry-go-round! The merry-go-round!

ERIC: They do have something in common, don't they George?

JANE: (*Comes back a couple of steps.*) That's right. George, Eric and me It was like going to the fair. No planning, no squirming, no worms like with you. You can't expect everyone to be like you.

ERIC: Let us at least make believe we know what we're doing.

GEORGE: Right you are! That's what I've been trying to say all along. It's not new, it's not the first time. With all the excitement of something you don't know anything about. No, it's just the two of you. It's the same as before, same as this whole year, but this is the last time. May that year-old pile of straw still be flammable. And if you've gotta laugh while you do it, then laugh. Laugh me away. Tell the world to go to hell, but do it. Don't think of it as a penance, it's a bath!

ERIC: Are you still at it with your bath?

JANE: (*Going up the stairs*) We're off George.

ERIC: (*Almost upstairs.*) You'd do better to go to the Zanzi.

(*Silence. George is alone. He sits down on his chair at the table. Hail and wind start. Suddenly stop, when Jane appears at the top of the staircase with the baby in her arms.*)

GEORGE: What's wrong?

JANE: Here, my sweety-pie. (*To George.*) You wouldn't want the baby to stay on our pillow, would you? (*She lays the child in the crib.*)

GEORGE: (*Going over to the crib.*) She's a beauty.

JANE: Yeah, everyone at the day care center stares at her.

GEORGE: She's got Eric's nose.

JANE: You can't tell yet. It'll take shape later. (*She goes back to the staircase again and pats his hair.*) Oh honey, what did they do to you in there? (*Goes up the stairs.*) See you soon. (*He follows her with his eyes. She doesn't look back anymore. He sits down on the chair again. He very briefly rubs his knuckles in his eyes. Finds a fashion magazine on the dressing table, leafs through it, and throws it back down.*)

VOICE OF ERIC UPSTAIRS: George turn the radio up a little. (*George turns the knob. Static.*) Fix the sound George. (*George tries.*) Some more bass. The knob to the left. (*George does it right.*) Yeah, that's good.

(*George goes over to the crib, stares at the baby for quite a while, takes out his jackknife, opens the blade, holds the point of the knife against the baby. Over the music of the radio, hail, wind, and rattling tiles from above is heard. The latter sound is now the loudest. George throws the knife into the kitchen door with sudden violence, where it sticks in the wood. George now paces from left to right and back again, straight across the stage with measured step. The radio music fades away. Hail and wind. Silence. The rattling of a bunch of keys, steps, metal doors slamming shut. Footsteps of about five people, which suddenly stops. Silence. A metalic voice. "Dumont, Jules." A moan. "Dumont, Jules, we're not going to hurt you. Come on Jules. Come on out kid. The brothers are here. They'll take care of you." The voice of Jules, hoarse and plaintive: "Lord Jesus, why have you deserted me? Dear Lord!" Hail and wind. Doors slamming shut. An electric bell. Short rings. Voice of Dumont, shrilly: "Vermeersch, where are you? It's not fair, Jesus, dear Jesus, just for a piece of ass! Put that hammer away. And the nails. No vinegar in my eyes! Please Jesus! Say just one word and I'm cured!" A scream sounding like the one from George in the beginning. The metal doors slam, the wind blows. The screaming keeps up. Beneath it one hears the low, gurgling screaming of Jane. George stands frozen. All the noise is abruptly over. A long silence. The radio starts playing again. Jane comes down. Goes over to the hairdresser's chair and sits down. Eric follows right after. He drinks from his half-filled glass of wine.*)

ERIC: Did you hear her scream?

GEORGE: Yes.

JANE: And now? Is there anything else we can do for you Mr. Vermeersch?

GEORGE: You didn't fool me. (*George goes over to Eric and gives him a long stare. Goes toward Jane, takes a hold of her face by the chin.*) No.

JANE: (*Shaking herself free.*) Shut up. Don't ask us to tell you all about it besides. We're happy, you're happy. The high mass is over.

GEORGE: You're all clean now, the two of you. With your eyes shining.

JANE: (*Fast.*) We won't talk about it anymore. Okay?

GEORGE: I won't ask anything else.

ERIC: (*Cheerily.*) Good. We're just like we were before again. Entirely like before.

JANE: Yes.

ERIC: I've done my duty. No complaints, hm Jane?

JANE: No. We did what he asked.

ERIC: Well then, I'm off. Okay George?

GEORGE: Sure Eric.

ERIC: (*Near Jane.*) Goodbye Jane.

JANE: Do you want me to wake Lillie? So you can see her eyes?

ERIC: I've seen them. They're your eyes. It'll be quite a while before we see each other again. I may be old and gray by then.

JANE: Then so will I.

ERIC: I'll send you a check. As much as I can. G'bye, or like we say in France -- au revoir. (*Sings, trying to keep his spirits up.*) Au revoir, my dear officer, au revoir and forget me not, forget me not.

JANE: (*Choked up.*) You crazy loon you.

ERIC: George.

(*They come close. An uneasy embrace.*)

GEORGE: I'm grateful Eric. You have no idea. We'll see each other again, but sometime in the future. You understand, don't you kid? Lots of luck with the cards.

ERIC: I'll be needing it. Say, I was thinking, if you need a new t.v., I've still got a '68 Phillips. I can get you a big discount.

GEORGE: No Eric. We'll buy ourselves a new one. From a store.

ERIC: Yes of course. You'll have a good life at Northern Textiles. It's the American method, six warehouse clerks. And they've gotta be struck by lightning before they bend down and pick up a nail.

GEORGE: Oh yeah?

ERIC: Well, 'bye George. Be good.

JANE: Some of your shirts are still in the wash. Two. Nylon.

ERIC: I'll buy me a new set of clothes in France. (*Goes over to Jane, who comes closer, and caresses her cheek.*) Take care of yourself. (*They go toward the hall door. Eric stops at the crib.*) She's like a flower. Okay. Just like we said.

GEORGE: I won't see you out. The people in the street would really talk then.

ERIC: No need. Goodbye.

JANE: Au revoir.

(*Eric exits.*)

GEORGE: (*Goes to the kitchen door, pulls the jackknife out and puts it in his pocket.*) There. S'all over.

JANE: You'd better put that t.v. away. In the garden under the shed, with the wood. (*George takes the t.v. into the kitchen. The sound of the set being plunked down on the floor. Jane looks at herself in the mirror.*)

GEORGE: This corner sure feels empty now.

JANE: And quiet. Listen, you can hear her breathe. (*They listen.*) You'll get used to it George. It'll be easy. We've thrown two of them out now. First there was Christine, now him. It's a clean sweep all right. But it hurts.

GEORGE: Is there any of that coffee left?

JANE: (*Looking in the coffee pot.*) Yes.

GEORGE: The new cups are pretty nice. (*Drinks coffee.*) Don't you like the painting?

JANE: (*Looking at it with difficulty.*) Yeah, sure.

GEORGE: So long as we were together, the three of us, Jules felt all right. You   have a few laughs, you play cards. But when he was alone he was totally out of his element. They put him on bread and water, stuffed him full of valium, but he tore the whole place down. 'Cause he was afraid Jesus Christ was going to put the crown of thorns on his head, he said. (*Gets up, nearby the painting.*) It's as though he were about to call out. Eric said he's an artist. And it's the truth.

JANE: You mustn't ever say his name again.

GEORGE: Oh no?

JANE: No, better not to. (*Silence.*) I'll say his name just one more time. Eric. Eric was a good dancer. Eric's going to Rouen tomorrow. On the first train.

GEORGE: You mustn't eat yourself up in sadness.

JANE: (*Laughing very loud and shrilly.*) Did you hear me screaming?

GEORGE: Yes.

JANE: (*Nervously.*) We had you fooled. We both screamed, me the loudest. We hopped up and down on the mattress making the springs squeak, so that you'd hear it. We sat side by side like two kids on a seesaw. The whole room shook. The dance of the elephants!

GEORGE: Hanh? Nothing happened?

JANE: It didn't work out. It wasn't the right day for it.

GEORGE: You didn't even try?

JANE: It wasn't the right day knucklehead!

GEORGE: Friday!

JANE: You know a Honeywell machine better than your own wife. That day of the month.

(*Silence.*)

GEORGE: It's been so long.

JANE: (*Goes over to the baby. Comes back. Sniffles.*) We kept three feet between us. Ooooh, ooh, he shouted. (*Under her breath.*) And he hopped up and down like a schoolboy. He didn't hug me even once! (*Suddenly sobbing, screaming, stammering.*) We're gonna be happy George. The three of us. We won't let anyone or anything get to us. There's still so much in store for us, we're not that old yet. It's not that cold in here. We don't have a bathtub, not yet anyway, but they didn't cut our eyes out with a jackknife and our hands haven't been chopped off by a machine. We've got so much more than other people. We make a living, you and me. Why wouldn't we be allowed to be happy, you and me, in our house? If a young woman passes us on the street and you look at me, I'm not that much older, am I all used up? Not me. I'll do the best I can. I promise. Whatever you want. We can go to the Ardennes for Christmas on a bus chartered by the neighborhood. Whatever you say George. Now that you got past Our Lord together with that customs inspector of yours there in jail, I can get down on my knees too. Just say the word. I can say a short prayer too.

(*Getting down on her knees by the sofa.*) Was it right here that you were with her? (*Recites in a high grating voice:*)

> Worms, worms, go to,
> Jesus of Nazareth bids you
> To eat the earth
> But not its fruits.

(*Sobs, bent over.*)

GEORGE: Come on, let's go Jane, it's late.

JANE: (*Gets up again.*) It's a quarter to eleven.

GEORGE: What time do you usually go to bed?

JANE: About 11 if there's nothing on t.v.

     (*Silence. She sniffles. He passes her the red towel.*)

GEORGE: Here. Blow your nose.

JANE: (*Takes the towel and folds it. Takes out a handkerchief and blows her nose. She goes towards the dressing table, moves the chair.*) Sit down. I'll cut your hair a little. So you'll look decent enough to go to work tomorrow.

GEORGE: Tomorrow. (*He sits down, looks at himself in the mirror.*)

JANE: (*Runs her fingers through his hair.*) It's so greasy. I'll wash it first.

(*The electric bell rings very loudly. Neither of them hears it. Jane starts combing his hair. The ringing suddenly stops.*)

CURTAIN

SERENADE

Translated By
David Willinger and Lucas Truyts

I. THE TENT

(The garden behind a country house. Dusk. Evening sounds: far-off automobiles, birds. Invisible hands put up a small khaki army tent using ropes. A light goes on in the tent. Indistinct young voices become audible. Then, after a little while the voices of one girl and two boys can be distinguished, giggling excitedly.)

FIRST BOY: Make way for Balthazar, Lord of the Demons!

SECOND BOY: Arkabella, o you sword strokes, come into my paws.

GIRL: Why, Nightcrawler? What did I do wrong?

SECOND BOY: You hurt my dick, lucky Lady Kymri!

GIRL: Where are my pants?

FIRST BOY: Put that big bad boner away, Starjammers!

SECOND BOY: 'm dark and dangerous Dragonfang. Ugg! This here's my golden saber, squaw!

GIRL: Oh, Lockheed, not those quack-beams again!

FIRST BOY: Down Rachel Phoenix, down before the Great Devourer.

SECOND BOY: Yes, Rachel Phoenix, let us have a peek at your secret valley.

(Muffled shrieking and horsing around. Monica, the young mother of one of the boys, steps out onto the porch, leans over the railing, and calls out absent-mindedly.)

MONICA: Boys . . . come in and eat. We've got swiss cheese sandwiches with calcium and egg white and vitamins . . . and calories . . . .*(She hears the childrens' muffled giggles and says more softly:)* Boys . . . it's getting dark. *(She listens.)*

FIRST BOY: The sly slider.

SECOND BOY: The cantankerous tuba. *(Spluttering and puffing)*

GIRL: *(Hawks and spits)* How'll that do ya, ranch hands?

FIRST BOY: No way!

GIRL: *(Cooing)* His golden saber's all melted.

SECOND BOY: My nightcrawler's lying there like the living dead, which is the signal for . . . One more time, Rachel Phoenix.

GIRL: No, Bald Barber, enough is enough.

SECOND BOY: No pity. The gushing geyser knows no pity.

(Overheated little shrieks. Monica rubs her belly against the railing, fixated on what's taking place out of sight; she starts at seeing Marie, a neighbor, standing on the other side of the hedge.)

MARIE: Is Walter over there with you?

MONICA: Sssh! Quiet! *(Marie comes over to the porch.)*

MARIE: What's wrong? You're as white as a corpse.

MONICA: New cream . . . Revlon.

MARIE: Are you cold?

MONICA: Quiet, Marie. *(Her teeth are chattering.) (Every now and then, a growl.)*

MARIE: *(Only now seeing the tent.)* Is Walter in there?

MONICA: Don't you recognize his voice? Your own child.

MARIE: What's going on in there?

MONICA: They're . . . playing.

MARIE: What are they doing to Walter?

MONICA: *(Fiercely)* He has to find out about it sometime. He's old enough. And what are you doing here anyway, Marie? Did I call you? Did I ask you for anything?

MARIE: You've never spoken to me that way before!

MONICA: Get out of here, girl! Back to your own side of the hedge!

MARIE: *(Starts making for her house.)* Walter!

MONICA: *(Fiercely)* Leave him alone! Let the boy be!

MARIE: You're at it again. You've been hitting the bottle again, and you promised, you swore . . . at Christmas. . . .

MONICA: Get out of my garden! How dare you? On a night like this.

MARIE: Is this Bart's birthday?

MONICA: *(Screaming)* Yes! That's right, yes, his birthday!

MARIE: Well, in that case . . . You ought to give Bart more vitamins. The last time I saw him, the rings he had under his eyes! Vitamin B.

MONICA: Is that supposed to be good for the eyes?

MARIE: Yes, but even more for the intestines.

MONICA: *(Sighs)* Thank you Marie.

MARIE: Has Walter been trying to wangle more pie out of you? Don't give him too much; a quarter pound at most. Bear in mind his liver.

MONICA: *(Sighs)* Yes I will, Marie.

MARIE: *(Going)* And not too late now.

(Monica swings one leg over the railing; straddling it, she rocks back and forth and listens. The voices in the tent can be made out every now and then.)

FIRST BOY: Don't be so rough!

SECOND BOY: Fairy-tale Princess.

GIRL: Please, please.

FIRST BOY: The excaliber in the murderworld.

SECOND BOY: Keep it up, Soldier Johnny.

(Monica rocks and sings softly.)

MONICA: Lockheed and Rachel and Baby Jerome
        Frolicking far from home.

(The light in the tent goes out. Monica comes down off the railing, goes toward the tent, from which the sounds have stopped. Then she sees her husband, Albert, standing on the porch. She goes over to him.)

ALBERT: I took the 6:15. I didn't want to at first 'cause all the scum in the world takes the 6:15; they sit there smoking and come into first class without a ticket--or anyway, with a second class one, but then I thought I'd rather come and fuck you on the kitchen table than hang around the station. . . . Why don't you say "Now! There's nothing I'd like better, Albert, light of my life!"

MONICA: I can't have you now, Albert.

ALBERT: You don't have me.

MONICA: I don't want you. Not tonight. Go into the kitchen and open up a can of Heinz Minestrone with fragrant little chunks of meat, Italian style.

ALBERT: When I come flying to you like a homing pigeon!

MONICA: Fly into the kitchen, Albert.

ALBERT: You love me less and less, Monica. It hurts me too. I can't help but notice it. While . . . for me . . . for me, it's the other way around. My love's been getting more ardent ever since our unfortunate engagement.

MONICA: It's the evening of . . . .

ALBERT: *(Pressing)* Come with me into the kitchen.

MONICA: . . . of the fruit.

ALBERT: Yes, yes, that's right. *(He gets very close to her, until he's up against her back.)*

> Oh lovely mother of my son Bart,
> Here in the orchard sauntering,
> Away to the kitchen, let me kiss your little rose,
> 'Ere it perish from languishing.

MONICA: Go away. You've got no business doing here. Not now.

ALBERT: Oh my slimy chick pea,
> My dirty columbine,
> My grimy eglantine.

MONICA: Not now, maybe later.

ALBERT: Isn't there anything besides Minestrone? No Won-ton? I want to squeeze another child out of you, Monica! *(He exits)* Tonight.

(Monica goes over to the tent, squeezes herself inside, closes the flap behind her. Cheers and roars break loose. Monica shouts; "The wild witch is here!" A stately aria by Handel is heard, and at the same time a boy calls out:"Mommy Monica, Mommy Monica." Shrieking with laughter, the Mother answers:"With her noisy harmonica!" Cheers.)

2. IN 1870

> *(King Ludwig II of Bavaria is waltzing in the garden with a young courtier, in Tyrolean garb. A young Duchess, seeing them, circles about them. She is drawn to them as to a magnet, but fights against the feeling and conceals herself as best she can. They don't notice her.)*

DUCHESS: *(Reciting)*
> O, if only I wouldn't dog your heels,
> Your egglets and your ice,
> But in silence bear my cross and steal
> Ever to your paradise.
> That is my feeble power,

You cause my nipples to shine
As with a smile your lover you shower
O bear down on me, into mine.
And you refuse to even glean
That it's for you I yelp.
It's of your grace alone that I dream
As I make love to myself.
With both my mouths weep I long and loud,
Just like your basest mutt,
O, my royal one so proud,
Strike me then O graciousness now,
Yes, hit me on my butt!

(She turns away, her forearm shielding her eyes; she stares hysterically off into space.)

O, moon perverse,
It's all getting worse.
Why O why was I born?
Yes in vain was my slit ever shorn!

(She can't help herself, goes right up to the two dancers, and squeezes in between them. All three then waltz; they kiss each other. But Ludwig II and the courtier are too much under each others' spell. She desperately attempts to arouse their interest, caresses them, licks them. To no avail. A flock of cawing crows sweeps down into the garden. She takes fright. Breaks loose and comes downstage. For a full thirty seconds she looks terribly cross-eyed.)

3. MISS WILDWORLD

(Glaring spots up. A girl parading around in a dark blue swim suit. Music blaring. Applause. She tries to make a good performance out of it, but she's not that hot. She waves to the audience and goes and sits.

An ultra-fashionably dressed female interviewer comes on stage and shouts: "Candidate Number 8! Monica!" Applause. She shouts: "Second round. Intelligence Test." The Interviewer sits down facing Monica. She taps on the microphone and fidgets a bit.)

INTERVIEWER: *(In an exaggeratedly intimate tone of voice)* Well, Monica, make yourself comfortable. We're going into the second round. FIrst question: Is there a man in your life?

MONICA: Yes, there is. Johnnie Van de Wetering. He's the quarterback for the Bruges Football Team *(Heavy applause)* He started out as left guard. Now he's . . . was . . . the quarterback.

INTERVIEWER: Is he watching you tonight?

MONICA: Is that the second question?

INTERVIEWER: Yes.

MONICA: No, he isn't watching. There's no t.v. in his room. But my father is taping tonight's show.

INTERVIEWER: But Johnnie can still . . . I mean, he doesn't have to stay in his room, does he?

MONICA: He's in the hospital.

INTERVIEWER: Oh, how terrible. Nothing serious, I hope?

MONICA: Aah . . . no . . . yes.

INTERVIEWER: Oh, I see. It's delicate. Third question: Are things going all right between you? From the physical point of view, to be specific.

MONICA: That sure is a funny question.

INTERVIEWER: You don't have to answer. But then, of course, you can't score any points for the question.

MONICA: That's true. I'm madly in love with Johnnie . . . from the physical point of view too . . . but recently--it was on my birthday. He started fingering me. I said, "Johnnie, leave me alone."

INTERVIEWER: That can happen to anyone. Sometimes we're just not in the mood. That's entirely normal, nothing to worry about.

MONICA: That's what I thought. But he kept right on feeling me up and schmoozing. "Let's have a look at your cherry," he says. I say,"No, Johnnie, my mind's on something else at the moment." "And it's your birthday," he says. I say, "Well, maybe that's why." "Well then I'll give you something to look at, " he says, and the dear fellow whips out his prick and it was blue. The whole erection was painted dark blue from top to bottom. His team color. I say, "Johnnie, now I'm really not in the mood, because you'll get me all blue inside." "Take a look then, Doughnut," he says, and May God strike me dead if it isn't true, but he'd painted an M right on the tip of his prick, a neatly drawn golden M with my gold nail polish that used to be fashionable a few years back, he must have been working on it quite a while, a beautiful M, a capital M, well then I went to get the axe, if you know what I mean, I thought it was so wild, and on my birthday too, who would ever do a thing like that for you on your birthday? So I said, "Well, come on then, Johnnie." So what if I am blue inside? You only have one birthday. One a year, I mean.

INTERVIEWER: *(Under the spell of the story, she drops her professional demeanor)* And then, and then?

MONICA: Then, he was at it on the living room sofa when he suddenly stops his ramming and he says, "What's the problem? Your mind's on something else, ain't it?" And I say, "I just told you! I don't feel nothing. This don't count for nothing." And he says, "You're thinking about somebody else!" I say, "What gives you that idea?" And he kept on nagging: "Come on, say it, who you're thinking about." I say, "Johnnie, I'm not thinking of anyone else, and if I were thinking about someone, it would only get you mad on my birthday." "No," he says, "we're good friends, but that narrow-minded I've never been." And I say, "Fine, then here it is. I can't help thinking about Mando." He's the quarterback for the Liège football team, the one that wears an earring, a silver earring, really wild, and Johnnie takes a swipe at me! "Mando!" he screams, and he takes another swipe.

INTERVIEWER: A swipe for the earring! Hahaha! *(All present laugh.)*

MONICA: *(Shoots a look around, surprised.)*

INTERVIEWER: And then? And then?

MONICA: I say, "Boy, if that's how it's gonna be, you might just as well put your balls back in storage. I've had enough for one night." Being made miserable doesn't turn me on. I can't get into it.

INTERVIEWER: If sado-masochism is really what's at issue here, then there's got to be mutual consent.

MONICA: *(Not listening)* Then he gave me another slap, and then I broke his knee. I jeopardized his whole future with the Bruges team. With the poker next to the fireplace that he'd lit for my birthday. Actually, I was aiming for his blue prick, but I was too far-gone. You know what I mean, don't you?

INTERVIEWER: And is that poor boy who barely escaped the worst possible fate the same one that's lying in his hospotal room now, all on his lonesome?

MONICA: I'm going over there pretty soon. We're back on good terms. Because I'm still head over heels in love with him.

From the physical point of view too. Just not on my birthday.

INTERVIEWER: Fourth question: Imagine you got the highest score and became Miss WildWorld; what's the main difference it would make in your life?

MONICA: If I become Miss WildWorld, I'm gonna move. And then I'll take in my kid brother, Walter, because the way that boy lives now is no life at all. He came down with encephalitis when they vaccinated him.

INTERVIEWER: And is Walter tuned into the Commercial Free Network tonight too?

MONICA: He's not allowed! My father won't let him! Because it'd get him much too over-excited *(cries out)* and his brains would start smoking . . . sizzling . . . and . . . and then, we'd really be out of the ballpark. *(gets upset)*

INTERVIEWER: Don't get nervous, Monica. We're just about ready. The jury won't take it amiss that you let your emotions show a bit, isn't that right, gentlemen of the jury? They're shaking their heads no! Thank you, gentlemen of the jury.

MONICA: Our Walter isn't difficult. My father says how difficult he is ten or twelve times a day, but Father forgets that he and Walter used to be the best of pals. *(Silence)* They were like pancakes and syrup together over the breakfast table back then! Both of them in their flannel pajamas, and then Father would drop his spoon. He'd say, "Pick it up, Monica." And Walter would shout, "Didn't you hear what Father just told you?" And the two of them gave each other a wink, and there I was eating butter cookies with hot chocolate, which was my favorite thing in the world, and then I got under the table and couldn't help seeing those four flannel pants legs and these two unspeakably smooth, pink pricks with their heads sticking straight up in the air and now I think chocolate milk's the dirtiest thing on earth, especially when there's a thick, dry, brown skin on it, just give me a King-size Coca Cola any day.

INTERVIEWER: Unh unh unh. Monica, no brand names! The jury won't like that. You could get points taken off for that.

MONICA: *(Not listening, getting more and more excited)* And now my father says that one of these days he's going to hold a pillow over Walter's face while he's sleeping, that it would be better for us all, but now there are three of us and then there'd only be two of us, and I don't want any part of that and that's why I'm telling all of Belgium and Holland about that pillow so that all Belgium and Holland will have it on video-tape, Father, and if anything should happen to Walter, you bastard, you'll be the first to be handcuffed and thrown right into the paddy wagon, head first; and then we'll have a good laugh.

(A fanfare starts playing, drowning her out. The Interviewer gets up. The spotlights focus elsewhere. Monica looks all around, bewildered. A shrill bell rings.)

INTERVIEWER: And here comes our Candidate Number Nine: Teresa Van Dierendonck.

4. IN A ROOM

(A man and a woman, both about seventy, are sitting watching t.v. The sound isn't on. The man is looking fixedly at the screen, while slowly pulling off his left sock. He picks at his toes. He is apparently deaf.)

WOMAN: If you don't put that sock back on in the next ten seconds, of your own free will, all by yourself, I'm going to get the electric knife and saw your ten disgusting toes right off, all ten of them. One, two, three, four, five, six.*(She makes wild movements and points at his naked toes, but he doesn't notice.)* *(Hollering)* Put your sock back on. *(No reaction)* One, two, three, four . . . .

(She gets up and puts the sock back on his foot. He keeps watching t.v. She stands in front of the t.v. set and lifts up her dress. He keeps watching the same as if it were the t.v. Dejected, she lets her dress down and goes back and sits.)

MAN: *(Abruptly)* Is the sound on or not?

WOMAN: *(Shakes her head.)*

MAN: Why not? Who's gonna be Miss WildAss? That dreary one there? Wanna bet? The jury likes 'em dreary. Turn up the sound. Then you'll hear if the tame one's the winner.

WOMAN: *(Shakes her head)*

MAN: Or would you like to hear me instead? *(He bursts out in a raucous fit of laughing, coughs, pants. Stops.)* Can you hear me? Listen. My stomach. *(Imitates the sound in his stomach.)* Listen. *(He makes rattling, gutteral sounds.)* I get it from my grandma. Throat's closing. It'll never open again. Never again. *(Roaring laugh breaks off suddenly.*

Silence.) Sometimes I can hear just fine. Only it's inside. I sometimes hear my left ball shifting, trying to get away from the other one; it's trying to climb, climb back up inside where it's warm.

WOMAN: Warm! *(She imitates his raucous laugh. Silence.)* You told me I had to keep my eyes closed. The whole time. I wasn't supposed to look at you. I closed my eyes. I heard you scraping. I said, "Can't you shave? Then it wouldn't scratch like that." That's where the skin is softest. "Witch," you said. I turned you into a frog a bunch of times. I blew you up with a straw. Until I was out of breath. But you never exploded. I said, "Put the garbage can outside, because my back is killing me." That was when you could still walk okay. The garbage can kept on stinking. Right over to the neighbors. My little sister Miriam said, "Marie, Mother didn't bring us up to be this way." You said, "Marie, I'd swim to the end of the sea, right between the jellyfish, if you marry me before Christmas." I said, "Yes, honeybuch, yes my darling, yes my beloved sweetheart." I kept saying it all night, the night was long. You said, "Keep your eyes closed, don't look at me." *(Silence.)*

MAN: The steering column: worn out. Brake drum: clogged. Cracks in the front axle. The crooked wheel turning loose. The tires emptying out. I can hear the whole thing.

WOMAN: The last time I called you "sweetheart," by accident, you looked at me like I was an idiot sitting at the table, you took your dentures out of your mouth, you laid them on the kitchen table.

MAN: *(Panting, fast)* The goods of this world are not in themselves bad. They become bad through bad usage.

WOMAN: You said, "My first wife would bite the nails off my toes. All night long."

MAN: A circle 'round the sun. Glory. *(Panting rapidly again)* Four-cylinder engine goes down, keeps on going down, the intake valve opens, open like Marie, the cylinder fills right up to the brim, the spark-plug sparks up, psst, the gas keeps burning, still going, bzzzz. *(He makes a bunch of plopping, blowing, shrill sounds, faster and faster, more and more violent.)*

WOMAN: You said, "Marie, you got the nicest pair of buttocks in Vilvoorde."

MAN: *(Dies with his eyes open.)*

WOMAN: *(Gets up, pulls off his socks, sits down next to him, and plays with his toes.) (Wearily)* The majority of accidents occur in the home. *(Gets up, closes his eyes, goes over to the phone, dials a number.)* Miriam . . . . Good . . . . That beginner's class at the night school. I've been thinking. I'll go with you, Mondays and Wednesdays, right. I'm starting it, Miriam, one and a half pounds of thick wool yarn, jersey knitting, one needle purling on the top side, one needle straight on the underside . . . . Size forty two! That boy of yours does keep on growing . . . . Miriam . . . that dishwasher, I've been thinking. I'm gonna buy it after all, that model that doesn't need an air vent. All you got to do is open the window a crack. I know, Miriam, the neighbors told me . . . . *(Looks at the Man. His eyes are wide open again.)* I'll call you right back. *(To the Man.)* Don't look at me. Keep your eyes shut.

> *(She closes his eyes again. Then, she takes off his pants, empties the pockets. She turns up the sound on the t.v. "Passion" by Rod Stewart. She sways to the beat. With a huge pair of scissors she starts cutting the pants to shreds.)*

5. ON THE TRAIN

> *(An empty compartment. A young woman with a hot dog in her hand enters and sits down. The train starts up. A man sinks down into a seat near the door, worn out. He has been running hard. While he is catching his breath, he sees the Woman. He gets up and comes over to sit down across from her. She takes the hot dog out of the bun and nibbles at it.)*

MAN: I saw you at the market place not so long ago. Along with a man in a white raincoat. Was that your father? Not your husband, was he ? No, he was well over fifty. He looked like a geography teacher to me. *(She looks outside.)* You've got hazel nut eyes. Not the color, but the shape. You don't see those very often anymore, hazelnuts.

WOMAN: They're mainly used in the chocolate industry.

MAN: That's for sure. *(Silence)* The breast section is also in order. *(Points at the nipples.)* Tip-top. Tip and top. No bra. That's what I like to see. Pure nature. Friend of mine just passed away. Was sitting watching t.v., handicapped, and boom. He'd only smoked one unfiltered cigarette after supper. *(Silence)* Wearing panties? Bet you are. Large or small?

Small. Salmon-colored? Salmon-colored. *(Silence)* Tasty, hunh, that hot dog? Hot dogs are tasty. The first bite is the best, right? Are you doing it on purpose, hmm, eating that hot dog so slowly? Well, I know how women are. *(She gives him a withering look, as she downs the rest of the hot dog. He turns away and then looks right back at her again.)* Sure is something, hm, being on a train at night? No other passengers. No conductor either. He's sitting up front, in first class, going over the t.v. listings in the newspaper, eating candy. Doesn't budge from that spot. No wonder the railroad's going bankrupt. Only brave souls dare to ride the trains this late. Heavy drinkers, people with tattoos. I've got a tattoo too. In a place I only show to hazelnut girls. *(He places his foot right alongside her.)* One goose says to the other goose, "Come with me to the poultry store. There's a whole bunch of naked chicks hanging around in the window." *(Silence)* Where are you headed? Don't tellme, because you might say "Dordrecht," and then you'd have to get off at the next stop and that's coming up very soon and I couldn't take it. I wouldn't stand for it. You can't do that to me. I go by the name of Marcus. What name do you go by? Don't answer, because you might say Mary Lou or Nicole or Monica and I wouldn't be able to take that. Gotcha! *(All of a sudden, he grabs the purse off her lap.)*

WOMAN: Give me back my purse.

MAN: Not until I've had a good look around for . . . goodies. *(Opens the purse, sniffs around in it.)* Hidden goodies. Wafts from the Orient. *(She snatches the purse back. Silence. He makes a move for the purse. She pulls it away. He teases her by making as though he were going to grab her purse again. Leaning back.)* Now you see how kind and peace-loving Marcus is. It's all because my friend died. Was watching t.v. His wife was sitting right there. Boom. *(Silence.)* Amanda with almond eyes. Amanda, will you let me pamper you? Oh, child of my heart, would I ever take care of you. I'd let my fingertips glide very slowly up the inside of your thighs to where the skin is the softest. You'd . . . you'd . . . *(He takes a magazine out of his pocket, "Candy;" hot-bloodedly leafs through it and reads)* Her clitoris was drenched in the oil that was dripping out of her wham-banged slit." Oh, Amanda, if you'd only let me, broad of my heart, I'd . . . .

WOMAN: Do it then.

MAN: What do you mean?

WOMAN: Enough beating around the bush. Go ahead. Ruin me.

MAN: Here?

WOMAN: Sure, the conductor's sitting reading the t.v. listings.

MAN: You mean it too.

WOMAN: *(Lifts one knee up. She rubs his crotch with her other foot. Taken aback, the man retreats.)*

MAN: I'm drunk. I'm not here. I'm dreaming this. *(Silence. She keeps staring at him.)* My fiancée would never do a thing like this. She's a real hot number, I won't deny that, but something like this . . . never. Not even a whore would do this without demanding to be paid in advance. You little rascal. *(She makes a grab for his crotch, unzips his fly, and sticks her hand inside.)* Ah! Have you lost your mind? *(He jumps up and runs down the aisle.)* Conductor! Come here, please, second class. *(Very rapidly)* Conductor, I'm thirty two years old, meat dealer, specialty horsemeat, secretary of the St. Francis Checkers Club. Tonight, I will admit, I had one glass of port too many, you can give me a breath test, that's because a bosom buddy of mine kicked the bucket, I'm a lieutenant in the reserves and engaged. Conductor, I demand that you write up a report, that you throw this bitch right off the train, where are you hiding Conductor? Is it always like this on this line? Is the railroad company trying to bring in a little money on the side with prostitution because it's going bankrupt?

(As he's shouting, she has come slowly towards him. The train seems to speed up tremendously. He flies before her approach. She goes over to him again, and as his back is up against the toilet door, she makes a grab for his crotch. She tugs with all her might. She pulls the penis right off his body. The train thunders on.)

MAN: *(Staring at his bloody crotch.)* I knew it. It was foretold. *(The woman goes and sits down. She looks outside. With the same devil-may-care as just before, she takes a bite out of his penis. The man staggers towards her, sits down opposite her.)* My geography teacher warned me about this. He can read the stars. It was in my stars. *(Feebly)* Is it tasty, at least? The first bite is the best, isn't it? Even so, you've still got hazelnut eyes. I don't answer to the name Marcus. I lied to you. I don't have a tattoo either. Pull the emergency brake, would you? Amanda? No? Please? Won't you?

(The trace of a smile passes over her face.)

6. WHISPERS

> *(Dusk is falling yet again. "Sérénade Mélancolique" by Tchaikowski. Three women are sitting next to each other.)*

FIRST WOMAN: My Cousin Frank, thirty years old, and all of a sudden comes down with the mumps. Not so uncommon, not so horrible. Already had two children.

SECOND WOMAN: I've got an I.Q. of 150. Property is theft. I want to be part of the opinion-making process. And still I've got hazelnut eyes. Not the color, but the shape.

THIRD WOMAN: In the park. It was raining, same as now. And this little guy comes up and walks next to me. Old, old, old, and fragile and beet red and filthy with mountain-climbing shoes on. The leather was full of cracks. My heart melted. "Angel," he says, "angel" and he walks off the path and keeps looking at me and droops, falls, lies spread out, his arms, squirms, tosses and turns with his little white crusty legs in the air, waving those mountain-climbing shoes around and those little pink nylon socks. "Angel," he says,"come on and take a dip on top of me, don't be embarrassed, just let yourself drop."

FIRST WOMAN: In the park?

THIRD WOMAN: I was too young.

SECOND WOMAN: And I did nothing but push and moan and puff and press and then it popped right out. I looked at it. It wasn't my child, not on your life. I pushed it right back inside. The doctor slapped me on the hands. The nurse tugged on my hair.

THIRD WOMAN: "Rita, Rita, I'm coming in." Rita, that was my grandma. "Rita, I'm coming in," my grandpa screamed. But she'd been dead for years. "Do you suffer carniphobia?" the doctor asked. Grandma didn't understand, 'cause she'd left school when she was fourteen and worked hard as a housemaid after that. The doctor asks her if she's got an aversion to meat. "Yes," Grandma says, I haven't been able to stand the smell of meat lately. And whenever I smell meat roasting, I could just throw up." "Thank you very much ma'am." That's the first symptom of cancer of the stomach, carniphobia, but the doctor didn't say a word about it. "Rita, Rita, I'm coming in!" Grandpa shouted and he dragged me down into his bed. "Lie down, Rita, I'm coming in."

FIRST WOMAN: And did he get in?

THIRD WOMAN: I was too young.

FIRST WOMAN: Maniac.

THIRD WOMAN: *(Yells)* Property is theft. But not now. Not in the slightest. I'd like to be the proud owner of four, six, maximum eight breasts. Eight sucking babies hanging off. Or they could be kittens. They hurt though. The best, actually, would be eight chopped-off mens' heads.

FIRST WOMAN: *(Quickly)* Patrick comes home, been gone for three weeks. Honduras or Uruguay, somewhere around there, drops down into the Breuer chair, lights up his Corona. "Glenfiddich straight up," he yells and then he says, "Honey, what a beautiful shot, what a brilliant shot!" No, it wasn't in Uruguay, but somewhere in the neighborhood. "Honey, a shot taken at the very moment that guy is being executed. One second after the order's given, a split-second before the bullets hit the black man in the chest." It was Bolivia, I think. "You have no idea, honey," Patrick says, "the look on that man's face in my Hasselblad and right after, when he was already dead, but the stare stayed in my SMC Pentax Reflex Zoom Six Hundred Eight Hundred Milimeter, eight-twelve, that stare *(Slower)*, you get that stare on your face sometimes, you know too." And with my dumb brain, I say "Thanks, Patrick, thanks a lot."

SECOND WOMAN: Gerard asks, "What gets you really turned on, what gets you really wet and dripping?" I say, "Nail polish peeling off."

THIRD WOMAN: The smell of horsemeat. Carniphobia? Are you out of your mind?

FIRST WOMAN: Together? Yes, yes, yes. It must, it should, both at the same time in one fell swoop. But still, it's the duller and less substantial together. When the other one has the same, the only thing that's yours too, then it's the same, identical, ditto. No, not together. You first, little fella, you first. Then me. And how!

7. AT THE HOTEL EDEN

> (A smartly dressed, refined gentleman is lying on his bed in a hotel room and is staring up at the ceiling. In the hallway, a girl singing Rod Stewart's "Passion." He

gets up, goes to the door, and motions to her.)

MAN: Is this the Hotel Eden?

WOMAN: Yes sir.

MAN: Is it an accomodation recommended by the Rotary Club, the Association for Large-Sized Families, the Freemasons, and the Flemish Motoring Club?

GIRL: Yes sir.

MAN: Come inside. Sit down over there. This morning, when I went to wash up, I found a hair stuck to my bar of hotel soap. What have you got to say to that? A dark hair. Dark as a maid-servant's. *(She raises her hand to her hair-do.)* No, it was shorter and curlier. Both elegant and inviting. That little hair was yours.

GIRL: But sir . . . .

MAN: May I ask whether I am supposed to interpret this as a deliberate act on your part, albeit obscure to me? Had it any connection with your serenade I heard just now? Or was this evensong not intended for my ears?

GIRL: *(At sea)* I don't know sir.

MAN: Bawling British tunes in the hallway and doesn't even know for whom? Ought I to believe that, or ought I to conclude, rather, that these were signals intended for the repellent, pimply popsinger who, if I may give credence to the daily gazette, is likewise lodging at the Hotel Eden, and that you, preposterous little groupie that you are, were hoping he'd storm out into the corridor and shout, "Who, oh who is that warbling there? You? Come into my arms, come into my nest, and as of tomorrow, you're in my band, in the gleam of the floods, wearing plastic underwear, doing back-ups with my three other lovers, the Mexicali Rosettes, cheek to cheek, singing *(Sings)* 'Oowaah, oowaah!' into the mike."

GIRL: You're kidding around sir.

MAN: Never. Never. Never say never. How old are you?

GIRL: Twenty three.

MAN: Ah. *(Gasps for breath. An intense sorrow comes over him; in a broken voice)* Are you a Pisces?

GIRL: A Pisces?

MAN: Ram?

GIRL: No. No. Excuse me sir. *(Starts to get up.)*

MAN: *(Sternly)* Sit right there! You come from the country?

GIRL: Two years ago . . . .

MAN: You came to the city, chock-full of hope and ideals, to take classes at the Conservatory of Music, and then, six months later, you were kicked out when the principal couldn't stand the sight of you anymore, since he'd come down with a case of blues as a result of your depriving him of your miraculously pure mons veneris. You didn't want to go back to the old folk's homestead, your wounded, righteous pride forbid you. Without a penny in your pocket you roamed the length of the city harbor, weighing the possibility of selling your twenty three-year old body but, being squeamish about venereal diseases, you fled to the heart of the city and fainted right in the municipal park, from which a Turkish cook's mate wafted you away to the Hotel Eden, where he was employed and where you now while away your days in servitude, homesick, in spite of it all, for the sweet rural night air, the countryside, the green oats, the milk cans, the crows. Ah, the countryside. Common sense. If I'd been raised by two dirt-poor grandparents out on the moors, I'd have become a saint. Here. *(He gives her a thousand franc bill.)* Will that suffice?

GIRL: *(Stuffs it into her pocket)* You are a saint sir.

MAN: I'm quite perfect; that's another matter.

GIRL: Excuse me sir.

MAN: We know nothing, my girl. Nothing of the world and nothing that is not of the world.

GIRL: You've got something there, sir.

MAN: Am I capable of loving my fellow man?

GIRL: Oh yes, sure.

MAN: Stupid cow! *(Silence)*

    (He comes over to her, lifts her up and sniffs at her neck.) Sweat from the alienating work, the soiled beds, the towels full of blood, the perfidiously growling vacuum cleaner. *(He gives her another franc bill.)*

GIRL: Thank you, sir. *(She takes off her dress, folds it neatly, and stands and waits in her slip.)*

MAN: There's a mardi gras in my soul each and every day, my girl. Would you like to get married?

GIRL: With you, sure, of course sir. In the sight of the law and in church.

MAN: Fine. *(She starts to come toward him.)* Sit down, I told you. *(Silence)* My lawfully wedded wife's name was Monica, like Saint Augustine's mother. She is no more.

GIRL: Aww.

MAN: *(Imitating her.)* Aw. Aw. Aw. Who gives a shit? Mountains in Patagonia burst open and haven't the slightest idea that my Monica ever existed. *(Silence)* Are all people so afraid? Or am I the only one?

GIRL: I am too, sir. *(Silence)*

MAN: All that pain, all those days. Are you a Gemini? No? My wife was a Pisces, with Ram rising, a lousy combination. She danced "Giselle." Perfection. *(He goes over to the closet, produces a white tu-tu, and hands it to the girl.)* Take off your shoe and put this on. *(She does so. He looks on.)* Infante. If we must be buried anyway, then we ought to be allowed to wear what we like for the occasion, oughtn't we? Monica coughed and spit up. Blood spouted over her poor tits. She kept right on dancing. All that pain, all those days. Infante. *(He turns on the cassette player and takes off his coat. Takes off his shoes and starts to dance to the music of "Giselle." She can barely keep from laughing. His dancing is clumsy and earnest.)* Come. *(He winks at her. She joins in; surprisingly elegant and light; he lets go of her, throws tens of thousand franc bills on the floor, drops into an easy chair, and watches her dancing round about the furniture. He quietly talks gibberish.)* Never again, never again. They laughed at me in all those capitals, through every Swiss province, there I was, her shadow. Her ribs, rippling as though by chance. The bridle across my snout. And all my languages instruments, begging. Never again. In the realm of the dead. Her silken thighs, trapped in the ice. "Look at me," she said, and I drank from her mouth. Both eyes wide open. And she, tired of petting, coughed and coughed. I lost her. *(Yells at the girl.)* Pliez! Un, deux, trois, pliez! *(He slides down off his chair and falls, face down; she takes fright.)*

GIRL: Sir, sir. *(Runs to the bathroom and comes back.)* Are there any pills anywhere? In your suitcase? Shall I call a doctor?

Is it epilepsy, sir? Say something. I want to help. *(She lifts him up and places him back in the easy chair.)* It's not my fault. *(She opens the top of his shirt; he lets her. Airplanes fly over, very low.)*

HE: What day is it today? *(A sudden panic overtakes him.)* Is it a war? WAR?

SHE: Not yet, sir.

HE: *(Jumps up, looks in the nighttable, in his coatpockets.)* Where's my passport? *(Extemely agitated and uncertain, he runs up and down, and then out of the room. She turns off the cassette player. Kneels and gathers up the scattered bills.)*

8. IN ANOTHER ROOM OF THE HOTEL EDEN

(A Singer, in her sixties, is on the floor, doing physical exercises. Push-ups. A young Nurse is looking on.)

NURSE: Twelve and thirteen and fourteen, come on, five to go.

SINGER: *(Drops back onto the floor.)* Sehnsucht, end of the line.

NURSE: You've got to, Miss Tilly.

SINGER: No. *(She starts to get up. The Nurse pushes her back down with her foot.)* But it'll give me bulging arms, loaded with muscles and clumps that won't look at all good in an evening gown.

NURSE: Come on, fourteen, fifteen. You want to look good at the Red Cambodia Ball, don't you?

SINGER: I can't do any more. Have mercy. *(She gets up with great difficulty.)* I'm dying, I'm so hungry, I'm dying, I'm so sleepy, I'm dying, I'm so horny. All for Cambodia. And what do you get in return? Peanuts. *(She hoists herself into an easy chair.)* Give me a cigarette.

NURSE: Out of the question. You've already had three today. They're bad for your voice.

SINGER: That's true. You're such a sweetheart. It's a good thing somebody's looking after me. *(Silence)* The body is one thing, but the soul's a whole other ball of wax. When I do exercises, my body thinks it's terrible, but it does realize that it's for it's own good. But not my soul. It gets no benefit out of it, it doesn't want any part of it, it doesn't feel good about it. I'll have to give the matter some thought again and put it down in my memoirs.

NURSE: Oh well, you're never going to write them anyway--your "memoirs."

SINGER: Just you wait. The whole book is marked down here. *(Points to her forehead.)* The only thing to do is write it.

NURSE: Are you going to put everything in that book?

SINGER: Everything. I haven't lived for nothing, chérie. They'll be stunned. I know a couple . . . that'll have a stroke. I'll start it next week. First draft in pencil, then a neat second draft, and then I'll have my Cousin Solange type it up. She's behind me a hundred percent. because she thinks that she's mentioned in my will, the idiot! It'll have everything in it. From start to finish, from the outermost surface to the deepest depths. "Serenade" by Tilly.

NURSE: Tilly?

SINGER: First name only, like Vincent.

NURSE: *(Brings her a box of chocolates.)* Here. This'll give you some courage.

SINGER: *(Rummages through it, stuffs one right in her mouth.)* How many calories are there in one piece of chocolate?

NURSE: A couple thousand.

SINGER: What? Now you tell me.

NURSE: Otherwise they'll get mouldy.

SINGER: You sound just like a war baby.

NURSE: You can't let food go to waste.

SINGER: Then give me another. The white one with the nut.

NURSE: No, not that one. That one.

SINGER: *(Eats the chocolate the Nurse had indicated, then sighs, satisfied.)*

NURSE: And now the eyes. One, two, one, two, one, two, one, two. *(The Singer opens and closes her eyes in time. Airplanes fly overhead very low.)*

SINGER: There's a war on the way.

NURSE: Does it scare you?

SINGER: I'm not scared of anything. My conscience is clear. I'm not scared of anyone or anything. *(Stops blinking her eyes.)* The Germans pointed their bayonets at my chest. But then, they let 'em drop and went away. I had the ability to make men melt just by staring at them. Even Germans in uniform.

NURSE: Doesn't Mr. Hector scare you?

SINGER: Even if he were a hundred Minister of Public Works, he wouldn't intimidate me, the creep.

NURSE: What did he do now?

SINGER: *(Dignified)* He screwed me in a way more customary in Mediteranean nations.

NURSE: Did it hurt?

SINGER: *(Bursting with laughter)* Au contraire, ma chérie. *(Serious)* But you don't do a thing like that without a lady's prior consent.

NURSE: *(Hands her another chocolate)* So that's the Minister of Public Work's deep dark secret.

SINGER: *(Secretively)* No. That isn't his deep dark secret. *(Eats the chocolate.)* Ugh, this one is bitter.

NURSE: Bitter dark chocolate. *(She shudders.)*

SINGER: No, just plain bitter.

NURSE: *(Hands her one with caramel filling.)*

SINGER: Thank you, dear. You're a real sweetheart. Strict, but a sweetheart nonetheless. It feels like I've always known you and you've only been here one week.

NURSE: Five days. *(Silence)*

SINGER: "Serenade" by Tilly. At first I wanted to call it "Evening Song," but that sounds more like the name of a country house.

NURSE: *(Oblivious)* Are you going to include things about other politicians?

SINGER: About friend and foe alike. The Benelux nations will tremble. My swan song. About the Minister's chief of staff, who always did it standing up. About directors of operas in which I triumphed, Valladolid, Bucharest, Tenerif, about one minister, who happens to still be in office, that used a knitting needle . . . but you'll read all about it. You'll be the first, because "Serenade" is for you. *(Sings in a marvelous alto voice)* "Sissisi, ce n'est qu'une serenade, sissisi, serenade sans espoir." *(Silence)* I feel so sleepy.

NURSE: You know, you could dictate your memoirs. Or talk into a tape recorder.

SINGER: Then I'd have to buy a machine of that sort.

NURSE: Oh, I could lend you my tape recorder.

SINGER: Oh yeah? Okay. *(Dictates)* Chapter One. How it grew. I, Rosa-Maria Van Ekeren, later known as Tilly van Eck, was born in Varsenare in the year . . . and so forth. Does that sound clear enough for a machine of that sort?

NURSE: You could hear every syllable.

SINGER: I took elocution lessons. *(Her eyes fall shut, she murmurs)* When I was seven . . . I'm seven and I wanna pee like a boy. I go up to the little green door on that big wooden board with the hole in it. Through the moon I can see the frost on the apple trees. And it works, it steams, it spurts straight into the hole, and in the hole I can see the most beautiful shimmering colors like the wings of a dragonfly and my skinny legs start to tremble, I'm in heaven. I am the master over everything. This will last for the rest of my life. That's just the way that men pee. *(She falls asleep. The Nurse goes to the door and looks out into the corridor, inquiringly, comes back and shakes the Singer's shoulder.)*

SINGER: *(Sings)* Tomorrow, tomorrow, tomorrow.

NURSE: Don't go to sleep yet. Not yet. Tell me about Hector De Jonghe, the minister.

SINGER: *(Her eyes still closed)* Love of my life, Hector. You'll never find a bigger creep.

NURSE: *(Takes the half-asleep Singer's pulse)* What happened last month here in the Hotel Eden? On Friday the twelfth? In Room Eleven?

SINGER: *(Grinning in her sleep)* He had to pay for a new mattress. *(Mumbles something incomprehensible.)*

NURSE: *(Takes a tape recorder out of her apron pocket and holds it to the Singer's mouth)* Why?

SINGER: *(Softly)* A spanking new mattress. Hector. Write a check.

NURSE: Why a new mattress?

SINGER: The one in Room Eleven was full of blood; it was soaked right through with blood. It dripped out onto the carpet. Luckily the carpet was red. Hector hollered like . . . like . . .

NURSE: Like . . .?

SINGER: *(Tenderly)* . . . like a little boy, a little Indian.

NURSE: And was it your blood?

SINGER: Who else's? *(Wakes up, all of a sudden)* Hey? Hey? Who? *(The Nurse immediately stuffs three chocolates into her mouth. She doses off again.)*

NURSE: Does it happen often? Has it been going on for a long time?

SINGER: Since Easter on the Canary Islands. When he was an agricultural attaché. He weighed eighteen pounds less.

NURSE: Nobody ever knew about it?

SINGER: Not even my own husband.

NURSE: And there was always blood?

SINGER: Not always . . . no . . . sometimes. Hector goes wild at the sight of blood. He wallows in it and . . .he shouts . . . like a little Indian. *(She dozes off and snores. A Man in a raincoat comes into the room. The Nurse gives him the tape recorder and the box of chocolates. The Man takes pictures of the sleeping singer.)*

SINGER: This chief of staff always wants to do it standing up. In the ocean too. My Cousin Solange says, "But Auntie, then how can you tell when he's coming?" Of course you do. The water is cold and then--all of a sudden--it gets warmer inside, you do notice the difference, you idiot. The chief of staff fell over backwards and drowned in the surf. No. *(Smiles)*, of course he didn't drown. *(Hums)* Tomorrow, tomorrow, tomorrow. *(The others stand there staring at her.)*

9. THE LITTLE BRIDE

> *(A girl in a white wedding dress, white lace gloves, veil, and so on comes on stage. "Sérénade Mélancolique." She is obviously looking for someone, but her heart isn't in it. She sees a shabby man in dirty clothes lying on a subway grating, fumes rising up out of it.)*

BRIDE: I've lost my husband. All of a sudden he up and ran away from the Hotel Eden. On the first day of our honeymoon. How do you like that? Now I've got to send thank you notes to relatives and acquaintances without his name on them! I must have done something wrong, that's for sure, but I'm racking my brains what it was. The doorman at the hotel told me he saw Patrick coming out of the elevator with a deadly grin on his face. A deadly grin, that's what the man said, a mere simple doorman. These days doormen see more than ordinary people, it comes with the territory, but still . . . a deadly grin, I ask you. We're still on our honeymoon and already a deadly grin, I ask you. *(The Bum lets fly a resounding belch.)* First we went to the hotel. Checked in and had the baggage taken up. No time to so much as comb my hair, but we had to hurry-scurry over to the graveyard where all the famous corpses are buried. Not even time enough for a regular coffee, oh no, all the graves, with the Michelin and the Paris guidebook in hand. Next, we hurry-scurry over to the Louvre, where the prettiest paintings on earth are. And then hurry-scurry back to the hotel, where we were supposed to get some rest before going to the Folies Bergère like we planned. "Planned," I said. *(Silence.)* I'm resting up and he's kissing. So far, so good. Till he says, "Honey, put your white wedding dress on, will you?" I put my dress on. He frowns with his eyebrows touching. Like this. I say, "What's wrong Patrick, aren't you feeling all right? The Paris air? The garlic?" Mind you, I hadn't caught one whiff of garlic, but it's in all the guide books. Paris smells of garlic. All I smell is Wimpy's. "I've got to go," Patrick says. I say, "Then go." He says, "I already went." I say, "Then go again." He says, "I sit and wait and nothing comes out." I say, "It'll pass." "What do you know about it," he says, barks. I say, "Patrick, I know a whole lot about it, if you ask me." And I say the following: *(Ambles over to the Bum and graciously recites.)* I have often noticed that all things of this world hinge on some eminent person's opinions and will, be it a king, prime minister, or high official. Now then, this opinion and this will hinge on the way live animal spirits penetrate the cerebellum and medulla oblongata. These animal spirits depend on the bloodstream; that blood depends on the manufacture of chyle. This chyle is manufactured in the mesenteric network; the mesentery is attached to the intestines by means of extremely thin threads; the intestines--if I may so express myself--are full of shit. Despite the fact that each intestine is encased in three strong pellicles, it is still as riddled with holes as a sieve, because everything in nature is equipped with an opening and no grain of sand is so tiny but it doesn't have five hundred pores. Well then, what happens with a constipated man? The tinnest, most delicate elements of his shit combine with the chyle in the Azygos Veins, go to the Portal Vein, and into the Paquet Resevoir. They travel through the muscles beneath the collar bone and enter the heart of even the most decent men and most gracious of women. It is the dew of the dried shit which runs throughout their whole body. Once this dew inundates the basic tissue, the blood vessels, and the glands of a splenetic person, then his bad humor grows cruel. The whites of his eyes grow fiery; his lips stick together. The color of his face assumes turbid pigments. This is more important than one may imagine, Patrick. Constipation has been the cause of some of the bloodiest scenes in history. That's what I said and then Patrick ran away. With a deadly grin on his face.

(The Bum belches again. The Bride goes over to him; he sees her legs and he lets his dirty, mangled fingers slide along her legs.)

BRIDE: You don't trust me either.
You're going to run out on me too.
Trust me.

*(He pulls her down to the ground, growling and sneezing and belching. He fingers her thighs, pulls up her dress, beneath which she is wearing very elegant underwear. They roll on the ground.
The sound of surf.)*

10. GRANDPA

(A Grandfather, who bears a strong resemblence to the Bum from the previous scene, is warming his hands over the flames of an open hearth. He is blind. On the sofa lies--in a Balthus position--a girl dressed as a child of ten. Silence.)

GRANDPA: I won't say another word. Any normal person talks for two hours of each day. On an average. Nine-tenths of his life, a normal man keeps his trap shut. I'm a normal man.

GIRL: Once upon a time . . .

GRANDPA: I won't say another word.

GIRL: Once upon a time . . .

GRANDPA: Once upon a time, there was a house. It's still there.

GIRL: My father's house.

GRANDPA: In my father's house there are many rooms. And all the rooms smell of horsemeat.

GIRL: You can see out through the windows.

GRANDPA: That's the way it usually is, it's seen to beforehand. And then you see the windows of other rooms in other houses belonging to the same father.

GIRL: And you really can't see anything besides that?

GRANDPA: Every once in a while you can see a sniff-sniff.

GIRL: *(Triumphantly)* A rabbit!

GRANDPA: With its best little friend, a quack-quack.

GIRL: A little duck!

GRANDPA: And the sniff-sniff pushes his little belly against quack-quack's little ass and they make tiny little sniff-quacks. It's been seen happening by scientists, it's been documented. But if you want to see it taking place, you've got to get up early and stay by the window all day long and watch until your little eyes turn red and start to burn, and do it for who-ole we-eks, since you've got to try really hard if you want to see anything. Get that into your heady-weddy, Monica, night and day, day and night. What you can also see--but that's mainly in winter and on Thursdays--is a woman with a check-ered shawl in front of her face and a garbage can under her arm. If you watch real close, then you'll know who that gar-bage can is.

GIRL: Mo-ni-ca.

GRANDPA: That's right. Kissums, Monica.

GIRL: *(Blows a kiss in his direction. Silence.)*

GRANDPA: All living beings have the scent of the Lord.

GIRL: Me too.

GRANDPA: You too. But only after a while, not before you've suf-fered from b.h.--broken heart.

GIRL: Suffered from a broken heart.

GRANDPA: And you get really sick from that, Monica.

GIRL: If it gets too bad, I'll swallow all of Mama's sleeping pills in one gulp.

GRANDPA: That's okay. But not before you've asked the Lord for his approval.

GIRL: He'd never approve of it.

GRANDPA: You don't know that. First ask Him and then wait for His answer! Wait. Don't shout "Hello, hello" right away.

GIRL: He never answers.

GRANDPA: You don't know that. *(Silence.)* Meanwhile, go from one room to the next in my father's house--or in my case, you totter--from one hallway to the next, go up the stairs, go down the stairs, from the attic, with the spiders, to the base- ment, with the rats. And listen. Then one day--in not too long a time either--He shall whisper, "Come, my broken, worn-out little child, come." But no matter what, you can't see Him without . . . without . . .?

GIRL: Without dying.

GRANDPA: There's a good girl. Kissums, Monica.

(She blows a kiss in his direction.)

GIRL: Once upon a time . . .

GRANDPA: Rooms sighing; wooden floors that split open like a shin- bone on a soccer field. Doors that squeak like a little sniff- sniff. There's somebody with big bare stinking feet walking by and when you turn around he's gone, but he's there, and you here him breathing like a quack-quack, hiding from the horny old sniff-sniff. And you stick out your hand and it's as though you were rummaging around in a tray full of little wet fish, but you can't pull your hand out, no, you've got to wait until your hand lets go and stops shaking. Then you know you've touched the wing of . . . of . . .

GIRL: . . . of the flying fish,the angel of death.

GRANDPA: . . . of the angel of death. *(He is dead tired.)*

GIRL: There's no t.v. in any of those rooms.

GRANDPA: Poor, poor Monica. *(He buries his head in his hands.)*

GIRL: Poor, poor Grandpa.

(Blood runs out of his mouth. She goes over to him and wipes it off with a routine gesture.)

GRANDPA: Has the sun already set? The pink in the trees?

GIRL: It's evening.

GRANDPA: Then it's all right, then. Warm air currents. A cyclone would be better.

GIRL: What's a cyclone?

GRANDPA: A roar rose up in the heavens . . .

GIRL: Yes, yes, Grandpa!

GRANDPA: . . . like a mighty swift wind and it filled all the rooms, in which they were running around like demented arf-arfs. Tongues of fire appeared and came down upon them. And they spoke Esperanto. *(Silence.)*

GIRL: Tell me about the rooms.

GRANDPA: Staircases overgrown with moss, chinese lanterns without any candles, daring ladies perched on the bannisters, rocking back and forth, the smell of dead horses. In the basement, where the leper and one-eyed rats live, lie rotten potatoes, that even the rats don't want, and busted suitcases, covered with dust. I was in room Eleven. *(Shouts.)* No one has ever escaped from Room Eleven! Are you listening? Can you hear me? Bitch! Where are you?

(He gets up out of his chair with great difficulty and gropes tensely about in the void, running straight into a wall. She observes him and walks cautiously around him. Blood runs out of his mouth. He flails about wildly. Then remins motionless, listening.)

GIRL: *(Whispering)* Once upon a time . . .

GRANDPA: There was so much and so often and seen it all, all those dead things . . . but I'll see His glory, His glory. And you won't, never will!

(He takes his coat and shirt off. His back is covered with scabs and blisters. He bends forward. He kneels. Blood is running out of his mouth. She soundlessly goes over to him and sticks her index finger into his mouth. He sucks the finger. She exits. He keeps on sucking for a long time with his mouth open.)

11. THE EVENING NEWS

T.V. LADY: And now, boys and girls, the Ardennes Rifle Brigade is passing by, staunch and cheerful men, sturdy men with hearts of gold, from the Ardennes Mountains . . . in their-padded parkas the color of autumn leaves . . . with all their plus-fours, pleated at the waist, flies standing open . . . so that the summer evening breeze that's blowing down the street and park, making our flag wave, has free reign up and down its staff . . . . I can make out four, five, eight gorgeous erections which, if I were only a few years younger, would have made my face turn red with awe . . . the dimensions of some of those vital parts compare favorably with the tightly laced skis the owners are carrying on their shoulders . . .

And there, driving up, boys and girls, comes the bullet-proof Cadillac of His Eminence. The limousine is stopping in front of the palace. His Eminence has a serious look on his face which suits the occasion, as he is about to solemnly inquire of Prince Hubert if he will take Princess Alexandra till death do them part. His Eminence is having some difficulty getting out of the car. The Cadillac appears to be equipped with a children's lock. But it is working. The prelate . . . ah . . . . we might have guessed . . . following his Holiness's example, His Eminence will kiss the ground . . . he is getting down onto his knees, bending forward, so that through the slit in his robe, that reaches up to his hips, we observe some rather racy underwear . . . I think it's Cacharel . . . no, he doesn't kiss the earth, but he's picking up a very sweet little *duck* that's lost in the crowd, lifting it up to crotch level . . . and . . . oh, no. . . . Boys and girls, I can see the cameras are now pointing towards the tops of the park's century-old trees and it's a good thing too . . . His Eminence is taking . . . no . . . is taking the tiny quack-quack . . . the way men who live in Meditteranean countries take . . . I'm very sorry. *(Music: "Sérénade Mélancholique.")* At the palace they are waiting for the Minister of Public Works in vain . . .

Rumor has it that the Minister . . . *(Softer)* . . . was found on a blood-covered mattress in Room Eleven of the Hotel Eden in a masturbatory position. . . . Neither the physician for the Ministry of Public Works nor the top contender from the Liberal Party was able to snap the Minister out of his dumb stupor. . . . His eyes were bloodshot as well and were cast reproachfully in the direction of the cathedral. *(Airplanes pass over quite low. The trememendous din of a stampeding mob.)* But what's happening? The crowd . . . has noticed . . . in the distance . . . the far-off armored Mercedes belonging to the princess Alexandra . . . the faces of the crowd seem as though whipped by a tremendous downpour . . . a storm . . . a cyclone of grateful ecstasy. . . . I can just make out the graceful white hand of Princess Alexandra waving . . . *(interference in the broadcast)* but our technical equipment is getting trampled, our cables are being squashed underfoot, the palace is being stormed . . . an old man is coming up cursing and belching to our microphone . . . I can make out the features of my Grandpa . . . he's shouting something from the Acts of the Apostles . . . heaven itself deterred. *(Interference)* Before I get ripped to shreds here . . . I just want to say, boys and girls, let's hope

that all's well that ends well . . . it's all in the game . . . this is
Monica Lefevre. . . . Back to the studio.

12. PENTHESILIA

PROTHOE: What is to become of you?

PENTHESILEA: I do renounce the law that binds us women.
    And I follow him, his youth.

PROTHOE: My Queen, what do you mean? You mean . . .?

PENTHESILEA: What? Why, of course!

PROTHOE: One word then, sister-heart, here in your ear. . . .

PENTHESILEA: No. For now I will step down into my breast
    As into a mine and there will dig a lump
    Of cold ore, an emotion that will kill.
    This ore I temper in the fires of woe
    To hardest steel; then steep it through and through
    In the hot, biting venom of remorse;
    Carry it then to Hope's eternal anvil
    And sharpen it and point it to a dagger;
    Now to this dagger do I give my breast. *(Plants the dagger in her
        breast)*
    So! So! So! So! Once more! Now, it is good.
    (She falls and dies.)

PROTHOE: She's dead! She has followed him.
    A brittle thing, ye gods, is humankind!
    She that lies broken here, a few hours since
    Swept proudly in her course among the peaks.

*(Black-out, applause, ovations. The footlights come up. Penthesilea
comes forward and greets the audience. Achilles gets up, shakes
hands with Prothoe and comes to bow to the audience.)*

PENTHESILEA: *(Comes further downstage, bowing again and
        again; in a whole other rhythm than before)* Ladies and
        gentlemen . . . I'd like to thank you tonight . . . thank you.
        (Starts to weep) There aren't words . . . I can't say it. . . .
        Never could . . . but now less than ever. . . . Ladies, dear
        ladies, before I go . . . since you'll never see me again, it's
        too hard, it's too much . . . never again . . . that's why I want
        to thank you . . . Achilles! *(She throws herself into his arms.
        Embarrassed, he pushes her away.)* . . . And Prothoe
        (Embraces her) and . . . where is she, where? *(She sear-
        ches, dashes off into the wings, and drags out the High
        Priestess, who bows with difficulty and greets the audience*

wearing an impressive Byzantine robe.) Here's the High Priestess . . . she's so shy. . . . She doesn't dare come greet you . . . and that's why I'm doing it for her . . . since she's been through so much lately . . . emotionally, I mean . . . what with that test-tube baby . . . They've helped me so much, these three . . . with my diction . . . could you hear me up there? Ooohh! *(Wails vehemently once again.)* Thank you . . . thank you, I'd like to thank Marie-José, who did my eyes . . . and Leonie for the dress that expressed what was happening inside Penthesilea better than my words and acting ever could. . . . I thank Aunt Nelly, who stood up to the whole family and always believed in me . . . *(Wails)* . . . in the craft of theatre. . . .

(Achilles, having had enough, affably smiles and bows to the audience and drags her off. Black-out. She can be heard sobbing and shouting, "Thank you, thank you." A little worklight is turned on. The High Priestess is still standing there. She goes to sit down and looks at the audience.)

HIGH PRIESTESS: Then, they let me go home, after all the hostilities, I mean after the operation, and the little egg stayed behind at the lab, and one of those real young doctors with an afro asked, "Mrs. Wijnstekers, do you have the feeling that you've left something behind here, something that belongs to you?" I said, "Why, no, I don't feel emotionally attached to that egg. Is that serious? I mean, it's my egg all right, but I don't feel emotionally attached to it." And then I finally came back to Noordkapellen. It's so pretty out there. You can see the freeway from our bedroom. I fell asleep on account of all the emotion and in the morning I felt around next to me and Pete wasn't in bed with me. I looked out the window, it had been snowing all night, it was so beautiful, everything whiter than white, like it always is after a snowfall, Pete was walking in the snow in his bare feet. He walks in the snow so long that he gets an erection and yes, same as usual . . . he ran into the house . . . up the stairs . . . to me . . . to me . . . to me.

13. IN THE DRESSING ROOM

(Achilles sitting in front of the mirror in a theatre dressing room, taking off his makeup. Penthesilea enters and squeezes out of her period dress.)

PENTHESILEA: Are you out of your mind?

ACHILLES: Pretty kettle of fish!

PENTHESILEA: I wanted to thank the people, Mr. Vandam.

ACHILLES: I noticed.

PENTHESILEA: I couldn't help it. I had to do it. It came straight from the heart.

ACHILLES: I wonder what they'll write in the Standard tomorrow. Klaas Tindemans will think it was part of the play. A reflection of the power struggle between people, with the language as an autonomous unit, and using you as an interchangeable aleatory vessel for the text.

PENTHESILEA: You are out of your mind.

ACHILLES: It was un-pro-fes-sion-al, Monica.

PENTHESILEA: One time . . .

ACHILLES: That you'd block my face with those rippling peasant arms of yours during my death scene, o.k., that's to be expected, but during the curtain call. . . .I stood there like a door frame for minutes at a time. You forget who I am.

PENTHESILEA: Never, Mr. Vandam. *(She sits in front of the mirror in a dressing gown.)*

ACHILLES: Using the opportunity to upstage a fellow actor.

PENTHESILEA: You do it too.

ACHILLES: What do I do?

PENTHESILEA: Use the opportunity.

ACHILLES: When?

PENTHESILEA: Every single preview up to now. Six times.

ACHILLES: I?

PENTHESILEA: Why do you think I'm "rippling' my "peasant arms" at that particular moment?

ACHILLES: At what moment?

PENTHESILEA: When you're lying there dying. What are you doing when you're lying there dying.

ACHILLES: I caress your right cheek. I turn stage right and say *(Declaiming)* "Penthesilea, my love, is this the Feast of the Roses you promised me?" and I prepare to die.

PENTHESILEA: You caress my cheek and what do you do with your other hand?

ACHILLES: I lean on it; otherwise I'd fall over backwards.

PENTHESILEA: No, Mr. Vandam, with the thumb of your other hand you bear down with all your might into my crotch.

ACHILLES: I? What makes you say that, woman? With my thumb?

PENTHESILEA: Yes, with that leathery proletarian thumb and that nicotine-stained nail you press and squeeze between my legs.

ACHILLES: You forget who I am, Monica.

PENTHESILEA: And I know precisely why you do this. Because you were given notice a week ago, and because this is your last season.

ACHILLES: *(Giving a start)* How do you know that? Who else knows? Have you spread the news, you lousy gossip?

PENTHESILEA: I told no one, Mr. Vandam. The director told me, and I'm not supposed to tell anyone. That's why you've been so crabby the whole week. That's why you're taking revenge out on me with your thumb.

ACHILLES: Let's say I'd do such a thing . . . in the heat of the moment. *(Suddenly enraged.)* What? I? Edmond Vandam doesn't do such things. Edmond Vandam fucks the same as when he was twenty, young lady, two times in a row with a five minute break in between! Vandam has no need of his thumb to get *his* rocks off, young lady. And even if my thumb did that, even so, you ought to consider it an honor and thank both Mr. Vandam and his thumb before the audience for whole minutes at a time.

(Silence; she takes off her make-up.)

PENTHESILEA: Why do you do this to me? Why me of all people? I, who venerate you.

ACHILLES: You? Ha! You who venerate me!

PENTHESILEA: Like a father.

ACHILLES: Ha!

PENTHESILEA: Like the first actor of this land that you are. You're the only one in your class. *(Silence.)*

ACHILLES: I'll keep an eye out for that thumb.

PENTHESILEA: Yes, do that!

ACHILLES: And if it should stray, I'll rein it in.

PENTHESILEA: Oh, all right, if you find it absolutely necessary for

that scene, if it really helps you with your acting . . .

ACHILLES: I believe I do find it necessary. Unconsciously. Otherwise I wouldn't be doing it.

PENTHESILEA: All right Edmond, I won't mention it again.

ACHILLES: What? Did I hear you aright? Edmond? How do you like that? Hel-lo! Young lady, have we ever gone to a whorehouse together?

PENTHESILEA: No.

ACHILLES: Then will you kindly refrain from calling me by my first

name?

PENTHESILEA: I'll never do it again, Mr. Vandam.

(She goes to the door, locks it, and comes back. She sits down at the make-up table, right under his nose, takes his hand, looks at his thumb. Without the emotional tone of the scene, she says, "For now I will step down into my breast as into a mine and there will dig a lump of cold ore, an emotion that will kill." *She slowly presses his thumb into her.)*

14. THE SUPERMARKET

> *(We hear shmaltzy Muzak. Three elegant women cheerfully enter a department store. As they pile various wares into their carts, and as they inspect and examine other wares, a choreography emerges, during which they do little dance steps, stroke one another, pick at one another and romp about.)*

FIRST WOMAN: Vitala! Aha! Vitala stabilizes my weight, stabilizes my weight slowly but naturally. What's more, it stablizes my desperate superflous fat. Wow!

SECOND WOMAN: Mimala! It's the most sa-tis-fy-ing! Hurray! Mimala distends my stomach enormously. *(She sticks out her stomach.)* Mimala is hard to digest, ergo a person is less hungry.

THIRD WOMAN: Honey, may I activate your intestinal system with Muralox?

FIRST WOMAN: Only because it's you.

SECOND WOMAN: Ravishingly beautiful. What a love! *(She holds a bra in the air.)* The new lovejoy must get its shape from the whistling of the wind.

(A Man in a dark suit, wearing sunglasses, enters. He doesn't react to the ladies at all, nor they to him.)

MAN: Renée? How I met Renée? At night classes.

THIRD WOMAN: Do you trust nature, pussy-wussy?

FIRST WOMAN: Tired? Oh, honey. Nervous? Oh, darling. Let me systematically care for your neuro-muscular system.

SECOND WOMAN: Pretty and soft as silk. Your veins expand.

MAN: We had something to eat together. Later, I bought a book of poems. I asked Renée to recite them so I could get them on my tape recorder.

FIRST WOMAN: *(Grabs Second Woman, bites and kneads her, giggling.)* A little beating, mixing, kneading, grinding, grating. Do you know what you are? You're my assortment fan of tasty little ideas.

SECOND WOMAN: And you're my robot with electronic speed adjuster.

MAN: Renée had soft pale skin.

THIRD WOMAN: Fluffy with criss-crossed woollen fibers.

MAN: On Thursday, July 11, Renée sat down in front of the tape recorder and started reading.

FIRST WOMAN: Hats off at the sight of such a nice big piece of tuna. Fresh vegetables fall right in love with it.

MAN: I was amazed that she felt nothing at all of what was about to happen.

FIRST WOMAN: Soft and creamy, bittersweet.

SECOND WOMAN: Heartwarming, a romantic climax.

MAN: Then I put the silencer on my gun. Then I shot her in the neck. *(A shot.)*

FIRST WOMAN: Little doll of mine, shinier than a mirror. A morning ode to the most womanly part of you.

SECOND WOMAN: Crack, crunch, cream, de-li-cious. *(A shot over the amplifiers. Many echoes.)*

MAN: I laid Renée's corpse down on the floor. I took a bite of it, but the skin wouldn't tear.

SECOND WOMAN: Crispy. Amber and topaz. For your many golden years. For your many golden hairs.

THIRD WOMAN: What can you absolutely not do with a shawl? Untransformable. Imperishable. Long-lasting shine; oh, rose of mine.

MAN: With a kitchen knife, I cut off the parts I prefer: the thighs and the buttocks.

FIRST WOMAN: Green is the color of adventure. Green is the odor of the evening hour.

MAN: I'd had a few pieces of that to eat.

FIRST WOMAN: Noble and natural and fiber-secure.

SECOND WOMAN: In a twinkling not one microbe remains and you smell entirely of pine trees.

MAN: Then I cut loose her breasts, her lips, her nose, her vagina, her ankles, and I ate them, either raw or fried in a pan with salt, pepper, and mustard.

THIRD WOMAN: The subtle combination of beauty fluids chases away time's treacherous little wrinkles.

SECOND WOMAN: That's what I like to see. My hair doesn't split!

MAN: While I was eating her up, I thought violently of Renée. I tried to connect her image with the peices of meat I was chewing on. And it tasted delicious to me because she was it. *(The three ladies' exuberance modulates.)*

FIRST WOMAN: The whole gamut of elbow bands, supportive ankle bands, knee bands, wrist bands.

SECOND WOMAN: Life-loving people enjoy all good things. That's why I enjoy you.

FIRST WOMAN: Now, with you and the pressure cooker, to bed. By love saved and wed.

MAN: In order to forget Renée, I took about thirty color polaroid shots of the cutting and eating. With self-unlocker. In place of music, I endlessly played with the tape of her voice, reciting the poems.

SECOND WOMAN: *(Three times, profoundly.)* That fragrant journey towards yourself.

THIRD WOMAN: *(Same.)* Pretty on a low budget.

MAN: This love-meal lasted two days. Then I sawed Renée into even more pieces with an electric knife. I dumped her clothes and her innards into several different garbage cans. The rest I put into two suitcases. Then I took a cab to the woods.

FIRST WOMAN: *(Almost sadly.)* Beauty is ageless.

SECOND WOMAN: *(Same.)* Real warmth comes from within.

THIRD WOMAN: *(Same.)* Find the way of free choice.

MAN: I admitted everything and then I stretched out on a bench at the police station and fell asleep.

(A strong light slowly fades up. It comes from t.v. spotlights. The Three Young Ladies go up to a microphone. Almost whispering.)

FIRST WOMAN: That obviously racy taste that adds the final touch to the bouquet of an harmonious Château in such a perfectly refined way.

SECOND WOMAN: Mommy, when I'm big, mother dear, I'll give you all the pants in the world.

THIRD WOMAN: The passion with which each coffee bean is selected is the eternal fire that accompanies man on his journeys all over the world, over all the oceans, in search of the noblest and purest conquest.

FIRST WOMAN: Amber and topaz, the golden years for your golden hairs.

CURTAIN